JUDGING DEMOCRACY

The New Politics of the High Court of Australia

The High Court is taking an increasingly important role
in shaping the contours of democracy in Australia. In
deciding fundamental democratic questions, does the
Court pursue a consistent and overarching democratic
vision? Or are its decisions essentially constrained by
institutional and practical limitations? *Judging Democracy*
addresses this question by examining the Court's recent
decisions on human rights, citizenship, native title and
separation of powers. It represents the first major political and legal examination of the Court's new jurisprudence and the way it is influencing democracy and
the institutions of governance in Australia.

A foreword to the book has been written by the former
Chief Justice of the High Court, Sir Anthony Mason.

Haig Patapan is a Research Fellow in the Key Centre for
Ethics, Law, Justice and Governance at Griffith Univers-
ity in Australia. He formerly taught in the School of
Politics and Public Policy at Griffith University, and was
recently a postdoctoral fellow in the Law Faculty,
Queensland University of Technology.

RESHAPING AUSTRALIAN INSTITUTIONS

Series editors: Geoffrey Brennan and Francis G. Castles, Research School of Social Sciences, Australian National University.

Published in association with the Research School of Social Sciences, Australian National University.

This program of publications arises from the School's initiative in sponsoring a fundamental rethinking of Australia's key institutions before the centenary of Federation, in 2001.

The program will publish the work of scholars from the Australian National University and elsewhere who are researching and writing on the institutions of the nation. The scope of the program includes the institutions of public governance, intergovernmental relations, Aboriginal Australia, gender, population, the environment, the economy, business, the labour market, the welfare state, the city, education, the media, criminal justice and the Constitution.

To my Parents

JUDGING DEMOCRACY

The New Politics of the High Court of Australia

HAIG PATAPAN

Griffith University

CAMBRIDGE
UNIVERSITY PRESS

PUBLISHED BY THE PRESS SYNDICATE OF THE UNIVERSITY OF CAMBRIDGE
The Pitt Building, Trumpington Street, Cambridge, United Kingdom

CAMBRIDGE UNIVERSITY PRESS
The Edinburgh Building, Cambridge CB2 2RU, UK
40 West 20th Street, New York, NY 10011–4211, USA
10 Stamford Road, Oakleigh, VIC 3166, Australia
Ruiz de Alarcón, 13, 28014 Madrid, Spain
Dock House, The Waterfront, Cape Town 8001, South Africa

http://www.cambridge.org

First published 2000

Printed in Australia by Brown Prior Anderson

Typeface New Baskerville (Adobe) 10/12pt. *System* QuarkXPress® [PH]

A catalogue record for this book is available from the British Library

National Library of Australia Cataloguing in Publication data
Patapan, Haig, 1959– .
Judging democracy: the new politics of the High Court of Australia.
Bibliography.
Includex index.
ISBN 0 521 77345 8
ISBN 0 521 77428 4 (pbk).
1. Australia. High Court – Political activity.
2. Democracy – Australia. 3. Political questions and
judicial power – Australia. 4. Courts of last resort – Political
aspects – Australia. I. Title. (Series: Reshaping
Australian institutions).
347.94035

ISBN 0 521 77345 8 hardback
ISBN 0 521 77428 4 paperback

Contents

Foreword

By The Hon. Sir Anthony Mason, AC KBE

This book examines the interpretive methods and judicial approaches adopted by the High Court in its more important constitutional and public law decisions (including *Mabo (No 2)* and *Wik*) in the past decade or so. The examination is undertaken with a view to evaluating the role of the Court, how it sees itself and how it is to be seen as an institution which has an uneasy and ill-defined relationship with the other arms of government.

A more appropriate title may have been 'Judging the High Court'. The subtitle 'The New Politics of the High Court' seeks to convey, in its own way, that the author is focusing his attention on certain aspects of the Court's jurisprudence which have consequences for its relationship with the legislature, government, the community and not least for the Court's legitimacy and acceptability. These aspects of the Court's jurisprudence include the move from literal interpretation of the Constitution towards a more progressive interpretation, the implication of rights (albeit limited in range) in the Constitution, the acknowledgment that judges engage in incidental law-making, native title and the separation of powers. The author succeeds in bringing out the nuances of the judges' treatment of these topics as well as the tensions which underlie that treatment, the consequential external perceptions of the Court and the possible impact of those perceptions on the Court.

The discussion identifies interesting and important issues which merit close consideration. Although the author's views on the Court and its work are contestable on various points, the discussion is valuable and thought-provoking.

I conclude with a caution to the reader. The High Court is not a monolithic institution. It is at any time a group of seven justices who are obliged to hear and determine, according to their individual judgment, particular cases. The justices may have conflicting views on the role of the Court as well as on the principles of law which should govern the case in hand. It would therefore be a serious mistake to assume that, in deciding a case, the Court as an institution embarks upon any general policy with a view to achieving a particular goal, political or otherwise, external to the disposition of that case.

Acknowledgments

It is my pleasure to acknowledge the many debts incurred in writing this book. My principal debt is to the Queensland University of Technology for the postdoctoral fellowship that made this book possible. The Law School at QUT was a genial and generous host, supporting my research and making me feel more than welcome. I wish to thank in particular Malcolm Cope, Dean of the Faculty of Law, Phillip Tahmindjis, the Head of the Law School, Bill Lane, and the members of the Public Law Concentration. Special thanks are also due to Francis Castles and Peter Cane, Research School of Social Sciences, for their warm hospitality during my all-too-brief visiting fellowship to the Australian National University.

I am grateful to Bernard Clarke, John Kane and Mark Mourell for their insightful comments on earlier versions of the manuscript. In joining trenchant criticism with generosity of spirit they demonstrated the true virtues of scholarship. Finally, I wish to welcome William and acknowledge my special indebtedness to Annabel, for her patience, wise counsel and unquestioning support. Of course, some debts can never be repaid. As a token of my appreciation it is my honour to dedicate this book to my parents, Vartkes and Mercedes Patapan.

An earlier version of chapter 2, Politics of Interpretation, appeared in the *Sydney Law Review* (vol. 22, no. 2, 2000). The arguments in chapter 6, Separation of Powers, were first developed in the *Australian Journal of Political Science* (Vol. 34, No. 3, 1999).

Preface

This book is in part a response to the Australian High Court's invitation for what it has called 'informed criticism' of its decisions. Informed criticism in this case required more than the usual categories or dichotomies – of activist/deferential, progressive/conservative – that tend to dominate commentary, not because they tend to partisanship and therefore inaccuracy, but because they are often inadequate intellectual tools that do not do justice to the fundamental legal and political changes we need to consider in evaluating what I have termed the new politics of the High Court.

Though welcoming the invitation to criticise, I am well aware of the considerable obstacles in the way of such a task. The principal difficulty, of which the Court is acutely aware and which it has attempted to address by various means, is the problem of specialisation. We know more and more about less and less. Specialist knowledge and disciplinary expertise are increasingly imposing boundaries on deliberation, debate and discussion. The problem is arguably exacerbated in Australia by the strict demarcation between law and politics. This has made writing for general readers as well as for students of law and politics especially challenging.

I have assumed that the burdens of office should not rest only on the shoulders of judges. Democratic government requires a sharing of the burden, not least through thoughtful debate and reflection that is the inevitable, indeed characteristic, feature of good citizenship. It is in this spirit and with this intention that I have endeavoured to understand the way the High Court is judging democracy.

CHAPTER 1

The New Politics of the High Court

In 1831, a 25-year-old French aristocrat, Alexis de Tocqueville, journeyed for nine months through America, meeting presidents, politicians and scholars. The eventual result of his travels and observations was his classic *Democracy in America*, a comprehensive and insightful work that examined in depth America's social, political and judicial institutions. Tocqueville saw in America the nation where the democratic revolution – an irresistible and universal advance of equality that seemed to be sweeping all before it – had been most fully and peacefully realised, where the sovereignty of the people had been put into practice in a direct, unlimited and absolute way. 'I admit', he wrote, 'that I saw in America more than America; it was the shape of democracy itself which I sought, its inclinations, character, prejudices, and passions; I wanted to understand it so as at least to know what we have to fear or hope therefrom.'[1]

As a *juge suppléant* or substitute judge, Tocqueville had the necessary experience and knowledge to evaluate with unparalleled clarity the nature of judicial power in America and thereby the influence of modern democracy on judicial authority. He was particularly struck by the unique power of the American judiciary to base its decisions on the Constitution rather than upon the laws. The right of judges not to apply laws they considered unconstitutional gave them great political influence, since few laws could long escape judges' searching scrutiny for constitutional inconsistency. Tocqueville observed that the 'American judge is dragged in spite of himself into the political field. He only pronounces on the law because he has to judge a case, and he cannot refuse to decide a case.'[2] Therefore, an 'American judge, armed with the right to declare laws unconstitutional, is constantly intervening in political affairs'.[3]

The political nature of this judicial authority obliged Tocqueville to investigate the extent to which the power of lawyers and the judiciary was

1

consistent with democracy. He began with the observation that 'hidden at the bottom of the lawyer's soul one finds some of the tastes and habits of an aristocracy':

> Men who have made a special study of the laws and have derived therefrom habits of order, something of a taste for formalities, and an instinctive love for a regular concatenation of ideas are naturally strongly opposed to the revolutionary spirit and to the ill-considered passions of democracy.[4]

Tocqueville concluded that, in societies where lawyers are held in high regard, their temper will be conservative and antidemocratic. Hence his remarkable claim that 'it is at the bar or the bench that the American aristocracy is found'.

The existence of such an aristocracy within a democracy was not, however, a contradiction, according to Tocqueville. On the contrary, he argued that democratic government favoured the political power of lawyers because when 'the rich, the noble, and the prince are excluded from government, the lawyers step into their full rights, for they are then the only men both enlightened and skilful, but not of the people, whom the people can choose'. As for the lawyers, though their tastes naturally draw them toward aristocracy, 'their interest as naturally pulls them toward the people. Therefore lawyers like democratic government without sharing its inclinations or imitating its weaknesses, a double cause for their power through it and over it'. For Tocqueville, lawyers were the natural liaison between the aristocracy and the people:

> The legal body is the only aristocratic element which can unforcedly mingle with elements natural to democracy and combine with them on comfortable and lasting terms. I am aware of the inherent defects of the legal mind; nevertheless, I doubt whether democracy could rule society for long without this mixture of the legal and the democratic minds, and I hardly believe that nowadays a republic can hope to survive unless the lawyers' influence over its affairs grows in direct proportion to the power of the people.[5]

Tocqueville considered the courts the primary means by which the legal body checked and thereby sustained democracy. He also acknowledged the reach and extent of the legalistic spirit beyond the court precincts. Lawyers, as the only enlightened class not distrusted by the people, were called on to fill most public functions; political questions sooner or later became judicial disputes, which meant that legal language came to dominate political controversy. Thus the spirit of the law infiltrated the whole people:

In the United States the lawyers constitute a power which is little dreaded and hardly noticed; it has no banner of its own; it adapts itself flexibly to the exigencies of the moment and lets itself be carried along unresistingly by every movement of the body social; but it enwraps the whole of society, penetrating each component class and constantly working in secret upon its unconscious patient, till in the end it has molded it to its desire.[6]

The Australian High Court as a Political Institution

It is intriguing to speculate what Tocqueville's reflections would have been had he visited one of the newer democracies, Australia. Indeed, Tocqueville had a definite though indirect influence on Australian democracy, primarily through John Stuart Mill whose *On Liberty* was a response to Tocqueville's diagnosis of tyranny of the majority and whose writings exercised great theoretical influence on Australia's founders. In addition, the Englishman James Bryce toured America in imitation of the great Frenchman, to observe and record the character of the institutions and people of what he called the 'Land of the Future'. His reflections were published in 1888 in *The American Commonwealth,* a book that was regarded by the Australian founders 'with the same awe, mingled with reverence, as the Bible would have been in an assembly of churchmen'.[7]

In one respect, Tocqueville would have found himself on familiar ground in Australia. The Constitution drafted by the Australian founders closely followed the American model, especially in the establishment of a strong and independent federal judiciary. Like the US Supreme Court, the Australian High Court exercises the power of judicial review to determine the constitutionality of laws. As a result, the Australian High Court inevitably intervenes in the political arena, though, just as in America, the political nature of its decisions was consistently denied for a long time. Until very recently the High Court regarded itself, and was generally considered to be, solely a legal institution. It was not until Brian Galligan's ground-breaking 1987 work *The Politics of the High Court,* which chronicled the reception and implementation of judicial review in Australia, that the political nature of the Court was examined in depth.[8]

The politics of the High Court appeared unpolitical because legislation was impugned indirectly: the validity of laws was raised in the course of disputes before the Court in the context of specific cases rather than as matters of general principle, and only when the Court was apprised of a matter. In this way the limits of the judicial power obscured the political nature of the Court's decisions. As Tocqueville noted, 'when a judge attacks a law in the course of an obscure argument in a particular case, he partly hides the importance of his attack from public observation'.[9] Yet a cursory survey of the High Court's decisions during the twentieth century clearly reveals the fundamentally political nature of the Court's constitutional jurisprudence. Its 1920 decision concerning the validity of a log of claims served on Western Australian State enterprises by the Amalgamated Society of Engineers effectively gave the Commonwealth arbitral control over national wages and foreshadowed a significantly greater scope for all federal legislative powers.[10] By upholding the Commonwealth's wartime income tax legislation in 1942, the Court allowed the Commonwealth to implement nationally uniform taxation, ousting the States from the field of income tax. Later decisions on excise completed the Commonwealth's fiscal dominance.[11] In a series of decisions between 1945 and 1949, the Court undermined the Australian Labor Party's postwar reconstruction program that had envisaged national ownership of airlines and banking, and a comprehensive system of social services.[12] In 1982, a dispute over the validity of a contract entered into by the Aboriginal Development Commission resulted in the validation of the Commonwealth *Racial Discrimination Act 1975*, establishing a new foundation for the recognition of the rights and claims of indigenous Australians.[13] The Court's 1983 rejection of Tasmania's challenge to the Commonwealth *National Parks and Wildlife Act 1975* that prohibited the construction of a dam in a World Heritage listed area, expanded the Commonwealth's external affairs power, reconfiguring environmental politics in Australia and thereby fundamentally altering the legal foundations of Australian federalism and giving greater recognition and impetus to Australian nationhood.[14]

These decisions show a politics of the Court that Tocqueville would have immediately recognised, where major political questions are determined in the course of often obscure argument concerning the validity of specific enactments. They also confirm that the judicial review exercised by the Court was essentially based on the federal division of powers secured by the Constitution. Even a case ostensibly about freedom of speech and association, the *Communist Party* case (1951), was decided on the basis that the Menzies government's *Communist Party Dissolution Act 1950* which sought to dissolve the Communist Party and declare that affiliated groups and organisations were unlawful, was beyond the Commonwealth's defence power.[15] Indeed, the High Court's principle of interpretation that parliamentary powers were to be construed broadly and generously meant that the few specific rights contained in the Constitution were given limited scope. For example, the Court gave a restricted reading to the constitutional provisions that secured religious freedom,[16] right to trial by jury[17] and non-discrimination based on State residence.[18]

The New Politics of the High Court

A major theme of this book is that the Australian High Court has moved beyond this familiar Tocquevillean terrain. It is now engaged in a 'new' politics, a role that has important consequences not only for the Court itself, but also for the character of Australian politics. The new politics is largely due to institutional changes that have increased the already significant power of the Court. Tocqueville saw the US Supreme Court as hedged in by a number of restrictions, most importantly the ability of government to amend the Constitution and thus 'reduce the judges to obedience'. In the case of the Australian High Court, however, this restriction has been more apparent than real. Though the Australian Constitution can be altered by referendum, the remarkable lack of success of such attempts (only eight of the forty-four proposals that have been put to the voters since Federation have succeeded) has meant that the High Court's interpretation of the Constitution is practically con-clusive, making the Court a more dominant power in society than its American counterpart. This power has been augmented by new pro-visions that allow appeals only with the Court's leave, so that the High Court can select the civil cases that appear before it. The effect is to change judicial review from a passive to an active form of legislative veto, a significant – albeit slow and indirect – power.

Just as important as this institutional change, however, has been the alteration in the Court's jurisprudence. Though not easy to demarcate precisely, the crucial shift occurred during the time that Sir Anthony Mason was Chief Justice of the Court (1989–95). Sir Gerard Brennan, who succeeded Sir Anthony as Chief Justice, was widely seen as less inclined to pursue the innovative and ambitious jurisprudence of the Mason Court. Nevertheless, the period of the Brennan Court (1995–98) involved a consolidation rather than an abandonment of that juris-prudence. The changes implemented during that time probably set the essential outlines of the jurisprudence that will be pursued by the current Gleeson Court, and beyond.

The Mason Court's announcement that it no longer 'declared' the law, that it in some sense made the law and had always done so, seemed to dislodge its jurisprudence from the legal restraints of case-by-case adjud-ication to a jurisprudence that pronounced on general principles. The price of this, as predicted by Tocqueville, was a Court exposed to partisan politics:

> If the judges had been able to attack laws in a general and theoretical way, if they could have taken the initiative and censored legislation, they would have played a prominent part on the political scene; a judge who had

become a champion or adversary of a party would have stirred all the
passions dividing the country to take part in the struggle.[19]

As a result, judicial independence, the nature of judicial appointments
and the make-up of the Court have become matters of increasing
political salience, debate and contention.

The nature of the new politics of the High Court can be seen in certain
recent decisions that have attracted unprecedented political scrutiny and
criticism. In some decisions, the Court has discerned implied constitutional rights such as the right of political speech and freedom of
movement. In others it has reinterpreted the common law in order to
recognise native title, compelling a reconsideration of indigenous politics in Australia. The Court has also relied on the separation of powers
entrenched in the Constitution to establish important procedural rights.
Generally, it has become a much more visible, vocal and public institution. An overview of the High Court's recent jurisprudence would indicate that the Court has augmented its federal judicial review with a
judicial review that confronts, engages and delineates questions concerning rights and freedoms, citizenship, representative and responsible
government, indigenous culture and politics, and separation of powers.
To an unprecedented extent, the Court has been prepared to decide the
character and to shape the contours of democracy in Australia.

But if the High Court is now willing to, in effect, 'judge democracy',
we are compelled to ask whether its constitutional interpretations and
common law decisions evince a coherent and comprehensive democratic
vision of the Australian polity. Or are its decisions *ad hoc*, determined by
the litigation before it, subject to the contingencies and exigencies of the
Court as an institution influenced and limited by the discretion of
individual judges, and constrained by the very process of adversarial
adjudication?

This book explores these questions by examining the major themes
that the Court has established and is pursuing in the course of its judgments. Our task is to reflect on this jurisprudence, to sound the Court's
decisions in order to understand the nature of the new politics and its
implications for democracy in Australia. Consequently each chapter is to
some extent self-sufficient, and stands alone as an in-depth exploration
and analysis of the different facets of the Court's jurisprudence. The
conclusions and lessons derived in these chapters are summarised and
compared in the final chapter, that assays the claim that the High Court
is judging democracy.

More specifically, chapter 2, 'Politics of Interpretation', examines what
the Court means when it claims to make the law. The Court's apparent

abandonment of the common law declaratory theory raises questions concerning the principles of interpretation it relies on when formulating the common law and reading the Constitution. These seemingly abstract questions in fact point to very real tensions between a law-making judiciary and theories of parliamentary or popular sovereignty. They disclose the Court's changed perception of its role within the regime and its assumptions about the nature and character of change in Australian politics.

The High Court's jurisprudence of rights and freedoms is examined in chapter 3, 'Politics of Rights'. The Australian Constitution contains few express rights. When the High Court held that various rights were implied in the terms of the Constitution or the institutions provided by it, the decision was greeted with surprise and, in some cases, condemnation. What were the nature and scope of the implied rights that the Court had discovered? Examining the theoretical foundations of these rights helps us to discern the substance and content that the Court gave to the notion of representative democracy, and to understand the character of liberal constitutionalism it sought to introduce into Australia.

Chapter 4, 'Democracy and Citizenship', traces the Court's decisions regarding representative and responsible government. The Court has dealt with questions concerning the franchise and voting rights and, importantly, the tensions between the requirements of one-person–one-vote and electoral divisions based on historical and cultural considerations. In so far as these matters give rise to contending formulations of citizenship, sovereignty and democratic participation, examining these cases helps to determine the concept of citizenship and therefore of democracy favoured by the Court.

Mabo inaugurated the Court as a new locus, and judicial politics as a new means, for asserting the claims of indigenous Australians. Though strictly speaking not constitutional decisions, the native title cases are *constitutive* in the sense that they involve the make-up of the regime. Thus chapter 5, 'Native Title and the High Court', is a detailed analysis of the judgments that acknowledge and develop native title in Australia, highlighting the Court's concept of the common law, civilisation and progress, showing how its rhetorical reformulation of these concepts influenced the politics of reconciliation in Australia.

Chapter 6, 'Separation of Powers', investigates the extent to which the High Court has shaped the meaning and content of separation of powers in Australia and thereby implicitly redefined judicial independence and the conventional boundaries between the legal and the political. It does so in the context of two theoretical foundations of separation of powers – the Blackstonian and that of the *Federalist Papers* – and their democratic presuppositions. It pays particular attention to the tension inherent in the concept of judicial independence when the judiciary is explicitly acknowledged as a law-making body.

Finally, chapter 7, 'Judging Democracy', draws together the ideas, arguments and themes explored in the previous chapters. It outlines the extent to which the new politics of the High Court can be said to represent and articulate an integrated and comprehensive change of direction in Australian constitutionalism, and the theoretical and practical limitations on the Court's ability to pursue such a goal.

It is hard to avoid the evidence: the Australian High Court is now taking an increasingly public and prominent role in Australian politics. The aim of this book is to understand the character of the new politics of the High Court, and in doing so ascertain the democratic vision of a Court that is now willing to judge democracy.

Notes

1 Tocqueville, Alexis de 1969, *Democracy in America* (ed. J.P. Mayer), New York, Doubleday & Co., author's introduction, 19.
2 ibid., Book I, ch. 6, 102–3.
3 ibid., Book I, ch. 8, 269.
4 ibid., 264.
5 ibid., 266.
6 ibid., 270.
7 La Nauze, J.A. 1972, *The Making of the Australian Constitution,* Melbourne, Melbourne University Press, 273. According to Deakin (cited in La Nauze, *Making of the Australian Constitution,* 19), 'An authority, to whom we have often referred since 1890, an authority to whom our indebtedness is almost incalculable, is Hon. Mr Bryce'. At the 1897–98 Constitutional Convention Bryce's *The American Commonwealth* lay on the parliamentary table throughout the proceedings: see La Nauze, *Making of the Australian Constitution,* 273.
8 Galligan, Brian 1987, *The Politics of the High Court,* Brisbane, University of Queensland Press. See also Solomon, David 1992, *The Political Impact of the High Court,* Sydney, Allen & Unwin; Solomon, D. 1999, *The Political High Court: How the High Court Shapes Politics,* Sydney, Allen & Unwin; Zines, L. 1997, *The High Court and the Constitution,* 4th edn, Sydney, Butterworths.
9 Tocqueville, *Democracy in America,* Book I, ch. 6, 100–1.
10 *Amalgamated Society of Engineers v Adelaide Steamship Co Ltd* (1920) 28 CLR 129.
11 *South Australia v Commonwealth* (1942) 65 CLR 373; *Victoria v Commonwealth* (1957) 99 CLR 575; *Ha v New South Wales* (1997) 189 CLR 465.
12 See Galligan, *Politics of the High Court,* ch. 4; *Australian National Airways Pty Ltd v Commonwealth* (1945) 71 CLR 29; *Bank of New South Wales v Commonwealth* (1948) 76 CLR 1; *A-G (Victoria) v Commonwealth* (1945) 71 CLR 237; *British Medical Association v Commonwealth* (1949) 79 CLR 201.
13 *Koowarta v Bjelke-Petersen* (1982) 153 CLR 168.

14 *Commonwealth v Tasmania* (1983) 158 CLR 1.
15 *Australian Communist Party v Commonwealth* (1951) 83 CLR 1.
16 *Krygger v Williams* (1912) 15 CLR 366; *Adelaide Company of Jehovah's Witnesses v Commonwealth* (1943) 67 CLR 116 cf *Church of New Faith v Commissioner of Pay-Roll Tax (Vic)* (1983) 154 CLR 120.
17 *R v Archdall* (1928) 41 CLR 128; *Kingswell v R* (1985) 159 CLR 264.
18 *Henry v Boehm* (1973) 128 CLR 482 cf *Street v Queensland Bar Association* (1989) 168 CLR 461.
19 Tocqueville, *Democracy in America*, Book I, ch. 6, 102.

CHAPTER 2

Politics of Interpretation

Implicit in each judgment of the High Court and at the heart of the judicial task is the question of how to interpret. In resolving this question the Court addresses more than a legal problem; it articulates its understanding of the legal system, the role of the Court in that system and, importantly, its vision of the regime as a whole. Therefore the question of interpretation has profound consequences for Australian constitutionalism.

One of the earliest and most important statements by the High Court on the proper way to interpret is found in its 1920 decision in the *Engineers* case. In *Engineers* the Court emphasised the importance of a literal and legal reading of enactments and thereby characterised its role as essentially that of declaring the law. The legal duty of interpreting and declaring the law, a vital aspect of the rule of law, was distinguished from the political role of making the law. Implicit in this view of interpretation was a political vision that located the legal task within a larger arrangement characterised by representative and responsible government, parliamentary sovereignty and a progressive parliamentarianism.

For various reasons, including changes in Australian constitutionalism and international developments, the Court has moved away from this method of interpretation. Its recent admission that it makes the law forces reconsideration of the Court's place within the legal system, and the new political vision entertained by the judiciary. Accordingly, the Court has been forced to resolve the tension between the rule of law and a law-making judiciary. This chapter argues that the Court has attempted to address this tension principally by resorting to a version of sociological jurisprudence and the notion of 'community values' as a guide and check on judicial law-making. Though the resort to community values appears to allow a neutral standard of interpretation, placing the judiciary in a subsidiary and instrumental role, I would argue that it does not resolve the problem of reconciling individual discretion with the demands of the rule of law. Perhaps more significantly, it seems that such a standard has opened the Court's jurisprudence to a range of fundamentally different political settlements, without allowing it the means to reconcile or negotiate between them.

Clear and Natural Meaning

The problem of how to interpret the Constitution was addressed by the High Court in its early years in the context of deciding the extent to which the Commonwealth and the States could control each other's operations. According to what became known as the doctrine of immunity of instrumentalities, the Court held that States could not control the operations of the Commonwealth and, reciprocally, some types of Commonwealth rules did not apply to the States.[1] Similarly, the implied doctrine of State reserved powers was relied upon by the Court to limit the powers conferred upon the Commonwealth Parliament.[2]

As the judgment of Chief Justice Griffith for the Court in *Baxters* case shows, these decisions presupposed a method of interpreting the Constitution:

> If it is suggested that the Constitution is to be construed merely by the aid of a dictionary, as by an astral intelligence, and as a mere decree of the Imperial Parliament without reference to history, we answer that that argument, if relevant, is negatived by the preamble to the Act itself . . . That is to say, the Imperial legislature expressly declares that the Constitution has been framed and agreed to by the people of the Colonies mentioned, who, as pointed out in the judgment of the Board in *Webb v Outtrim*, had practically unlimited powers of self-government through their legislatures. How, then, can the facts known by all to have been present to the minds of the parties to the agreement be left out of consideration?[3]

This way of interpreting the Constitution, which looked to American precedents, was prepared to take into account the political and legal context of the Australian founding, relying on the historical facts and circumstances to give meaning to the text.[4] Importantly, implicit in this method of interpretation was a political vision of a co-sovereign federalism that was largely consistent with the views of the Constitution's framers. This is not surprising given that the sitting judges – Chief Justice Griffith and Justices Barton and O'Connor – had taken part in political life, been delegates to the Constitutional Conventions and contributed to the drafting of the Constitution. For them the Constitution was more than an Act of Imperial Parliament; it represented a compact between States, an instrument of government.[5]

Engineers Case

This view of the Constitution was to change fundamentally with the High Court's decision in the *Engineers* case.[6] *Engineers* overturned the doctrine of implied prohibition as well as the doctrine of reserved powers. Significantly for our purposes, it formulated a new basis for interpreting the Constitution that was to exercise far-reaching influence on the High Court's jurisprudence.

In the *Engineers* case, Western Australian government enterprises had been served a log of claims by the Amalgamated Society of Engineers. When the Society commenced proceedings in the Commonwealth Conciliation and Arbitration Court, the government of Western Australia challenged the proceedings on the grounds that the federal Act establishing that Court could not apply to State government enterprises. Therefore, the issue was whether the Commonwealth's power to make laws with respect to conciliation and arbitration of industrial disputes was binding on the States. The High Court held that the Act establishing the Conciliation and Arbitration Court was a valid exercise of the power in the Constitution and that there was no basis to exclude the States from the operation of the Act.[7] On what grounds did the High Court reject its previous decisions? According to the majority, no clear principle emerged from the cases previously decided by the Court:

> They are sometimes at variance with the natural meaning of the text of the Constitution; some are irreconcilable with others; and some are individually rested on reasons not founded on the words of the Constitution or any recognised principle of the common law underlying the expressed terms of the Constitution but on implication drawn from what is called the principle of 'necessity', that being itself referable to no more definite standard than the personal opinion of the Judge who declares it.[8]

The need for consistent and impartial adjudication was undermined by recourse to implications in the Constitution:

> An interpretation that relies on 'an implication which is formed on a vague, individual conception of the spirit of compact' can only lead to divergences and inconsistencies because it is 'rebuttable by an intention of exclusion equally not referable to any language of the instrument or acknowledged common law constitutional principle, but arrived at by the Court on the opinions of judges as to hopes and expectations respecting vague external conditions'.[9]

In the *Engineers* case the High Court states that it is returning to 'settled rules of construction', which means giving words their 'natural' meaning:

> The one clear line of judicial inquiry as to the meaning of the Constitution must be to read it naturally and in the light of circumstances in which it was made, with knowledge of the combined fabric of the common law, and the statute law which preceded it, then *lucet ipsa per se*.[10]

The greater emphasis on the strict reading of the Constitution meant that the Court was limited as to the material it would rely upon in interpreting the terms of the Constitution. It adopted Lord Haldane's remarks regarding the 'golden rule or universal rule':

> In endeavouring to place the proper interpretation on the sections of the statute before this House sitting in its judicial capacity, I propose, therefore, to exclude consideration of everything excepting the state of the law as it was when the statute was passed, and the light to be got by reading it as a whole, before attempting to construe a particular section. Subject to this consideration, I think that the only safe course is to read the language of the statute in what seems to be its natural sense.[11]

A natural reading which resulted in consistent, definite and clear decisions required the Constitution to be interpreted as any other Act of Imperial Parliament.

To understand the decision in *Engineers*, it is important to recall that the Constitution as a federal arrangement was an American innovation that differed in a number of important respects from the then-dominant English understanding of law and constitutionalism. It was a fundamental, or 'constitutive', document in a way that was unknown in evolutionary English constitutionalism. Its establishment of a federal union with separate sovereign authorities was also an innovation in parliamentary tradition. And, importantly, it included federal judicial review, giving the judiciary power to overrule parliamentary enactments.[12] This form of judicial review, which required a novel form of adjudication, appeared to be contrary to the common law tradition. Whereas the Griffith High Court had been prepared to take up such a jurisprudence, the Court in the *Engineers* case, largely comprising lawyers who had not been involved in framing the Constitution and who had little political experience, wished to return to the settled rules of construction.[13] The High Court in *Engineers* declined to take on federal judicial review that could be construed as 'political'. In doing so it preferred the authority of the Privy Council to the American precedents, disengaging itself from the jurisprudence of the US Supreme Court. Thus *Engineers* can be seen as the

point where conventional rules of interpretation asserted their dominance over the innovation of federalism: the Constitution was seen not
as a constitutive enactment but as any other Act of Parliament, part of the
fabric of the law of the Constitution that preceded federation.[14]

The reference to the fabric of common law suggests that the Court in
Engineers returned to the common law form of adjudication. Classical
common law, as outlined in the works of Coke, Blackstone and Hale, was
unwritten, based on custom and usage. Thus, the common law represented the refined experience and wisdom of successive ages. The
superiority and hence the authority of the common law was founded
upon the 'artificial reason' of the law. Unlike the natural reason possessed by individuals, artificial reason and judgment of the law were
acquired by long study of the common law. Therefore, knowledge of the
laws of the land justified the judge's role.[15] Judges did not make the
common law; in the famous words of Blackstone, they are 'depositories
of the laws; the living oracles'. As oracles of the common law, judges did
not decide cases according to their own private judgments or sentiment
but in agreement with precedents, not making new law but maintaining
and expounding the old. If a judge's decision was manifestly absurd or
unjust the common law did not regard it as bad law, but rather as no law
at all.[16]

This self-understanding of the classical common law possessed a
number of strengths. It reconciled the competing demands of the rule
of law and judicial discretion. It was flexible enough to accommodate
change within a timeless common law. Significantly, in defending the
authority of the common law it justified the judicial role as an exercise of
a superior artificial reason, supplying a strong foundation for judicial
independence.[17] Nevertheless, classical common law was subjected to
sustained criticism, both political and philosophical.[18] Consequently, at
the time of Australia's founding classical common law contended with a
powerful Benthamite utilitarianism that rejected the justice and efficacy
of an immemorial common law.[19] Two of the most influential thinkers of
the time, Bryce and Dicey, were utilitarians who accepted the Benthamite
critique of the common law. Bryce was the pre-eminent authority – his
The American Commonwealth became the sourcebook on American government and federalism for Australia's founders, while his *Studies of History
and Jurisprudence* introduced the concept of flexible and rigid constitutions to constitutional thought.[20] Dicey, a colleague of Bryce at Oxford,
wrote the influential *Introduction to the Law of the Constitution*, which was
relied upon by Australia's founders and became the seminal text on
constitutional law in England and Australia. In the *Law of the Constitution*
Dicey distinguished between rules that are enforced by the Courts, which
are called laws, and customs and conventions. The laws of the Constit-

ution are animated by two principles, the sovereignty of Parliament and the rule of law. Dicey's formulation of parliamentary sovereignty, the rule of law and the dependence of conventions upon the law of the Constitution exercised a major influence on the High Court.[21]

The Diceyan distinction between the political and the legal, which can be traced to the influence of Bentham, can be seen clearly in the *Engineers* case. According to the Court the doctrine of 'implied prohibitions' is incapable of consistent application because:

> 'necessity' in the sense employed – a political sense – must vary in relation to various powers and various States, and indeed, various periods and circumstances. Not only is the judicial branch of the Government inappropriate to determine political necessities, but experience, both in Australia and America, evidenced by discordant decisions, has proved both the elusiveness and the inaccuracy of the doctrine as a legal standard.[22]

To abandon legal standards, to venture into political issues – 'a labyrinth to the character of which they have not sufficient guide' – is to accede to the personal opinions of the judge who declares the law; in effect, it is to deny the rule of law.

The demarcation between the legal and the political did not preclude Dicey from accepting that judges make laws, even though judicial lawmaking had a number of limitations.[23] But over time the High Court went beyond Dicey on this issue, by claiming that judges did no more than declare the law. This was arguably a return to the common law declaratory theory, albeit incorporating a new positivism. To Dicey, such a stance was explicable in terms of the legalism that was the spirit of federalism, and the natural tendency of modern judges to prefer certain and fixed rules over laws which are liable to modification. The substantial general appellate workload of the Australian High Court may also have been a contributing factor.[24]

The difference between the 'legal' and the 'political' justified the role of the judiciary as a neutral expositor of the law. It also presupposed a political settlement. In the *Engineers* case the Court assumed not only the common law but also a common sovereignty of the Commonwealth and responsible government.[25] A sovereign Parliament was the essential counterpart to a judiciary that relied on legal reasoning. The judicial role was limited because of the availability of political remedies:

> the extravagant use of the granted powers in the actual working of the Constitution is a matter to be guarded against by the constituencies and not by the Courts . . . If it be conceivable that the representatives of the people of Australia as a whole would ever proceed to use their national powers to injure the people of Australia considered sectionally, it is

certainly within the power of the people themselves to resent and reverse what may be done. No protection of this Court in such a case is necessary or proper.[26]

Therefore the Court's reassertion of 'settled rules of construction' in the *Engineers* case was a confirmation and endorsement of the primacy of parliamentary, responsible government – indeed, one presupposed the other.

Political Consequences of the Engineers Case

The decision in the *Engineers* case was subsequently regarded by the High Court as a definitive statement on the principles of constitutional interpretation and as an authority for literalism and legalism.[27] Thus, the case had a profound political influence on Australian constitutionalism.

Its major political consequence concerned the way the case redefined the federal balance in Australia. A literal reading of the Constitution, combined with the view that the terms of the Constitution should be interpreted broadly, resulted in an expansive interpretation of federal powers at the expense of States' residual powers. A growing sense of Australian nationalism may also have contributed to the growth of central power.[28] The Court's subsequent decisions on taxation, excise, commerce and external affairs, to name a few, significantly shifted the federal balance in favour of the Commonwealth.[29]

The *Engineers* case also had significant political implications for the authority and legitimacy of the Court within the regime. A 'natural' reading of the text distinguished and characterised the legal method and was the essence of legal reasoning. Therefore a literal reading of the text justified judicial authority in Australia. In contrast, the resort to 'implications' betrayed an attempt to augment a clear legal reading with personal preference or opinion – it marked a movement from the legal to the unbounded political. As the adjudicator of federalism the Court faced questions that were inherently political and potentially divisive, yet it was essential for judicial office to be, and appear to be, impartial and unbiased, both for the authority of the Court and for the safety of the federal Constitution. The principles of interpretation adopted by the Court in the *Engineers* case were meant to meet this challenge. By limiting its decisions to the legal aspects of the case the Court solved the apparently intractable problem of partiality. The political role of the Court was incidental, or indirect – it was political in the way a judge deciding a case of breach of contract could be said to be political. Adjudication by the Court was a legal act, removed from the complexities and dangers of the political debates on the wisdom or expediency of legislation.[30]

In deciding major federal disputes the Court was no more than an umpire, applying the rules determined by another. In the words of Sir Owen Dixon on the occasion of his swearing-in as Chief Justice, 'the Court's sole function is to interpret a constitutional description of power or restraint upon power and say whether a given measure falls on one side of a line consequently drawn or on another'.[31] Reminiscent of Tocqueville's account of the role of the judiciary in America, the overturning of State or Commonwealth legislation by the High Court was not considered to be a political act: it was no different from the interpretation and application of any other Act of Parliament.

As we have seen, this justification of judicial review presupposed a legitimate forum that would consider the wisdom and expediency of legislation. The political settlement assumed in the *Engineers* case – sovereignty of Parliament, representative democracy, responsible government – was the foundation and justification of the Court's jurisprudence. In turn, this political vision was given texture, substance and authority by the decisions of the High Court, which gave as much authority to Parliament as possible.[32] The American 'suspicion' of government was rejected; constitutional grants of power were given extensive operation. As a consequence, civil liberties provisions that limited such powers were given a restricted reading.[33] The Constitution was seen as the barest structure necessary to found a federal union and accommodate a changing and growing body politic. It certainly was not a comprehensive constitutive enactment that attempted to limit government or secure inalienable rights. Rather, responsible government and the rule of law were the foundations of liberty. Though the extent to which this political vision accurately reflected the realities of Australian constitutionalism is contested,[34] few would deny its power and influence in directing the course of Australian constitutionalism.[35]

Reasons for Change

Recent decisions suggest that the Court is moving away from the principles of interpretation established in the *Engineers* case.[36] Before investigating the differing interpretive methods developed by the Court, and their political implications, it is necessary to understand the reasons for this change. Such an understanding brings to light the factors that influence the Court as an institution and explains how they have substantially moulded the character of the interpretive principles that the Court has favoured in recent decisions.

The move away from legalism and literalism can be traced to important changes in Australian constitutionalism that took place during the twentieth century. These changes had important institutional consequences for the Court, significantly reformulating its role within the polity. Australia's development into an independent sovereign state was a gradual process, signposted by major Imperial enactments such as the *Colonial Laws Validity Act 1865* (UK), the *Commonwealth of Australia Constitution Act 1900* (UK) and the *Statute of Westminster 1931* (UK). Perhaps the most important enactment, at least in terms of symbolism, was the passing of the Australia Acts in 1986, which formally terminated the power of the UK Parliament to legislate for Australia. These changes in Australian constitutionalism were mirrored in the increasing authority of the High Court within the Australian legal system.[37]

One of the most important changes was the gradual transformation of the High Court into the final court of appeal in Australia. Though the majority of founders intended the High Court to be a supreme court of appeal in Australia, appeals to the Privy Council in certain cases were retained in the Constitution as a result of compromises implemented when the Constitution was formally enacted in Westminster.[38] As a result the High Court was not a final court of appeal in Australia and appeals to the Privy Council, though few, were pursued by litigants. This meant that English judicial opinion, especially that of the House of Lords and the Court of Appeal, were considered authoritative in Australia. For example, in *Piro's* case, a decision handed down in 1943, the High Court held that in cases of conflict the decision of the House of Lords would be binding on the High Court, effectively placing the House of Lords at the apex of the Australian legal system.[39]

Twenty years later things had changed. In *Parker*, decided in 1963, the High Court announced its judicial independence and held that it was free to consider issues independently of English authority.[40] By this time strong nationalist sentiment regarded appeals to the Privy Council as contrary to the status of Australia as an independent nation, and legislation in the form of the *Privy Council (Limitation of Appeals) Act 1968* (Cth) and the *Privy Council (Appeals from the High Court) Act 1975* (Cth) limited the right of appeal to the Privy Council. As a result of these decisions, the High Court held in 1978 in *Viro* that it would no longer be bound by the decisions of the Privy Council.[41] The remaining avenue of appeal to the Privy Council was abolished by the Australia Act itself. By 1986 the High Court was effectively the final court of appeal in Australia.[42]

The independence of the Court was accompanied by changes that emphasised its role as a national court. The Federal Court of Appeal was established in 1976 with the specific purpose of freeing the High Court to decide constitutional issues and appeal cases of national importance.[43] A successful referendum allowed the enactment of the *Constitutional Alteration (Retirement of Judges) Act 1977* (Cth) which ended life tenure for judges, imposing a mandatory retirement age of seventy. Under the *High Court of Australia Act 1979* (Cth), the Court was given maximum independence to manage its building, staff and finances. The Court's increasing importance was symbolically confirmed with the construction of a new High Court building close to Parliament House in Canberra. The building, which was opened by the Queen in 1980, was also important for practical reasons: sophisticated court-reporting services using audio-visual resources were installed in the building, as was the Court's extensive library.[44] Its procedures also reflected its growing stature at the apex of the federal legal system as well as a general court of appeal in Australia. The Court was now in charge of its own docket. By 1984 most appeals 'as of right' (automatic permission to appeal) were eliminated, and special leave to appeal would be granted by the Court only in cases that raised issues of public importance or important questions of law.[45] The Court also looked different – as a constitutional court it decided that its judges would no longer wear traditional wigs.

At the time of these changes the Court continued to insist that it was no more than an impartial adjudicator of the law, declaring the common law without making it. Desirable changes to the law were to be left to Parliament.[46] This stance contrasted with developments in other courts of final jurisdiction in the common law world. The most important source of change for the judiciary in those other jurisdictions was the adoption or entrenchment of Bills of Rights, which fundamentally transformed their jurisprudence, altering their methods of interpretation as well as their role within the polity. The European Court of Justice and the decisions of the European Court of Human Rights had a major influence on the interpretation of law in the United Kingdom, undermining the strength of the declaratory theory to such an extent that by 1972 the judicial members of the House of Lords were willing to admit publicly the reality of judicial creativity. Lord Reid claimed that the declaratory theory was an 'open sesame' form of interpretation, a 'fairy-tale' no one believed any more.[47] In Canada, after a false start in 1960 with the Canadian Bill of Rights, the entrenchment of the Charter of Rights and Freedoms in 1982 justified the Supreme Court in adopting a new jurisprudence of human rights. In America the decisions of the Warren Court in the 1960s placed the Bill of Rights at the forefront of its jurisprudence. Similar developments could be discerned in India, Ireland and New Zealand.

In contrast, the Australian High Court appeared to stand outside the mainstream of changes to courts of final jurisdiction. Part of the problem was the fact that Australia did not have an extensive constitutional Bill of Rights – various attempts to entrench such a Bill were singularly unsuccessful.[48] Despite lacking a Bill of Rights, Australia was increasingly committing itself to a number of international human rights covenants and conventions. The gradual opening up of the Australian legal system to the world and the increasing importance of human rights in international law exposed the High Court to international influences. As a court of final jurisdiction, the High Court became the institution that would mediate international changes, requiring it to adopt a more extensive and profound role in the adjudication of constitutionalism in Australia.[49]

These developments, combined with the absence of a Bill of Rights, compelled the judiciary to reconsider the adequacy of Australia's political institutions of governance in protecting human rights. The orthodox theoretical framework of responsible government and parliamentary democracy that protected individual rights and thereby justified a limited role for the judiciary no longer seemed valid. The reality of party government, executive dominance and the administrative state appeared to represent an unchecked and unaccountable power in Australian politics. Thus the Court's abandonment of the declaratory theory and its turn to a jurisprudence of individual rights and freedoms, a jurisprudence that saw the Constitution as a constitutive enactment, was justified as much by an acknowledgment that the political settlement that protected civil liberties and therefore justified judicial deference no longer operated in Australian political life, as by international developments.[50]

These factors would not, by themselves, be sufficient to account for the changing direction in the Court's jurisprudence. What made them decisive was a theoretical perspective predicated on the need to accommodate change. Here it is necessary to acknowledge the powerful influence of Roscoe Pound, Julius Stone and sociological jurisprudence in the development of the High Court's view of its role within the regime.

Sociological jurisprudence came of age in America in the first decade of the twentieth century, at a time of declining faith in the economic and social philosophy of *laissez-faire*. The increasing need for state involvement and the subsequent demands for regulation were acknowledged in the writings of Roscoe Pound by the recognition of the reality of conflict and the primacy accorded to social interests. He also recognised that the pace of social change led to a need for reform in political and legal fields. Yet Pound's emphasis on laws as rules preserved the notion of law as an autonomous phenomenon; it preserved the practitioners' perception of the law. From this perspective law is seen as an instrument with normative or purposive content – the task of legal theorists and practitioners is to intervene when the legal system is malfunctioning, when there is a gap between the goals of law and their social consequences.[51]

Pound's sociological jurisprudence and his pragmatic theory of justice and law were developed and applied by Julius Stone in his major works, *The Province and Function of Law* (1961), *Human Law and Human Justice* (1965) and *Social Dimensions of Law and Justice* (1966).[52] According to Stone, in any given society at a given time individuals are asserting interests as worthy of protection by the law of that society. It is not possible to distinguish or rank these claims for interests, because all demands are good. Thus in any given society the legal system represents an attempt to adjust the interests of individuals with each other and with the interests asserted on behalf of society and the state, with the least possible sacrifice to the whole. Law is a compromise or reconciliation of the range of demands; justice is an adjustment of relations and ordering of conduct that will make the goods of existence go as far as possible with least friction and waste.[53] Here we see the egalitarian bias of sociological jurisprudence – all demands merit attention, the aim is to maximise interests.

The concept of law as social control or social engineering has important implications for judging. Judges do not apply clear and definite rules because there are limits to formal logic in legal reasoning. As Stone notes, all judging is to this extent indeterminate and relies on creative judicial law-making; judges always take 'policy' considerations into account.[54] How is a just decision to be reached? Judging as an adjustment of interests requires resolving interests so that the solution does least injury to the scheme as a whole. The first step is to observe the interests that are being pressed for recognition by the law. This comprehensive picture will reveal 'jural postulates', fundamental principles presupposed by the interests and demands. Jural postulates are a rationalisation of these claims but cannot represent all of them. The postulates are employed to alter the legal institutions of a particular society, to bring them into harmony with the actual demands made in that society. The jural postulates applied to interests will also set up a 'scheme of interests' which will enable a number of *de facto* claims to be eliminated. Judging can be described as evaluating conflicting interests in terms of the scheme of interests as a whole.[55]

Though sociological jurisprudence has been subjected to extensive criticism, for our purposes it is sufficient if we note important themes in the theory concerning interpretation.[56] The first concerns the ascertainment and status of demands and interests. Demands and interests are articulated in, and assume, a civilisation in a certain time and place. Yet the formulation of time and space for evaluating demands remains fundamentally elusive.[57] As well, the apparent reluctance to evaluate interests by accepting all demands as good (that is, to be pragmatic rather than *a priori*) becomes questionable when it is seen that the majority of interests are to be accommodated, a process that is more than a quantitative exercise.[58]

Moreover, 'jural postulates' and the 'scheme of interests' seem to suggest that there are fundamental principles within the law, that bringing the law into harmony with contemporary conditions improves the law. But jural postulates and schemes of interests do not have such a fundamental status, so that unless a progressive civilisation is assumed there is no reason to think that harmonising the law has any higher claim than that of consistency. This difficulty is acute during a period of transition where one set of postulates is no longer accepted and the others are speculative.[59]

Finally, justice understood as resolution of conflict seems to deny any substantive content to claims of right – pragmatic justice appears to be no more than procedural justice. Yet Pound's evaluation of the practical implications of such an interpretation reveals a distinctive vision of an American regime in 1919.[60] As Hunt notes, 'Poundian theory is the reflex of the conservative progressivism of Theodore Roosevelt, explicitly structured within the framework of a capitalist economy and seeking to give a new "socialised" form to the traditional individualistic creed'.[61] A similar vision is reflected in Stone's concerns with a postwar settlement between individualism and socialism.[62] Sociological jurisprudence, though claiming to have no inherent, natural or absolute 'values', discloses its social democratic inclinations through its emphasis on practical justice and social reform.

As professor of jurisprudence in the University of Sydney and later at the University of New South Wales, Stone was an inspiring teacher who had a lasting influence on generations of students.[63] As Justice Kirby has noted:

> Through Stone, Pound's practical and realistic approach to jurisprudence, entirely compatible with the spirit of English common law, found acceptance amongst the young lawyers of Australia and New Zealand in the 1940s, 1950s, 1960s and beyond. Those young lawyers came in time to positions of influence in the law and its institutions in the antipodes. It is only now that the impact of Stone's jurisprudential teachings upon lawyers of Australia is coming to full flower.[64]

One of these students was Lionel Murphy, who was Attorney-General in the Whitlam Labor government and was appointed to the High Court in 1975. In Murphy's judgments we see the first application of the principles of sociological jurisprudence by the High Court.[65] But Justice Murphy was unable to gain significant support on the Bench. This was partly due to his reluctance to persuade: in general his judgments were brief and tended to assert or declare rather than demonstrate the strengths of his position. His ambition and desire for reform inclined him towards undue haste, and he thought the justice of his position was a complete answer to, and would vindicate, the overturning of precedents. Though Murphy's long-term influence on the Court is contested, it cannot be denied that he shifted the boundaries of debate, facilitating the changes that were soon to be adopted by the Court. [66]

One of the earliest intimations of the forthcoming changes was the first Menzies Lecture in 1986 by Sir Anthony Mason, a student of Julius Stone at the University of Sydney who became Chief Justice of the High Court in 1987. In this lecture, which focuses on the problem of constitutional interpretation, we get a glimpse of the aims of the future Mason Court. [67]

According to Mason, the usual controversy that surrounds the High Court concerns the interpretation of the Constitution as a federal document – the limits of federal and State powers. But of greater importance for Mason is the dominance of what he calls the doctrine of legalism, which is based on the concept of parliamentary supremacy and the supremacy of the rule of law. The problem with legalism is that it may be a 'cloak for undisclosed and unidentified policy values'. As well, 'Legalism, when coupled with the doctrine of *stare decisis*, has a subtle and formidable conservative influence'.[68]

Mason advocates a new approach to interpretation, that he describes variously as a 'dynamic' or 'policy' approach. This method of interpretation requires judges to take into account community values, especially when interpreting a Constitution. Constitutions are not blueprints but a framework for government, and therefore should be interpreted dynamically and liberally. The difficulty with amending the Constitution supports and justifies this view of constitutional interpretation. Perhaps more fundamentally:

> Because policy-oriented interpretation exposes underlying values for debate it would enhance the open character of the judicial decision-making process and promote legal reasoning that is more comprehensible and persuasive to society as a whole. This development would lead to a better understanding of constitutional judgments and, no doubt, to a greater capacity and willingness to criticise them. But criticism is a small price to pay if the approach is one that contributes, as it seems to have done in the United States, to a stronger sense of constitutional awareness on the part of the community and a more accurate appreciation of the issues arising for decision.[69]

Dynamic interpretation will change the formal rules of statutory interpretation: sovereignty of the people will replace Imperial sovereignty;

extrinsic material will be allowed in interpreting the terms of the Constitution; the Constitution will not be confined to its meaning of 1900, it will be read as an 'instrument of national government'.[70] These changes in interpretive technique will not fundamentally alter the Court's jurisprudence of federalism because dynamic interpretation is unlikely to arrest the decline in State authority. It will, however, provide a new focus for future controversy – fundamental rights. In his lecture, Mason implicitly raises the possibility that recourse to community values may lead to an American-style jurisprudence of rights. Though anticipating such a development, he makes it clear that he would prefer to have a formal Bill of Rights to authorise such jurisprudence.[71]

Dynamic and Progressive Interpretation

The recent decisions of the High Court show a marked shift in the Court's methods of interpretation. It is now prepared to take into account decisions in other jurisdictions and principles of international law. It sees the Constitution as more than an Imperial enactment, and is prepared to articulate the principles that are implicit in its terms or general structure. Perhaps most importantly, it has rejected the view that the Court merely declares the law, describing it as a 'fairytale'.[72]

The admission that the Court in some sense 'makes' the law has raised a number of difficulties. If indeed the Court makes the law then its impartiality, neutrality and lack of bias come into question. The difficulty this poses for the legitimacy of the Court is exacerbated by the argument that, in a democracy, law-making should only be undertaken by the representatives of the people. In fact, a judiciary that has authority to invalidate parliamentary enactments and appropriates the right to make laws appears to overturn the rule of law and assume supreme authority in the polity.

Community Values and the Common Law

There have been many attempts to formulate theories of interpretation that will justify the Court's role as law-maker. Though the declaratory theory retains some support, the dominant view on the Bench has been that it has a proper and legitimate role in repairing and keeping the law up-to-date with changing and fundamental community values.[73] The influence of sociological jurisprudence in this formulation is evident. Indeed, as we will note, the strengths and weaknesses of the Court's preferred formulation mirror those of sociological jurisprudence.

The community values argument appears to have a strong case in the interpretation and formulation of the common law. If the common law is viewed not as the declaration of an immemorial law but as judge-made law, then the role of judges as law-makers appears unavoidable. But if judges are no longer 'living oracles', if they exercise judgment to develop the law, are there any limits or constraints on judicial law-making? The Court's response has been to defend judicial law-making as repair and upkeep of the common law: judge-made law, an area of specialised (if not arcane) knowledge and expertise, should be altered by judges in order to keep up with the changes in society. Accordingly, common law judicial law-making relies not on the discretion of individual judges but on community values. If community values shape, guide and constrain the judiciary then it is possible to justify judicial law-making as a form of representative governance. By construing the community to include practitioners, scholars and the larger deliberative community, it may be possible to have more representative and therefore authoritative decisions by the Court. Clear judgments that are a consequence of public debate and discussion are more likely to reach an outcome that accords with the principles of the regime. At the very least they will have more significant support and acceptance in the community. As a consequence of adopting this method of interpretation the Court has been more willing to expose itself to what it considers informed criticism, making its judgments clearer and more accessible to the general public. It has been prepared to relax the rules of standing and broaden the range of interveners and *amicus curiae* (friends of the Court), especially in constitutional cases.[74] Judges have also been more willing to undertake extra-curial work, explaining the work of the Court by granting interviews, making public speeches and presenting papers at conferences.

Though this interpretive position offers a number of advantages to the Court, including justifying its judgments as a form of consensual elaboration of the direction sought by the community as a whole, there are a number of difficulties that recall the theoretical limitations of sociological jurisprudence outlined above. If, in referring to community values, the Court does not have in mind surveys and polling – the stuff of politics – but is more concerned with informed criticism and debate, the difficulty lies in evaluating the extent to which such criticism (whether through scholarly works, media commentary or even political criticism) may be said to represent the community. Perhaps the community holds no views on a matter, or its views are fundamentally divided. It is not evident that the judiciary is well-placed to discern community values, especially where the common law is not merely extended or applied by implication to related areas, but is radically altered or even overturned, as it was, for example, in the Court's decision in *Mabo*.[75] Political silence or inactivity may represent an impasse or indifference. In short, it is not always evident whether the judiciary is at the forefront or the rear of changing community values.

Moreover, who or what constitutes 'the community' is problematic in a larger sense. For example, the Court has stated that where there is uncertainty in the common law it may turn to jurisprudence from other countries and to international laws and conventions to inform its deliberations. Resorting to these international developments will certainly, over time, tend to produce an international common law and thereby a community of liberal-democratic regimes influenced and directed by their courts of final jurisdiction. But this would suggest that these courts are creating such a 'community' rather than taking their bearings from such communal values. Community values in this sense would appear to impose few restrictions on judicial law-making.[76]

The Court's attempt to rely on community values to justify its common law jurisprudence tends towards a definite political vision. It sees the regime as democratic, evolving and progressive, where change is determined by discussion, debate and deliberation. It justifies the judicial role as a sophisticated form of representative governance that is open to the concerns of an informed community. Importantly, it places the regime within an international community of like-minded and favourably disposed states that are evolving towards greater freedom. But within this understanding of the common law there persists a view that draws upon, or reintroduces, the classical common law.[77] For example, in *Mabo* the majority distinguishes between a common law that can be altered, and fundamental principles – such as the doctrine of tenures which Justice Brennan calls a 'skeletal' principle – that cannot be altered. The notion of a skeleton and thereby the body of the common law returns us to more ancient metaphors for the common law – a tree or stream that remains the same although changing over time.[78] This limitation on judicial discretion may perhaps be explained as no more than a jural postulate that guides and limits the recognition of interests. If so, it is a powerful reminder of how difficult it is to negotiate and distinguish between core and peripheral principles.

There is, however, a conception of the common law that does appear to radically limit the judicial task of progressive interpretation. According to a minority in the Court, there are deep and enduring values in the common law that cannot be altered by the judiciary, the Parliament or the people.[79] Though the claim that the common law is the foundation of the Constitution has been advanced before,[80] this view goes further by claiming that the legislative and executive power of Parliament is limited by common law rights, that the common law prevails over the Constitution. This suggestion is reminiscent of Coke's famous statement in *Doctor Bonham's* case that the common law will control Acts of Parliament, as well as his response to James I in *Prohibitions del Roy* that the artificial reason and judgment of the common law are superior to the natural reason of individuals.[81]

This argument can be said to reintroduce the common law and elements of the declaratory theory into the Court's jurisprudence. To the extent that the common law reconciles fundamental principles and change (acknowledging such a tension in its use of metaphors of tree or stream) it may be possible to retain an interpretation based on community values. However, where these fundamental principles are not conceived within the framework of the common law tradition, it appears they would limit, if not oust, a jurisprudence based on community values. Here the judiciary becomes the guardian of fundamental values, guiding and directing community values accordingly. The nature of the regime anticipated by such a theory of interpretation will depend on the character of the fundamental principles being interpreted. Where such principles reject parliamentary supremacy or popular sovereignty, or are not derived from 'nature' or 'humanity', this theory no longer necessarily favours or secures a liberal-democratic regime.

Interpreting the Constitution

The theoretical difficulties with the admission that the Court makes laws become more acute in the case of constitutional interpretation. How is the Court to interpret the Constitution? Clearly the answer to this question has far-reaching legal and political consequences, especially in Australia where few attempts at amending the Constitution have been successful and therefore the Court's constitutional decisions have assumed even greater importance, becoming for practical purposes the definitive interpretation and formulation of its terms.

The Constitution itself is silent regarding the way it should be interpreted. But the fact that it can only be altered by a majority vote of electors in the majority of States (section 128) suggests that in constitutional adjudication the Court has a duty to interpret and apply the law, not make it. That is, the founders' intentions, and the intentions of the electors who have amended the Constitution, should have a paramount role in interpretation of the Constitution. The High Court has to some extent accepted this argument, variously termed originalism or intentionalism, relying on the Constitutional Convention debates, drafts of the Constitution and other historical material to ascertain the meaning of constitutional provisions.[82]

The more prevalent view, however, has been that the Constitution is not a rigid blueprint, a detailed and exhaustive statement of the founders' intentions, but rather 'a set of general principles designed as a broad framework or outline for national government'.[83] The Constitution as a framework of government – as a living instrument – justifies a dynamic or progressive interpretation of its terms in the light of, and in accord with, community values and standards. From this point of view the framers' intentions become less important and in some cases seem like dead hands, 'reaching from their graves to negate or constrict the natural implications' of the Constitution's provisions or doctrines.[84] The debate between those who favour a progressive rather than an originalist inter-pretation of the Constitution need not be as intransigent in Australia as it is in America, especially if it can be shown that the founders supported a progressive interpretation. But looking at the founders' views would reveal, as noted above, that they were prepared to leave most matters of public import to the political processes, including in the Constitution only the minimal requirements of a federal union.

A dynamic or progressive interpretation of the Constitution raises profound questions concerning the legitimacy of judicial law-making. By taking into account community values and other fundamental principles when interpreting the Constitution, the judiciary can be said to 'con-stitutionalise' them. By transforming what was previously conventional or political in a broad sense into a justiciable matter, the judiciary in effect augments its authority and responsibility. For example, by construing the Constitution as more than a federal enactment the Court introduces into its general jurisprudence a judicial review based on human rights. Importantly, this process of constitutionalising exposes the Court to complex political, philosophical and social arguments that involve the very make-up of the regime, giving it the ability to alter the nature of the Constitution and thereby the potential to reorder or refound the regime. In this context we are forced to question whether dynamic interpret-ation, especially of the Constitution, effectively relieves the judiciary of the demands and constraints of the rule of law. Do the concepts of community (including, in its largest sense, international norms) or fun-damental values impose any significant limits on individual choice and discretion? These questions return us to the difficulties noted above concerning the formulation and use of jural postulates and scheme of interests in judicial law-making, inherent in the principles of sociological jurisprudence. To see how the Court has confronted them in practice it is necessary to consider its decisions on implied rights and separation of powers.

The consequences of resorting to community values and fundamental principles in interpreting the Constitution became evident in the series of controversial decisions on political speech handed down by the Mason Court. Though there is no explicit provision in the Constitution protect-ing freedom of speech, the High Court struck down Commonwealth and State legislation that unduly limited political discussion, on the grounds that political speech was essential for the system of representative demo-cracy guaranteed by the Constitution.[85] Thus these decisions, relying on the postulate of representative democracy, 'constitutionalised' the right of political speech.

Used this way, the concept of representative democracy appeared to give the judiciary a significant means of constitutionalising a range of other rights. In other words, dynamic or progressive interpretation appeared to provide a judicial *carte blanche*.[86] Aware of these criticisms, the Court subsequently moved away from the notion of representative democracy as the conceptual basis for interpreting rights, preferring to rely on specific constitutional provisions regarding the election of members of the House of Representatives and the Senate. Implications would have to be drawn from the structure of the Constitution or from the express terms derived by logical or practical necessity. [87]

Similarly, the Court has relied upon the concepts of separation of powers and the rule of law to impose limits on both the Commonwealth and the States, 'constitutionalising' aspects of criminal law including due process, fair trial and determination of guilt.[88] In these cases the Court has in fact relied on Chapter III (The Judicature), specifically section 71, of the Constitution to ground the notions of judicial power and the rule of law. Nevertheless, the potential for unbounded judicial discretion through the use of these concepts as interpretive principles is evident in certain minority judgments. For example, though there is no provision in the Constitution limiting Parliament's power to enact retrospective legislation, a minority in the *War Crimes* case held that the enactment of retrospective criminal laws could be considered a parliamentary usurpation of judicial power because it amounted to legislative judgment of guilt.[89] Similarly, Justice Gaudron in *Leeth* held that the concept of equal justice was fundamental to the judicial process: 'a concept which requires the like treatment of like persons in like circumstances, but also requires the genuine differences be treated as such'.[90] This formulation of equality before the law introduces the concept of substantive due process: not only will courts ensure procedural due process is observed, but now they are in a position to review the rationale for discrimination. By determining the character and scope of 'genuine difference' the Court becomes the arbiter of all legislation and determines the wisdom and efficacy of parliamentary enactments.

Like the Court's implied rights jurisprudence, these decisions reveal a Court concerned with its legitimacy, grounding its jurisprudence in the specific provisions or the structure of the Constitution. They also confirm the potential of a dynamic interpretation based on community values or fundamental principles to move from concepts such as representative democracy, separation of powers and the rule of law to larger claims that appear to impose no restrictions on judicial review.

What political settlement is implicit in such a dynamic interpretation of the Constitution? It cannot be denied that the Court has discerned in the Constitution and thereby established in Australia a form of representative democracy. In doing so, however, it has presented the barest

outlines of its view. There is little substantive content to the representative democracy depicted by the Court. It has put itself forward as a
defender of the Constitution, a protector of democratic processes, not
an advocate of any specific substantial democratic version of the regime.
As a variation of 'representation-reinforcing' judicial review, courts uphold the general structure of the regime and superintend the political
processes, while political life and all the substantive concerns of the
polity stand outside the purview of the judiciary. Not only does this
division legitimate the role of the judiciary, it provides almost unlimited
scope for democratic politics. Politics is to be left to politicians and
the direction it takes cannot be second-guessed or restrained by the
courts.[91]

This view arguably reproduces a more sophisticated version of the
political settlement effected in the *Engineers* case. But as the decisions
above show, neutral, process-based judicial review will slip into a more
substantive liberal-democratic jurisprudence.[92] This would suggest that
the Court's implied rights jurisprudence, though relatively restrained in
scope and ambition, nevertheless anticipates not only a representative
democracy that is progressive, enlightened and rational, but in some
instances a democracy that is limited by liberal rights and freedoms.

Sovereignty of the People

The other significant development in the Court's method of interpretation has been its view that sovereignty resides in, or derives from,
the people and therefore the Constitution is founded upon popular
sovereignty. It is arguable that from the beginning the Constitution
was based on the sovereignty of the Australian people: it was drafted
in Australia, debated in conventions, and finally adopted by means
of popular referendums. The acknowledgment in section 128 that the
Constitution can only be amended by the vote of electors confirms the
autochthonous nature of the enactment.[93]

As we have seen, this view was not accepted by the Court. Until the
passing of the *Australia Acts 1986* (Cth and UK) it held that the UK
Parliament retained power to legislate for Australia (for example by
passing the *Statute of Westminster 1931* (UK)), and British legislation
applying by paramount force could invalidate repugnant State legislation
pursuant to the *Colonial Laws Validity Act 1865* (UK). According to this
view, the Constitution was an Imperial Act of the British Parliament.

However, to a number of justices on the Court the passing of the *Australia Acts 1986*, which formally declared that the United Kingdom would
no longer legislate for Australia, marked the end of the legal sovereignty
of the Imperial Parliament (effectively making the United Kingdom a
foreign power)[94] and recognised that ultimate sovereignty resides in the

Australian people.[95] This argument appears to allow an easy transition from Imperial sovereignty to popular sovereignty, bringing constitutional interpretation up-to-date with the changes in political and legal developments. In this light popular sovereignty appears to be consistent with Burkean or Millian incrementalism, the result of keeping up with the evolutionary changes at the core of English constitutionalism.

But the move from Imperial to popular sovereignty is more than an incremental change. As a legal concept, sovereignty of the people is fundamentally different from Imperial sovereignty or the sovereignty of Imperial Parliament.[96] The shift from parliamentary sovereignty to sovereignty of the people is a theoretically radical departure with major legal and political ramifications. For the Court, sovereignty of the people introduces a more complex form of judicial review. The Court no longer simply ensures that the processes of parliamentary government are followed, it is now an institution that belongs to the people and exercises its powers for the people.[97] This gives greater legitimacy to the judiciary and, as a superintendent of the sovereign will of the people, the Court may elevate its role above other institutions, including Parliament.

In addition to augmenting judicial authority, the concept of sovereignty of the people introduces a different form of constitutionalism. If the Constitution derives its authority and legitimacy from the will of the people, it represents a radical constitutive formulation of the people's coming together. In this sense the view of the Constitution as a type of social contract draws upon different political and theoretical traditions with major consequences for the character of the regime. It may well be that as an expression of Lockean liberal constitutionalism the Constitution secures natural rights, limited government and representative government. However, sovereignty of the people also opens up a world of fundamentally different aspects of sovereignty, from Hobbes' sovereign to Rousseau's general will, and different political visions, from communitarianism to republicanism.[98] In these outer reaches the judicial task of interpreting and applying the law, of choosing the character of the political regime, becomes a delicate task more suited for the skills, abilities and discretion of a political philosopher and statesman.

Interpretation and Democracy

The High Court has abandoned its previous methods of interpretation and has declared that it now makes the law. Given the crucial importance of legitimacy for the judiciary, this admission has compelled the Court to reconcile its new role with the rule of law, to explain what law-making means for the judiciary. Hence its recent decisions are equally concerned with the proper basis for adjudication – the way the Court should interpret and develop the law – as with the substantive issues in each case.

In attempting to resolve the tension between judicial law-making and the rule of law, the Court has relied on a version of sociological jurisprudence. Though not abandoning the common law way of proceeding, this form of judicial law-making is justified as a legitimate way of bringing the law up-to-date with community values. Dynamic and progressive judicial review is seen as consistent with, and supplementary to, democratic governance. In this formulation the Court's law-making reflects the politics of the community; the judiciary do not have a democratic vision as such.

This apparently neutral and ministerial method of interpretation appears at odds with the presuppositions of sociological jurisprudence, namely, its separation of the legal and the political, its egalitarianism, its commitment to social democratic principles and its belief in change and progress. Therefore, contrary to the Court's claims, it would seem that dynamic interpretation does assume a vision of a democratic and representative regime. If, on the other hand, such a dynamic interpretation does not favour any specific political settlement, the Court's recent decisions suggest that the notion of community values may not in fact provide the anticipated check on individual judicial discretion. Minority judgments regarding the common law, implied rights, separation of powers and sovereignty of the people reveal the extent to which these concepts are sufficiently supple and complex to harbour divergent and in some instances irreconcilable positions. Perhaps these difficulties are no more than those faced by Pound and Stone regarding the ascertainment of interests, the establishment of community or societal values and their reconciliation with jural postulates or fundamental values. If indeed they are inherent limitations to the dynamic method of interpretation, they open the possibility of individual judicial preferences being implemented under the auspices of justice, progress and community demands.

In any case, the inherent pluralism of dynamic interpretation has introduced into the High Court's jurisprudence a greater willingness to appropriate a range of concepts, theories and ideas in trying to reach a just outcome. Such an apparently neutral method of interpretation has therefore led to the Court's adoption of fundamentally different theoretical frameworks and political settlements. For example, the need for a just outcome has meant that some justices have employed fundamental values of the common law at the same time as resorting to notions of popular sovereignty and the social contract theories of sovereignty. In other words, though the Court has proposed a representative and progressive democracy as a minimal political vision, its decisions also prefigure regimes based on common law principles, liberal democratic regimes based on popular sovereignty and potentially republican regimes relying on representative institutions. In short, its method of interpretation has made possible these different political visions without specifying the bases for choosing between them. The inability of dynamic interpretation to rank, arbitrate or negotiate between these different views represents its fundamental limitation as a method of interpretation.

The politics of interpretation can be seen in the specifics of judicial method, in the Court's understanding of its role in the Australian community and, in its largest signification, in the character of the Australian regime and constitutionalism it favours. The Court has acknowledged its increasing role in the shaping of Australian politics. In doing so it has opened itself to a world beyond legal authority and precedent, to unfamiliar historical, political and philosophical terrain. It has done so, however, without a distinct theoretical basis for negotiating the different notions of democracy it is confronting. How it faces these difficulties, and its success in meeting these challenges, will have major implications for Australian constitutionalism.

Notes

1 *D'Emden v Pedder* (1904) 1 CLR 91; *Railway Servants* case (1906) 4 CLR 488.
2 *Peterswald v Bartley* (1904) 1 CLR 497; *Union Label* case (1908) 6 CLR 469; *Huddart Parker & Co Pty Ltd v Moorehead* (1909) 8 CLR 330.
3 *Baxter v Commissioner of Taxation* (NSW) (1907) 4 CLR 1087 at 1093.
4 The Court's jurisprudence relied heavily on the decisions of the US Supreme Court, in particular the decision of Marshall J in *McCulloch v Maryland* (1819) 4 Wheat 316.
5 See Latham, Sir John 1961, 'Interpretation of the Constitution' in R. Else-Mitchell (ed.), *Essays on the Australian Constitution*, Sydney, Law Book Co., 1–48; Goldring, J. 1997, 'The Path to Engineers' in M. Coper & G. Williams (eds), *How Many Cheers for Engineers?*, Sydney, Federation Press, 1–44.
6 *Amalgamated Society of Engineers v Adelaide Steamship Co Ltd* (1920) 28 CLR 129.
7 The joint judgment of Knox CJ, Isaacs, Rich and Starke JJ was delivered by Isaacs J. Higgins J delivered a separate judgment agreeing with the majority. Gavan Duffy J dissented.
8 *Engineers* at 142.
9 ibid. at 145.
10 ibid. at 152.
11 ibid. at 149.
12 Warden, J. 1993, 'The Fettered Republic: The Anglo-American Commonwealth and the Traditions of Australian Political Thought', *Australian Journal of Political Science*, 28: 83; Stokes, M. 1986, 'Federalism, Responsible Government and the Protection of Private Rights: A New Interpretation of the Limits of the Legislative Powers of the Commonwealth', *Federal Law Review*, 16: 135; Galligan, B. 1987, *The Politics of the High Court*, Brisbane, University of Queensland Press, ch. 2.
13 Knox CJ, Rich and Starke JJ were lawyers with little political experience. As Goldring notes in 'Path to Engineers' at 39, Isaacs and Higgins JJ, who took

part in the framing of the Constitution, never ceased to look at the Constitution from the perspective of lawyers.

14 cf Meale, D. 1992, 'The History of the Federal Idea in Australian Constitutional Jurisprudence: A Reappraisal', *Australian Journal of Law and Society* 8: 25; Fraser, A. 1990, *The Spirit of the Laws: Republicanism and the Unfinished Project of Modernity,* Toronto, University of Toronto Press.

15 *Calvin's* case (1608) 7 Co Rep 1 at 3b; *Prohibitions del Roy* (1608) 12 Co Rep 1.

16 Blackstone, W. 1765, *Commentaries on the Laws of England,* Oxford, Clarendon Press, introduction, section 2.

17 See generally Lobban, M. 1991, *The Common Law and English Jurisprudence, 1760–1850,* Oxford, Oxford University Press; Simpson, A.W. 1973, 'The Common Law and Legal Theory' in *Oxford Studies in Jurisprudence,* Oxford, Oxford University Press; Twining, W. (ed.) 1986, *Legal Theory and Common Law,* Oxford, Blackwell; Davies, M. 1994, *Asking the Law Question,* Sydney: Law Book Co.

18 One of the earliest critics of the common law, anticipating many of the modern 'philosophical' objections, is Hobbes: see his *A Dialogue Between a Philosopher and a Student of the Common Laws of England,* as well as *Leviathan.* For a response to Hobbes, see Hale's *Reflections by the Lord Chiefe Justice Hale on Mr Hobbes his Dialogue of the Law.*

19 Postema, G. 1986, *Bentham and the Common Law Tradition,* Oxford, Clarendon Press.

20 Bryce, J. 1919, *The American Commonwealth,* 2nd edn, New York, Macmillan; Bryce, J. 1901, *Studies of History and Jurisprudence,* Oxford, Clarendon Press. With respect to the importance of these concepts for the High Court's understanding of sovereignty see, for example, *Clayton v Heffron* (1960) 105 CLR 214; *Union Steamship Co of Australia Pty Ltd v King* (1988) 166 CLR 1; *R v Kirby; Ex parte Boilermakers' Society of Australia* (1956) 94 CLR 254.

21 Dicey, A.V. [1885] 1915, *Introduction to the Law of the Constitution,* 8th edn, London, Macmillan; Dicey, A.V. [1914] 1926, *Lectures on the Relation between Law and Public Opinion in England,* 2nd edn, London, Macmillan. See generally *Chu Kheng Lim v Minister for Immigration, Local Government and Ethnic Affairs* (1992) 176 CLR 1; Sugarman, D. 1983, 'The Legal Boundaries of Liberty: Dicey, Liberalism and Legal Science', *Modern Language Review* 102; Loughlin, M. 1992, *Public Law and Political Theory,* Oxford, Clarendon Press; Patapan, Haig 1997, 'The Author of Liberty: Dicey, Mill and the Shaping of English Constitutionalism', *Public Law Review* 25: 211.

22 *Engineers* at 151.

23 *Law and Public Opinion in England,* Lecture XI and Note IV in the appendix. According to Dicey, the limitations of judicial law-making include the fact that the judiciary cannot openly declare a new principle; statutory principles cannot be simply set aside; established principles cannot be amended; judicial legislation can exhaust principles; and the law has a hypothetical character until confirmed by the highest court (Note IV).

24 Compare Galligan's claim in *Politics of the High Court* that legalism was an intentional rhetorical device employed by the Court. See in this context the debate between Galligan and Goldsworthy in (1989) *Federal Law Review* 18: 27–52.

25 Zines, L. 1997, *The High Court and the Constitution,* Sydney, Butterworths, ch. 1.

26 *Engineers* at 151–2.

27 See for example the judgments of Latham CJ in *South Australia v Common-wealth (First Uniform Tax* case) (1942) 65 CLR 373 at 409; the often-quoted praise of 'strict and complete legalism' by Sir Owen Dixon on his appoint-ment as Chief Justice ((1952) 85 CLR xiv); and the praise of 'legal reasoning' by Barwick CJ in *A-G (Cth); Ex rel McKinley v Commonwealth* (1975) 135 CLR 1 at 17. It should be noted, however, that the way these terms were subse-quently employed was distanced from strict literalism: see Zines, *The High Court and the Constitution*, 424–32; Booker, K. & Glass, Arther 1997, 'What Makes the *Engineers* Case a Classic' in M. Coper & G. Williams (eds), *How Many Cheers for Engineers?*, Sydney, Federation Press, 45–71.

28 *Victoria v Commonwealth (Payroll Tax* case) (1971) 122 CLR 353 at 396 per Windeyer J; Zines, *The High Court and the Constitution*, 14–15.

29 See generally Galligan, *Politics of the High Court*; Lee, H.P. 1992, 'The High Court and External Affairs Power' in H.P. Lee & G. Winterton (eds), *Aus-tralian Constitutional Perspectives*, Sydney, Law Book Co., 60–91. The *Engineers* decision regarding reserved powers has been followed in subsequent cases: see for example *Strickland v Rocla Concrete Pipes Ltd* (1971) 124 CLR 468. But the principle of intergovernmental immunities rejected in the *Engineers* case has since been revived: see *Melbourne Corporation v Commonwealth* (1947) 74 CLR 31; *Queensland Electricity Commission v Commonwealth* (1985) 159 CLR 192; *Re State Public Services Federation; Ex parte Victoria* (1995) 184 CLR 188.

30 See for example *First Uniform Tax* case (1941) 65 CLR 373 at 409 per Latham CJ; *Australian National Airlines* case (1945) 71 CLR 29 at 70 per Rich J; *McKinlay's* case (1975) 135 CLR 1 at 17 per Barwick CJ.

31 (1952) 85 CLR xii–xiv.

32 See Gageler, S. 1987, 'Foundations of Australian Federalism and the Role of Judicial Review', *Federal Law Review*, 17: 162.

33 *R v Federal Court of Bankruptcy; Ex parte Lowenstein* (1937) 57 CLR 765 regarding trial by jury; *A-G (Vic) Ex rel Black v Commonwealth* (1980) 146 CLR 559 on religious freedom; *Henry v Boehm* (1973) 128 CLR 482 cf *Street v Queensland Bar Association* (1989) 168 CLR 461 regarding equal rights of residents in different States. In general see Williams, G. 1999, *Human Rights under the Australian Constitution*, Melbourne, Oxford University Press; Hanks, P. 1992, 'Constitutional Guarantees' in Lee & Winterton, *Australian Constit-utional Perspectives*, 92–128; Mason, Sir Anthony 1986, 'The Role of Con-stitutional Court in a Federation: A Comparison of the Australian and the United States Experience', *Federal Law Review* 16: 1, 6–11.

34 See Irving, H. 1997, *To Constitute a Nation: A Cultural History of Australia's Constitution*, Cambridge, Cambridge University Press; Davidson, A. 1991, *The Invisible State: The Formation of the Australian State 1788–1901*, Cambridge, Cambridge University Press; Detmold, M.J. 1985, *The Australian Common-wealth: A Fundamental Analysis of its Constitution*, Sydney, Law Book Co.; Kercher, B. 1995, *An Unruly Child: A History of Law in Australia*, Sydney, Allen & Unwin.

35 For an indication of its strength see Menzies, Sir Robert 1967, *Central Power in the Australian Commonwealth*, London, Cassell, 52–4; Dixon, Sir Owen 1942, 'Address at the Annual Dinner of the American Bar Association', *Australian Law Journal*, 16: 192; Galligan, B. 1990, 'Australia's Rejection of a Bill of Rights', *Journal of Commonwealth and Comparative Politics*, 28: 344; Fraser, A. 1990, *The Spirit of the Laws: Republicanism and the Unfinished Project of Modernity*, Toronto, University of Toronto Press.

36 For the various views regarding this proposition see generally Coper & Williams, *How Many Cheers for Engineers?*; Craven, G. 1992, 'The Crisis of Constitutional Literalism in Australia' in Lee & Winterton, *Australian Constitutional Perspectives*; Williams, G. 1995, '*Engineers* is Dead, Long Live Engineers!' *Sydney Law Review*, 17: 62.

37 See generally Galligan, *Politics of the High Court*; Bennett, J.M. 1980, *Keystone of the Federal Arch: A Historical Memoir of the High Court of Australia to 1980*, Canberra, Australian Government Publishing Service; Sawer, G. 1956, *Australian Federal Politics and Law, 1901–1929*, Melbourne, Melbourne University Press; Sawer, G. 1963, *Australian Federal Politics and Law, 1929–1949*, Melbourne, Melbourne University Press.

38 The appeals to the Privy Council were favoured by the British Colonial Office, a group of colonial Chief Justices and retired judges, and English investors. See La Nauze, J.A. 1972, *The Making of the Australian Constitution*, Melbourne, Melbourne University Press, 173, 220–1, 248–9.

39 See *Piro v W. Foster & Co Ltd* (1943) 68 CLR 313.

40 *Parker v The Queen* (1963) 111 CLR 610. See also *Skelton v Collin* (1966) 115 CLR 94; Menzies, Sir Douglas 1968, 'Australia and the Judicial Committee of the Privy Council', *Australian Law Journal*, 43: 79.

41 *Viro v The Queen* (1978) 52 ALJR 418.

42 In theory, a right of appeal to the Privy Council remains under s. 74 of the Constitution. However, such appeals require a certificate from the High Court and the Court has since 1914 declined all such requests. In *Kirmani v Captain Cook Cruises Pty Ltd [No 2]* (1985) 159 CLR 461, the Court described s. 74 appeals as obsolete.

43 The constitutional role of the Court was anticipated by Sir Garfield Barwick as early as 1964: see Barwick, Sir Garfield 1964, 'The Australian Judicial System: The Proposed New Federal Court', *Federal Law Review*, 1: 1; Barwick, Sir Garfield 1979, 'The State of the Australian Judicature', *Australian Law Journal*, 53: 487; Bennett, *Keystone of the Federal Arch*, 82ff.

44 A competition to design the building took place in 1972–73 and construction began in 1975. The first hearing there took place in June 1980. The Court is now a major tourist attraction. Its website (http://www.hcourt.gov.au) is a popular and sophisticated introduction to the building and the work of the Court.

45 See O'Brien, David 1996, *Special Leave to Appeal: The Law and Practice of Application for Special Leave to Appeal to the High Court of Australia*, Sydney, Law Book Co.; *Judiciary Act 1903* (Cth), s. 35A.

46 See *Dugan v Mirror Newspapers Ltd* (1979) 142 CLR 583; *State Government Insurance Commission v Trigwell* (1979) 142 CLR 617; *Australian Conservation Foundation Inc v Commonwealth* (1980) 146 CLR 493; McHugh, M. 1988, 'The Law-making Function of the Judicial Process', *Australian Law Journal*, 62: 18 (Part I), 20–4.

47 McHugh, 'The Law-making Function of the Judicial Process'; Lord Reid 1972, 'The Judge as Law-maker', *Journal of the Society of Public Teachers of Law*, 12: 22; Lester, A. 1993, 'English Judges as Law Makers', *Public Law* 269; Sturgess, G. & Chubb, P. 1988, *Judging the World*, Sydney, Butterworths, 257–93.

48 See in general Charlesworth, H. 1993, 'The Australian Reluctance about Rights', *Osgoode Hall Law Journal*, 31: 195; Galligan, 'Australia's Rejection of a Bill of Rights', 344.

49 Bailey, P. 1990, *Human Rights: Australia in an International Context*, Sydney, Butterworths; Tenbensel, T. 1996, 'International Human Rights Conventions and Australian Political Debates: Issues Raised by the Toonen Case', *Australian Journal of Political Science*, 31: 7; Charlesworth, H. 1991, 'Australia's Accession to the First Optional Protocol to the International Covenant on Civil and Political Rights', *Melbourne University Law Review* 18: 428.

50 Mason, Sir Anthony 1989, 'A Bill of Rights for Australia?', *Australian Bar Review* 5: 79; Brennan, Sir Gerard 1992, 'The Impact of a Bill of Rights on the Role of the Judiciary: An Australian Response', paper delivered at a conference on Human Rights, University House, Canberra, 16 July; Toohey, J. 1993, 'A Government of Laws, and Not of Men?', *Public Law Review*, 4: 158.

51 See generally Hunt, A. 1978, *The Sociological Movement in Law*, London, Macmillan, ch. 2.

52 Stone, J. 1961, *The Province and Function of Law: Law as Logic, Justice and Social Control*, Sydney, Maitland Publications; Stone, J. 1966, *Social Dimensions of Law and Justice*, Sydney, Maitland Publications; Stone, J. 1965, *Human Law and Human Justice*, Stanford, Stanford University Press. For a bibliography of the published works of Julius Stone see Blackshield, A.R. (ed.) 1983, *Legal Change: Essays in Honour of Julius Stone*, Sydney, Butterworths, 335–44.

53 Stone, *Social Dimensions of Law and Justice*, 4.

54 See generally Stone, *The Province and Function of Law*, chs vi, vii, regarding fallacies of the logical form in legal reasoning. The specific fallacies include the legal category of meaningless reference, concealed multiple reference, competing reference, concealed circuitous reference and indeterminate reference.

55 ibid., 358–61; Stone, *Human Law and Human Justice*, ch. 9.

56 Refer to the critique in Stone, *The Province and Function of Law* generally, and Hunt, *The Sociological Movement in Law*.

57 Stone, *The Province and Function of Law*, 365–6; Stone, *Human Law and Human Justice*, 269–77.

58 Stone, *The Province and Function of Law*, 363–5; Stone, *Human Law and Human Justice*, 275–7.

59 Stone, *The Province and Function of Law*, 362–7.

60 ibid., 366–8.

61 Hunt, *The Sociological Movement in Law*, 39.

62 Compare the jural postulates outlined by Pound in Stone, *The Province and Function of Law*, 367, with the general discussion by Stone in *The Province and Function of Law*, chs xxi, xxii; Stone, *Social Dimensions of Law and Justice*, chs 6–8.

63 For an indication of Stone's influence see the essays in Blackshield, *Legal Change*; Walker, G. 1988, *The Rule of Law: Foundation of Constitutional Democracy*, Melbourne, Melbourne University Press, 175; Sturgess & Chubb, *Judging the World*, 13, 15; Star, L. 1992, *Julius Stone: An Intellectual Life*, Melbourne, Oxford University Press in association with Sydney University Press.

64 Kirby, M. 1983, 'Law Reform as "Ministering to Justice"' in Blackshield, *Legal Change*, 201. As Kirby demonstrates, Stone was also influential in shaping the course of institutional law reform in Australia.

65 To Murphy, not only did judges make law, they had a positive duty to do so – the judicial role supplemented the parliamentary and political. He argued that the Constitution was based on sovereignty of the people, and that it implicitly protected a number of fundamental rights including the right to

vote, free speech, movement and equality. See Ely, J. & Ely, R. 1986, *Lionel Murphy: The Rule of Law*, Sydney, Akron Press; Scutt, J. (ed.) 1987, *Lionel Murphy: A Radical Judge*, Melbourne, McCulloch Publishing; Hocking, J. 1997, *Lionel Murphy: A Political Biography*, Cambridge, Cambridge University Press; Williams, J. 1997, 'Revitalizing the Republic: Lionel Murphy and the Protection of Individual Rights', *Public Law Review*, 8: 27.

66 See generally Coper, M. & Williams, G. (eds) 1997, *Justice Lionel Murphy: Influential or Merely Prescient?*, Sydney Federation Press.

67 Mason, 'The Role of Constitutional Court in a Federation'. For similar views published around the same time consider McHugh, 'The Law-making Function of the Judicial Process'.

68 Mason, 'The Role of Constitutional Court in a Federation', 5.

69 ibid., 28.

70 ibid., 24–7.

71 ibid., 11–13.

72 Mason, Sir Anthony 1996, 'The Judge as Law-Maker', *James Cook University Law Review*, 3: 1; Gleeson, A.M. 1999, 'Legal Oil and Political Vinegar', Sydney Institute, Sydney, 16 March 1999; Craven, G. 1992, 'After Literalism, What?', *Melbourne University Law Review*, 18: 874; Craven, G. 1993, 'Cracks in the Facade of Literalism: Is there an Engineer in the House?', *Melbourne University Law Review* 19: 540; Fullagar, I. 1993, 'The Role of the High Court: Law or Politics?', *Law Institute Journal*, 67: 72; Lindell, G. 1994, 'Recent Developments in the Judicial Interpretation of the Australian Constitution' in G. Lindell (ed.), *Future Directions in Australian Constitutional Law*, Sydney, Federation Press, 1–46; Lane, P. 1996, 'The Changing Role of the High Court', *Australian Law Journal*, 70: 246.

73 See generally Preston, K. & Sampford, C.J.G. (eds) 1996, *Interpreting Constitutions: Theories, Principles and Institutions*, Sydney, Federation Press; Thomson, J. A. 1982, 'Principles and Theories of Constitutional Interpretation and Adjudication: Some Preliminary Notes', *Melbourne University Law Review*, 13: 597; Mason, Sir Anthony, 1995, 'Trends in Constitutional Interpretation', *University of New South Wales Law Journal*, 18: 237; Mason, Sir Anthony 1996, 'Courts and Community Values', *Eureka Street*, 6: 32; Brennan, Sir Gerard 1993, 'A Critique of Criticism', *Monash University Law Review*, 19: 1; Gleeson, M. 1997, 'The Role of the Judiciary in a Modern Democracy', Judicial Conference of Australia Annual Symposium, Sydney, 8 November.

74 *Bateman's Bay Local Aboriginal Land Council v Aboriginal Community Benefit Fund Pty Ltd* [1998] HCA 49 (6 August 1998); *Levy v Victoria* (1997) 189 CLR 579.

75 *Mabo v Queensland (No 2)* 175 CLR 1.

76 Kirby, M. 1995, 'The Role of International Standards in Australian Courts' in P. Alston & M. Chiam (eds), *Treaty-making and Australia: Globalisation versus Sovereignty*, Sydney, Federation Press; Saunders, C. (ed.) 1996, *Courts of Final Jurisdiction: The Mason Court in Australia*, Sydney, Federation Press, part II. For example, almost all human rights conventions were the result of compromise and negotiations during drafting and adoption. Therefore, there is a potential range of conflicting principles enshrined in each enactment, authority for a range of differing outcomes.

77 Of course, to abandon the declaratory theory is not to abandon the way common law proceeds in general, for example, the incremental nature of the adversarial system, the requirement and limitations of *stare decisis* or precedent, the need to hear cases and issue judgments, to take into account all

the procedural requirements of adjudication. In fact, these requirements have posed problems as well as offering the Court opportunities in developing its jurisprudence.

78 Sandoz, E. (ed.) 1993, *The Roots of Liberty,* Columbia, University of Missouri Press; Pocock, J.G.A. 1987, *The Ancient Constitution and the Feudal Law,* Cambridge, Cambridge University Press.

79 For an early formulation of this possibility see *Union Steamship Co of Australia Pty Ltd v King* (1988) 166 CLR 1. Deane and Toohey JJ rely on this argument in *Leeth v Commonwealth* (1992) 174 CLR 455 and *Nationwide News Pty Ltd v Wills* (1992) 177 CLR 1. For the majority view rejecting this see *Kable v Director of Public Prosecutions for the State of New South Wales* (1996) 189 CLR 51; Zines, *The High Court and the Constitution,* 418–20.

80 Dixon, Sir Owen 1965, 'The Common Law as the Ultimate Constitutional Foundation' in *Jesting Pilate,* Melbourne: Law Book Co.; *Uther v Federal Commissioner of Taxation* (1947) 74 CLR 508 at 521; *Cheatle v R* (1993) 177 CLR 541 at 552; Zines, *The High Court and the Constitution,* 400–2; Mason, Sir Anthony 1996, 'An Australian Common Law', *Law in Context,* 14: 81; Brennan, Sir Gerard 1991, 'Courts, Democracy and the Law', *Australian Law Journal,* 65: 32; Castles, A. 1982, *An Australian Legal History,* Sydney, Law Book Co., ch. 17.

81 *Doctor Bonham's* case (1610) 8 Co Rep 114; *Prohibitions del Roy* (1608) 12 Co Rep 63. For Coke's view of 'higher law' see Stoner, J. 1992, *Common Law and Liberal Theory,* Lawrence, Kan.: University of Kansas Press, chs 1–3.

82 See for example *Cole v Whitfield* (1988) 165 CLR 360; *New South Wales v Commonwealth* (1990) 169 CLR 482; Craven, G. 1990, 'Original Intent and the Australian Constitution: Coming to a Court Near You', *Public Law Review* 1: 166; Goldsworthy, J. 1997, 'Originalism in Constitutional Interpretation', *Federal Law Review* 25: 1; McCamish, C. 1996, 'The Use of Historical Materials in Interpreting the Commonwealth Constitution', *Australian Law Journal* 70: 648; Dawson, Sir Daryl 1990, 'Intention and the Constitution: Whose Intent?', *Australian Bar Review* 6: 93.

83 Mason, 'Trends in Constitutional Interpretation', 238; Mason, 'The Judge as Law-maker'.

84 *Theophanous v Herald & Weekly Times Ltd* (1993) 124 ALR 1 at 50 per Deane J; Patapan, H. 1997, 'The Dead Hand of the Founders? Original Intent and the Constitutional Protection of Rights and Freedoms in Australia', *Federal Law Review,* 25: 211.

85 *Nationwide News Pty Ltd v Wills* (1992) 177 CLR 1; *Australian Capital Television Pty Ltd v Commonwealth* (1992) 177 CLR 106; *Theophanous v Herald & Weekly Times Ltd* (1994) 182 CLR 104; *Stephens v Western Australian Newspapers Ltd* (1994) 182 CLR 211.

86 See the various articles in the Symposium on Constitutional Rights for Australia in (1994) *Sydney Law Review* 16: 1; Doyle, J. 1993, 'Constitutional Law: "At the Eye of the Storm"', *University of Western Australia Law Review* 23: 15; Horrigan, B. 1995, 'Is the High Court Crossing the Rubicon? A Framework for Balanced Debate', *Public Law Review* 6: 284; Blackshield, A.R. 1994, 'The Implied Freedom of Communication' in G. Lindell (ed.), *Future Directions in Australian Constitutional Law,* Sydney, Federation Press, 232–68; Williams, '*Engineers* is Dead, Long Live Engineers!'.

87 *McGinty v Western Australia* (1996) 186 CLR 140.

88 *Leeth v Commonwealth* (1992) 174 CLR 455; *Chu Kheng Lim v Minister for Immigration* (1992) 176 CLR 1; *Dietrich v R* (1992) 177 CLR 292; *Polyukhovich*

v Commonwealth (1991) 172 CLR 501; Hope, J. 1996, 'A Constitutional Right to a Fair Trial? Implications for the Reform of the Australian Criminal Justice System', *Federal Law Review,* 24: 173; Winterton, G. 1994, 'The Separation of Judicial Power as an Implied Bill of Rights' in Lindell, *Future Directions in Australian Constitutional Law,* 185–208.

89 *Polyukhovich v Commonwealth* (1991) 172 CLR 501 at 608 per Deane J, at 705 per Gaudron J.

90 *Leeth v Commonwealth* (1992) 174 CLR 455 at 502; Saunders, C. 1994, 'Concepts of Equality in the Australian Constitution' in Lindell, *Future Directions in Australian Constitutional Law,* 209–31.

91 Tucker, D. 1994, 'Representation-reinforcing Review: Arguments about Political Advertising in Australia and the United States', *Sydney Law Review,* 16: 274; Galligan, D. 1983, 'Judicial Review and Democratic Principles: Two Theories', *Australian Law Review,* 57: 69; Ely, J.H. 1980, *Democracy and Distrust: A Theory of Judicial Review,* Harvard, Harvard University Press.

92 See in this context Tribe, L. 1980, 'The Puzzling Persistence of Process-based Constitutional Theories', *Yale Law Journal,* 89: 1063; Ackerman, B. 1985, 'Beyond Carolene Products', *Harvard Law Review,* 98: 713; Berger, R. 1979, 'Government by Judiciary: John Hart Ely's "Invitation"', *Indiana Law Journal,* 54: 277.

93 Murphy J argued along these lines: see *China Ocean Shipping Co v South Australia* (1979) 145 CLR 172 at 236–7. See generally Detmold, *The Australian Commonwealth*; Winterton, G. 1986, 'Extra-constitutional Notions in Australian Constitutional Law', *Federal Law Review,* 16: 223, 235–8.

94 *Sue v Hill* (1999) 163 ALR 648.

95 *Australian Capital Television Pty Ltd v Commonwealth* (1992) 177 CLR 106 at 137–8 per Mason CJ; *Nationwide News Pty Ltd v Wills* (1992) 177 CLR 1 at 70 per Deane and Toohey JJ; *Theophanous v Herald & Weekly Times Ltd* (1994) 182 CLR 104 at 180 per Deane J; McHugh J, *McGinty v Western Australia* (1996) 134 ALR at 343-4. See Zines, *The High Court and the Constitution,* 393–7; Winterton, G. 1998, 'Popular Sovereignty and Constitutional Continuity', *Federal Law Review* 26: 1; Wright, H.G.A. 1998, 'Sovereignty of the People: The New *Grundnorm?*', *Federal Law Review* 26: 165.

96 As Zines, *The High Court and the Constitution,* 394–5 notes, British Parliament is a specific body that can exercise its will in the form of enactments and other ways that are different from the will of 'people', which requires representatives to implement its will. Secondly, unlike Parliament, the people cannot legally or practically control or direct the institutions created to carry out its will. Finally, the Commonwealth Parliament was not accountable to Imperial Parliament the way it is said to be accountable to the people.

97 Mason, Sir Anthony 1993, 'The Role of the Judge at the Turn of the Century', Fifth Annual AIJA Oration in Judicial Administration, Melbourne, 5 November, 29–30.

98 See generally Williams, G. 1995, 'A Republican Tradition for Australia?', *Federal Law Review,* 23: 133; the debate between George Williams and Andrew Fraser in (1995) *Federal Law Review,* 23: 362–77; Fraser, A. 1990, *The Spirit of the Laws,* Toronto, University of Toronto Press; Special issue 1993, *Australian Journal of Political Science,* 28; Hudson, W. & Carter, D. 1993, *The Republicanism Debate,* Sydney, New South Wales University Press; Cristaudo, W. 1993, 'Republic of Australia? The Political Philosophy of Republicanism', *Current Affairs Bulletin,* 69: 4.

CHAPTER 3

Politics of Rights

A defining feature of the new politics of the High Court is its human rights jurisprudence. Yet in augmenting its federal judicial review with decisions that discerned certain implied rights and freedoms in the Constitution, the Court was charged with improper activism and political adventurism. In fact, in elaborating an implied freedom of political speech the Court was said to be creating a right that was not in the Constitution, the first step in a larger and more ambitious judicial project to develop a comprehensive implied Bill of Rights.

Why was the Court prepared to undertake this apparently contentious jurisprudence? What was the character of the rights and freedoms being 'discovered'? What implications did these decisions have for the nature of Australian constitutionalism and democracy? This chapter will examine the Court's jurisprudence of rights and freedoms to confront, engage and respond to these important questions. It will do so by placing the Court's implied rights decisions within the larger context of Australian parliamentary tradition and the various unsuccessful attempts in Australia to entrench a Bill of Rights. These cases are contrasted with the Court's recent human rights decisions that are informed by international legal developments and therefore appear to be introducing changes to Australian constitutionalism.[1]

Rights and the Constitution

Though the Australian Constitution has a limited number of express rights, such as the requirement that Parliament acquire property on just terms (section 51xxxi), the requirement of trial by jury for indictable offences (section 80), freedom of religion (section 116) and limits on State discrimination based on residence (section 117), it does not have a

Bill of Rights.[2] This fact seems unusual given that the founders relied extensively on the American Constitution. Why did the founders not entrench in the Australian Constitution a version of the American Bill of Rights – the first ten amendments to the US Constitution?

An important starting-point in attempting to answer this question is the realisation that though the framers of Australia's Constitution drew extensively from American constitutionalism, particularly in relation to the innovation that was federalism, the Australian Constitution was seen as a continuation and development of English constitutionalism, an evolutionary advance rather than a break from 'Mother England'. English common law formed the backbone of the colonies, and institutions such as representative and responsible government were gradually transplanted and claimed as 'ancient rights and lawful liberties' by the colonists.[3] Though marking legal and political emancipation from English dominance, these measures in fact underlined the extent to which the colonies represented a continuation of constitutional traditions.

An essential aspect of this tradition was the 'conventional' dimension to Constitutions, which allows us to understand better the apparently unlimited and unconstrained powers given to colonial legislatures.[4] The absence of entrenched Bills of Rights and rights-based limitations on the exercise of power would seem to suggest that the colonists were unconcerned with the protection of civil liberties. In fact, the common law was regarded as one of the most important measures for the protection of immemorial rights and liberties. Though common law rights were subject to parliamentary control and therefore could be limited for the public good, this was not considered to pose a major threat to liberty because Parliament itself was seen as a manifestation and defence of another form of liberty – the right to be represented and participate, through voting, in the formulation of laws. To the founders, the executive and not Parliament posed the greatest threat to liberty.

This notion of rights can be discerned most clearly in the course of the Australian founding. Though the founders were prepared to entrench a federal Constitution which was 'written and rigid', contrary to the 'elastic' English model that had served well in protecting rights and privileges, they did not entrench a Bill of Rights. When we turn to the Convention Debates to discover why specific provisions were incorporated into the Constitution, we see that the few rights that were retained in the Constitution were considered either an aspect of federalism or a harmless confirmation of existing rights and freedoms.[5]

The founders' conception of rights, derived from English constitutionalism, drew upon, and encompassed, a number of philosophical traditions. These included the common law tradition as articulated in the writings of Hale, Coke and Blackstone, the Burkean notion of prescriptive rights, and the more recent concepts as developed by Bentham. But the dominant view of the founders was largely a utilitarianism that had been 'corrected' by Mill; the founders were Millian progressives rather than Benthamite utilitarians. To them, Parliament was to have unrestricted authority, untrammelled by constitutional limitations; its hands were not to be tied because it represented the primary means for addressing political problems as they emerged. Parliamentary supremacy and the rule of law protected freedom and made progress possible, allowing human beings to evolve and advance from barbarism and intolerance to enlightenment and civilisation. Community was not based on such abstract notions as nature, contract and citizenship; to limit Parliament by entrenching rights was to question the motives of Parliament and, implicitly, to assume progress was questionable.

Parliamentarianism

This theoretical perspective, based on parliamentarianism, the common law and traditional rights, persists as a powerful orthodoxy in Australia. For example, it was endorsed by Menzies, Australia's longest-serving Prime Minister and founder of the Liberal Party, as is evident from a series of lectures he delivered at the University of Virginia in 1967 after retiring from office. In *Central Power in the Australian Commonwealth*, a collection of those lectures, Menzies summarises his views regarding the absence of specific rights in the Australian Constitution:

> In short, responsible government in a democracy is regarded by us as the ultimate guarantee of justice and individual rights. Except for our inheritance of British institutions and the principles of the Common Law, we have not felt the need for formality and definition.[6]

That Menzies quotes at length Sir Owen Dixon's well-known speech delivered to the American Bar Association in 1942, reveals the extent to which this orthodoxy informed and dominated the judiciary. According to Sir Owen Dixon, the founders were not prepared to place fetters upon legislative action because:

> in Australia one view held was that these checks on legislative action were undemocratic, because to adopt them argued a want of confidence in the will of the people. Why, asked the Australian democrats, should doubt be thrown on the wisdom and safety of entrusting to the chosen representatives of the people sitting either in the federal Parliament or in the State Parliaments all legislative power, substantially without fetter or restriction?[7]

The views expressed by Sir Owen Dixon were shared by a number of judges who regarded Parliament as the proper arena for resolving political questions. To them the judicial task was purely legal, separable from the vagaries and uncertainties of the political by the certainty of the legal method. It is this spirit of judicial deference to the will of Parliament that accounts for the limited reading accorded by the High Court to the few constitutional provisions for rights and freedoms.

The strength and dominance of this theoretical perspective also account for the significant lack of success Australia has experienced in entrenching a Bill of Rights in the Constitution.[8] One of the earliest attempts to amend the Constitution to entrench rights and freedoms occurred in 1944, as part of the postwar reconstruction program proposed by Labor. After its sweeping victory at the polls in 1943, the Curtin Labor government put forward a wide-ranging proposal for increased Commonwealth powers. As part of the increased powers, three 'safeguards' were included: freedom of expression, extension of freedom of religion (section 116) to apply to the States, and a new provision to allow either House of Parliament to disallow regulations. The Constitution Alteration (Postwar Reconstruction and Democratic Rights) Bill of 1944 was rejected at referendum.[9]

The question of a Bill of Rights was not taken up again until the Whitlam Labor government gained office in 1972. Lionel Murphy, Whitlam's Attorney-General, began to implement a civil liberties platform, announcing soon after a Constitutional Convention in Sydney in 1973 that he would introduce into Parliament a statutory Bill of Rights embodying the main provisions of the UN Covenant on Civil and Political Rights. Given the opposition to the Human Rights Bill, it was abandoned in the lead-up to the 1974 election.

Labor's next attempt to implement a Bill of Rights took place in 1983 when the Hawke government was elected to office. The Attorney-General, Gareth Evans, proposed as a precursor to constitutional amendment a statutory Bill that would bind the States. It was to be weaker than Murphy's proposed Human Rights Bill, as it was to be largely declaratory and educational. Due to a mishandling of its announcement its tabling was delayed until after the expected election in 1984. After the election Evans was replaced as Attorney-General by Lionel Bowen, who initially opposed a Bill of Rights then pursued it with little enthusiasm. Bowen's draft Bill followed the structure of the Evans Bill but was even weaker than Evans', especially as it did not apply to the States and applied only to provisions enacted after its operation. Despite its limited reach the Bill was subjected to extraordinary attack in Parliament, and was abandoned after a filibuster in the Senate.

The unsuccessful attempts to enact a Bill of Rights, each progressively weaker, form the background to the only other attempt to entrench rights by amending the Constitution, the 1988 referendum. Based on the recommendations of a Constitutional Commission, the referendum proposal represented the least ambitious measure that had been put forward, seeking to extend to the States the constitutional guarantees that applied to the Commonwealth, namely the right of trial by jury, freedom of religion and just terms for the acquisition of property. This modest attempt suffered the worst defeat of any referendum proposal, winning less than 31 per cent support, effectively rejecting foreseeable attempts to entrench a Bill of Rights.[10]

Australia was one of the few common law countries that did not have an entrenched Bill of Rights. By 1980 twenty-four Commonwealth countries had adopted codes of fundamental rights; by the mid 1990s Canada, New Zealand, Israel, Hong Kong and South Africa had also adopted some form of Bill of Rights. The United Kingdom and Australia seemed to stand in defiant isolation.[11] Though this brief overview shows the continuing strength and powerful influence of parliamentarianism in Australia, it also highlights the nature of the challenges posed to that orthodoxy by competing traditions that have a different philosophical provenance.

Natural Rights and Human Rights

As a result of the continuing international prominence of human rights treaties and conventions and the popularisation of 'rights talk' in general, natural rights and human rights occupy an increasingly important role in Australian politics. Though the foundation of modern natural rights can be traced to Hobbes' decisive break from the scholastic natural law tradition, John Locke was the first to formulate a liberal constitutionalism founded upon natural rights. To Locke, the 'state of nature' is a state of perfect freedom and equality.[12] Although in the state of nature a person has all the freedom and right of nature, property in the state of nature is 'very unsafe, very insecure' because 'the enjoyment of it is very uncertain, and constantly exposed to the invasion of others'. Therefore, according to Locke, people are willing to quit the state of nature and enter into political society 'for the mutual *Preservation* of their Lives, Liberties and estates, which I call by the general name *Property*'.[13]

To Locke, the perfect freedom and equality, and the insecurity of property, found in the state of nature justified a liberal constitutionalism characterised by the rule of law and representative government with legislative, executive and federative powers. Importantly, since the aim of civil society is peace, safety and the public good of the people, if a government attempts to destroy the property of the people, or reduce them to slavery, the people have a right to resume and exercise their original liberty. Natural right and original freedom allow the people to dissolve governments; to Locke, political power is based on, and limited by, natural rights.[14]

The Lockean tradition was appropriated by Kant, especially in Kant's republican and representative constitutionalism where public right is a system of laws based on pure principles of right.[15] But in Kant's formulation of human rights we find the natural rights tradition extended and altered in fundamental respects. Kant, influenced by Rousseau, distinguishes between two forms of causality, one according to nature and the other according to freedom. Causality in the sensible world has a necessary or phenomenal character, determined by the order of nature. Causality in the noumenal sense acknowledges the idea of transcendental freedom, the possibility of human freedom and hence morality. The coexistence of radical human freedom with the natural necessity has major consequences for rights.

Kant distinguishes between rights derived from *a priori* principles (natural rights) and rights that proceed from the will of the legislator (positive or statutory rights). Rights as moral capacities are also divided into innate and acquired rights. According to Kant there is only one innate right: freedom 'is the only original right belonging to every man by virtue of his humanity'.[16] The innate right includes the right to equality, the right to be one's own master and the right to communicate. As a human right based on freedom, it makes possible a method for settling disputes regarding acquired rights. It also has important political implications: the rights of persons must be held sacred, whatever they may cost the ruling power. Thus the infinite worth and dignity of the human person justifies the pursuit of morality without recourse to calculation, the 'wisdom of serpents'; justice is to prevail though the world should perish.[17]

The Kantian formulation of rights reintroduced into rights-based liberalism the important moral dimension of autonomy and dignity. The primacy of our morality, and hence our infinite value as human beings, has come to influence the articulation of rights. It has widened the formulation of rights to include the right to equal concern and respect, and thereby elevated and augmented the responsibilities of the state. Equal concern and respect has allowed the development of social and economic rights, rights to self-esteem and group rights.[18] It has also made it difficult to distinguish such rights from positive rights, entitlements that are enacted by Parliament. Indeed, it is arguable that there is now a merging or confluence of the rights-based and utilitarian streams of liberalism.[19] Nevertheless, the persistent fundamental differences between the two traditions account for the difficulties Australia has experienced in entrenching a Bill of Rights. It also indicates that the Bill of Rights debate in Australia involves more than the best means for securing rights and freedoms, it concerns fundamental theoretical alternatives in liberal constitutionalism.

Consequences for Democracy

The philosophical differences between these traditions are evident in their different conceptions of rights, citizenship, authority, legitimacy and progress, to name a few. For example, rights-based liberalism conceives of rights as personal entitlements, as ontological givens. In contrast, the deontological tradition views rights as negative or residual, what remains after the law has defined the proper limits. Similarly, rights-based liberalism conceives of citizenship as an entitlement based on nature, reason or humanity. Thus it will favour a more inclusive, egalitarian and therefore expansive foundation for citizenship and sovereignty. In contrast, citizenship within the parliamentary tradition, if it is referred to at all (as it relies on the notion of 'subjects', not citizens), draws upon historical circumstances which may include representations of class, territory and interests, as well as evolving concepts of community.

Perhaps the most noticeable institutional difference in the traditions concerns the politicisation of the judiciary. The elevation of rights and freedoms to a constitutional and thereby constitutive status necessarily gives the judiciary the duty and responsibility to interpret and define rights in the course of adjudication, thereby shaping and determining the contours of the regime. Combined with the increasing importance, if not dominance, of 'rights talk', the judiciary has become a new avenue for political action and an adjudicator of the character of the regime. In these important ways, the Bill of Rights debate raised far-reaching and fundamental questions concerning Australian constitutionalism.

A Judicially Created Bill of Rights?

It is in this light we need to consider the Court's implied rights jurisprudence. As we will see, through a series of decisions the Court began to develop a regime of rights, discerned and elaborated from the terms and structure of the Constitution. In doing so the Court appeared to enter into the political debates regarding the merit of a Bill of Rights, instituting through judicial means what had been difficult to achieve by constitutional changes or federal legislation. From one perspective, its actions could be justified as an attempt to overcome the political impasse created by fractious and partisan politics, to implement something that was necessary for the development of liberal democracy in Australia. But from another vantage point, the Court appeared to be entering a debate that was at best inconclusive and at worst opposed to an entrenched Bill of Rights, declaring an implied Bill of Rights with the intention of gaining for itself the legitimacy and authority to strike down parliamentary enactments that it decided were inconsistent with, or contravened, such rights. Thus its intervention in rights appeared as bold as its subsequent decision on native title. Why was the Court prepared to embark on such a venture? What was it about the absence of a Bill of Rights in Australia that necessitated such a judicial response? To answer these questions it is necessary to consider a range of international, institutional and theoretical developments that formed the background to, and were influential in, the development of the Court's jurisprudence.

Australia's evolution into an independent sovereign state during the twentieth century coincided with the globalisation of the economy and greater international interdependence, brought about by technological advances and the recognition that cooperative solutions were needed in such areas as environment, drugs, health and crime. There was also an increasing international acceptance, as evident in international conventions, treaties and instruments, of universal human rights norms. Australia took an active role in the formulation and promotion of an international human rights regime. Australia's impressive international reputation for human rights is based as much on its work in the drafting and preparation of international human rights instruments, as on its ratification of an extensive range of conventions and treaties.[20] In sharp contrast to these developments, as we have seen, was Australia's apparent reluctance to entrench a Bill of Rights in its Constitution.

The High Court itself had previously attempted to overcome this disparity by its wide interpretation of the Commonwealth's external affairs power (section 51xxix) which facilitated the introduction of an international human rights regime into the domestic law as well as the development of the Commonwealth as an independent and sovereign nation.[21] Thus the Commonwealth had been able to enact legislation that incorporated treaty obligations such as the *Racial Discrimination Act 1975*, the *Sex Discrimination Act 1984* and the *Crimes (Torture) Act 1988*.[22] Perhaps the most subtle means for introducing international human rights principles into the domestic regime was Australia's accession to the first Optional Protocol of the *International Covenant on Civil and Political Rights 1966*, which allowed citizens to lodge complaints against the government with the UN Human Rights Committee, effectively allowing the Committee to scrutinise and criticise the Australian domestic regime on the basis of the Covenant on Civil and Political Rights. The Human Rights Committee is not a court, it cannot enforce its decisions and its decisions are not binding, but it can exert significant political influence by means of an adverse finding. For example, the first

Australian communication to the Human Rights Committee was by Nicholas Toonen, who claimed that Tasmania's criminal laws regarding homosexuality contravened the provisions of the Convention. The Committee's adverse findings were relied upon by the Commonwealth when enacting the *Human Rights (Sexual Conduct) Act 1994* to overrule Tasmanian legislation.[23]

However, these developments presented difficulties for the High Court. Changes in Australian constitutionalism had placed the Court at the apex of the Australian legal system; it was a final court of appeal responsible for the development of Australian law in the light of international developments. But the absence of an entrenched Bill of Rights, and the character of the Court's traditional jurisprudence – general appellate work and federal judicial review – made such a task onerous. This task was complicated by the international scrutiny and potential censure of such bodies as the Human Rights Committee, which could later review the Court's decisions and thereby question its authority, evaluating its jurisprudence on the basis of a human rights regime that it could not immediately influence and shape. The Court, aware of this anomaly, drew attention to it in its judgments. For example, Chief Justice Mason and Justice McHugh in *Dietrich* thought it was 'curious that the Executive Government had seen fit to expose Australia to the potential censure of the Human Rights Committee without endeavouring to ensure that rights enshrined in the ICCPR are incorporated into domestic law'.[24] Thus the Court's concern with the limitations on its ability to shape Australian law in conformity with international developments, and the problems this posed for its reputation and authority, may have influenced its decision to turn to a jurisprudence of implied rights.

But perhaps one of the most important reasons why the Court was prepared to undertake such a jurisprudence was its view that times had changed, posing new threats to democratic governance.[25] Chief Justice Mason, in an address to the Australian Bar Association in 1988, outlined the potential source of the new problems:

> The common law of the 19th century was directed primarily at governing the relationships between individuals. Landlord/tenant and contract law come to mind. The common law, a body of rules crafted by judges and susceptible to modification by legislatures, was well suited to regulating these relationships. However, the emergence of the omnipresent welfare state throws up problems of a different complexion. Government is now a major source of wealth and it participates in nearly every facet of social and economic life.[26]

In this light, human rights represented a force countervailing the exercise of totalitarian, bureaucratic and institutional power, 'widely identified as the greatest threats to the liberty of the individual liberty and democratic freedom this century'.[27] But a jurisprudence based on human rights would make political and moral questions justiciable, giving the judiciary greater authority. Was this consistent with democratic government? According to Chief Justice Mason, the realities of democratic governance justify such judicial review:

> If by democracy we mean majoritarian democracy and we assume, contrary to the fact, that every Act of Parliament is a reflection of the majority will then a Bill of Rights associated with judicial review is undemocratic. But, for various reasons (which include unequal voting rights and distorting political structure and practices) parliamentary decisions often fail to coincide with majority opinions. Sometimes they reflect the narrow goals of particular interest groups, including bureaucracy itself. At other times the majority will, as reflected in the statute, is no more than a selfish pursuit of the majority interest in disregard of the legitimate interests of the minority, what Alexis de Tocqueville called 'the tyranny of the majority'.[28]

Thus he employs two, not simply consistent, arguments to justify a judicial review based on rights. The first, a critique of process, argues that parliamentary decisions do not always reflect the majority view; the second claims that in some instances the majority view may be wrong or tyrannical.

Chief Justice Mason was not alone in his views. Justice Brennan endorsed Chief Justice Mason's position at a human rights conference in 1992, arguing that bureaucratic and institutional power may require new checks and balances:

> If the risk of discriminatory exercise of power to the disadvantage of minorities and the weak and the risk of oppressive exercise of power by the political branches of government are sufficiently grave, and if there is no other means available to avoid or diminish those risks, then a case can be made for casting on the Courts a supervisory role, albeit a role which is radically different from the role which Courts have been accustomed to exercise.[29]

It seemed that, beyond the international and institutional developments, an overarching theoretical concern with the protection of individual rights and democratic freedom, the defence of liberalism, justified and sustained the Court's attempt to introduce rights into Australian constitutionalism. To determine the theoretical foundations of this new jurisprudence, and the new role it presented to the judiciary, it will be necessary to turn to the High Court's implied rights decisions.

Implied Bill of Rights

As late as 1986 the High Court rejected the existence of an implied constitutional guarantee of freedom of communication.[30] But by 1988 the Court was hinting at a change in direction.[31] The Court's new jurisprudence was inaugurated in two decisions handed down on the same day, *Nationwide News* and the *Political Advertising* case.[32] In *Nationwide News* the Court held invalid a provision of the *Industrial Relations Act 1988* (Cth) that made it an offence to bring the Commission or its members into disrepute. Although all the judges in the case held the Act invalid, different theoretical bases and approaches were offered for the protection of fundamental rights. The elaboration and justification of these perspectives, as well as the resolution of which views would prevail, were outlined in greater detail in the *Political Advertising* case.

The *Political Advertising* case concerned the validity of Labor's *Political Broadcasts and Political Disclosures Act 1991* (Cth) which extended the disclosure rules on donations and amended the *Broadcasting Act 1942* (Cth), prohibiting the broadcasting of political advertising in election periods and requiring broadcasters to make units of time available, free of charge, to political parties and other groups and individuals. The enactment was defended by the Labor government as a way of addressing the potential for undue influence in raising the increasingly prohibitive sums needed for election advertising, especially on television.[33] The provision was challenged by New South Wales and television stations on the grounds that it affected State entitlements and contravened an implied guarantee of freedom of communication secured by the Constitution.

By a majority, the High Court held the provisions invalid because they infringed the right to freedom of communication on political matters implied in the system of representative government provided for in the Constitution. Representative government required the people's representatives to be accountable and responsible to them, something that was not possible without freedom of communication in relation to public affairs and political discussion. The specific provision undermined freedom of communication by favouring established political parties and their candidates; others were required to rely on the discretion of the Broadcasting Tribunal, even though the Act did not outline any criteria on how the discretion would be exercised. Thus a provision that was intended to improve the democratic processes, representation and accountability had exacerbated the problem of party politics, bureaucratic unaccountability and executive dominance. The Court's decision was a politically useful way for Labor to extract itself from the situation, allowing it to rely extensively on public broadcasting for the election of the Keating government.

The majority judgments in the *Political Advertising* case revealed a range of positions regarding implied rights. At one end Justice McHugh was prepared to accept a limited form of a right to political communication, not implied from the Constitution but derived from the electoral processes secured by section 7, which requires senators be chosen by the people of the State, and section 24 which requires members of the House of Representatives be chosen by the people of the Commonwealth. Chief Justice Mason accepted that the Constitution provides for a system of representative government and representative democracy, which in turn presumes an 'implied guarantee of freedom of communication, at least in relation to public and political discussion'.[34] Justices Deane and Toohey were prepared to go further, arguing that the implication of freedom of communication extends beyond the Commonwealth to other levels of government, especially the States.[35] The most extensive scope for implied rights was elaborated by Justice Gaudron, who, relying on the judgments of Justice Murphy and Canadian jurisprudence, stated:

> The notion of a free society governed in accordance with the principles of representative parliamentary democracy may entail freedom of movement, freedom of association, and perhaps, freedom of speech generally. But, so far as free elections are an indispensable feature of a society of that kind, it necessarily entails, at the very least, freedom of political discourse. And that discourse is not limited to communication between candidates and electors, but extends to communication between the members of society generally.[36]

Of the dissentients, Justice Brennan restated his view in *Nationwide News* that the legislative powers of Parliament were limited by an implied freedom to discuss political and economic matters essential to sustain the system of representative government prescribed by the Constitution. But he decided that the restrictions on advertising, except for those sections that burdened the functioning of the States, did not trespass upon implied constitutional freedoms.[37] On the other hand, Justice Dawson upheld the legislation because the Australian Constitution, contrary to the American model and with a few exceptions, 'does not seek to establish personal liberty by constitutional restrictions upon the exercise of governmental power'.[38]

In *Nationwide News* and the *Political Advertising* case the majority of the High Court had argued that the institutions secured in the Constitution presupposed and therefore gave rise to rights and freedoms. Freedom of political communication was one such right. But what was the scope of that right? Were there other related rights and freedoms, as Justice Gaudron appeared to suggest? If so, how would one evaluate, develop and indeed prescribe the character and range of such rights? The Court looked at these considerations in 1994 when it handed down its decisions in *Theophanous* and *Stephens*.[39]

Theophanous concerned a defamation action by Dr Andrew Theophanous, a Labor member for House of Representatives seat of Calwell, who had taken an active and prominent part in public discussions of immigration issues. He had taken proceedings against the Herald and Weekly Times Ltd and Bruce Ruxton, President of the Victorian branch of the Returned Servicemen's League, on the grounds that Ruxton's letter to the editor published in the *Sunday Herald-Sun*, entitled 'Give Theophanous the shove', was defamatory. The defendants argued that the implied constitutional freedom of communication provided a defence to the defamation action because it protected the publication of material discussing governmental and political matters. At issue was whether the common law of defamation, as supplemented by State legislation prescribing statutory defences to defamation actions, was subject to the constitutionally protected right of free speech.

In a joint judgment, the majority of the Court decided that there was an available defence to defamation proceedings, based on the freedom of communication implied in the Constitution. The constitutional defence required the defendant to establish that the material was published in the course of political discussion, that the defendant was unaware of falsity and did not publish recklessly, and that the publication was reasonable in the circumstances. Justice Deane, the fourth member of the majority, would have gone further. In his opinion the implied constitutional freedom allowed critics to make statements about the official conduct or suitability for office of holders of high public office, without fear of defamation actions. But as his opinions were not supported by the rest of the Court, he was prepared to agree with the majority view.

The effect of the decision was to alter the existing defamation laws by striking a new balance between free speech and the protection of an individual's reputation. According to the majority:

> the common law defences which protect the reputation of persons who are subject of defamatory publications do so at the price of significantly inhibiting free communication. To that extent, the balance is tilted too far against free communication and the need to protect the efficacious working of representative democracy and government in favour of the protection of individual reputation.[40]

Justices Brennan, Dawson and McHugh delivered separate dissenting judgments, though all three accepted the existence of an implied constitutional freedom of communication. Justice Dawson argued that the Constitution did not contain any guarantee of freedom of speech, and that it was not up to the courts to define the limits of responsible govern-ment.[41] To Justice McHugh, the freedom of political speech secured in the Constitution was connected to elections – any extension to general political rights was an exercise in political and not legal reasoning.[42] Justice Brennan distinguished between the Court's proper role in shap-ing the common law and the necessity for judicial deference in the interpretation of the Constitution. In his opinion, such constitutional rights and freedoms did not directly affect individuals.[43]

In *Stephens,* members of the Western Australian Legislative Council's Standing Committee on Government Agencies commenced defamation actions in the Supreme Court of Western Australia against the publisher of the *West Australian* newspaper. A number of articles in the *West Australian* had described interstate and overseas trips undertaken by the Committee members as 'junkets' and a 'rort'. In defence, the newspaper pleaded that the relevant articles were published pursuant to a freedom guaranteed by the Commonwealth Constitution and the Constitution of Western Australia. In a decision handed down at the same time as *Theophanous,* the same majority found that the defence to defamation proceedings based on the implied freedom of communication derived both from the Commonwealth Constitution and from the State Consti-tution of Western Australia.

The immediate and practical effect of *Theophanous* and *Stephens* was to alter the defamation laws in Australia, exposing politicians, public figures and persons engaged in activities that have become the subject of political debate and discussion, to greater public scrutiny. The use of defamation proceedings by public figures to limit criticism of political decisions was significantly curtailed. In achieving this, however, the Court advanced its implied rights jurisprudence in two important ways. It extended the reach of implied rights to the common law by deciding that the implied freedom of communication derived from the Common-wealth Constitution altered the common law, in this instance the com-mon law of defamation. Moreover, it was now clear that State laws were also subject to such implied rights, either because the implied freedom discerned in the Commonwealth Constitution extended to all political discussion, including discussion of political matters relating to govern-ment at a State level, or because such implied freedoms derived from the State Constitutions themselves.

But what did 'political discussion' entail? This question was addressed in another of the Court's implied rights decisions in 1994, *Cunliffe's* case.[44] The *Migration Act 1958* (Cth) prescribed a system for registering immigrant agents. Subject to exceptions, only registered agents (who were required to pay substantial fees for registration) were entitled to give immigration assistance, including assisting or advising on entrance applications. Though the majority of the Court held that these provisions did not breach implied constitutional limitations, Chief Justice Mason and Justices Deane, Toohey and Gaudron were of the opinion that the communications restricted under the Act came within the concept of political speech for the purposes of implied freedom.[45] It seemed, therefore, that 'political' would not be construed in a narrow sense – dealings with ministers and government officials, in fact public administration generally, would constitute political communication and discussion.

These advances in the Court's jurisprudence of rights were criticised by the government and scholars. The early decisions in *Nationwide News* and the *Political Advertising* case were described as undemocratic judicial activism and adventurism, though a few suggested that they did not go far enough.[46] The defamation cases were greeted as another instance of unwarranted judicial politics that altered the responsibilities of Parliament and the judiciary, an awkward and unjustified intrusion into the field of defamation law that purported to redefine the fine balance between freedom of speech and protection of reputation reached through lengthy common law and legislative fine-tuning. Moreover, *Theophanous* and *Stephens* appeared to introduce a radical innovation into Australian constitutionalism by allowing constitutional rights and freedoms to be employed as defences in private litigation, in this instance as a defence to defamation proceedings. Finally, the Court's reliance on representative democracy and democratic institutions to interpret implied rights and freedoms was said to introduce extra-constitutional and potentially arbitrary political principles in constitutional interpretation.

These criticisms were directly confronted by the High Court in its next major decision on rights, *McGinty*.[47] *McGinty* is a significant decision because it represented an attempt to extend the Court's implied rights jurisprudence beyond political communication to the related area of voting rights. Certain provisions of the Western Australian Constitution and the *Electoral Distribution Act 1947* (WA) provided for disparities between the number of voters enrolled in metropolitan and non-metropolitan districts for the election of members of the Legislative Assembly of Western Australia. The plaintiffs challenged the validity of these provisions, arguing that the principles of representative democracy were impliedly incorporated in the Commonwealth Constitution and the Constitution of Western Australia. As representative democracy requires universal adult suffrage, which includes the right to vote and equality of voting power, the principle of one-vote–one-value was also implicit in each Constitution.

A majority of the High Court (Chief Justice Brennan, Justices Dawson, McHugh and Gummow) rejected this argument. Though the Commonwealth Constitution secures representative democracy, the majority held that the quality and character of the nature of the representative democracy is neither fixed nor precise. To Justice Dawson, the Constitution provides minimum standards but does not purport to go further.[48] According to Justice McHugh, one-vote–one-value is not indispensable to representative government.[49] Justice Gummow acknowledges the importance of the principle but is prepared to defer to Parliament on the point.[50] Justice Brennan declines to decide whether the Constitution requires equality of votes because he denies that such implications can be applied to the States. On the question of whether the Western Australian Constitution secures such a principle, he states that the position in *Stephens* – that direct choice by the people implied freedom to discuss political matters – did not extend to equality of voting. Similar views are expressed by the other majority judges.

The minority judgments of Justices Gaudron and Toohey show the path the Court's rights jurisprudence may have taken. Justice Toohey contends that once it is conceded that the Constitution has established a system of representative democracy, it is possible to discern more than freedom of political communication. One-vote–one-value is seen as a minimal requirement of representative democracy.[51] Having examined the terms of the Western Australian Constitution, he concludes that representative democracy is preserved by the Constitution and therefore arguments with respect to franchise and electoral boundaries apply with equal force in Western Australia. Justice Gaudron agrees in general with that opinion, accepting that both the Commonwealth and Western Australian Constitutions provide for a system of representative democracy which in turn requires universal adult franchise and equality in vote.

In *McGinty* the majority of the Court declined to expand its jurisprudence of rights to the areas of citizenship and one-vote–one-value. Its reluctance, shown clearly in Justice McHugh's strongly worded judgment critical of the Court's decisions in *Theophanous* and *Stephens*, was partly based on a change in its method of interpretation. For the majority, representative democracy was not to be a 'free-standing' principle in the interpretation of the Constitution. Rather, the text and structure of the Constitution were to be given primacy in constitutional adjudication. Thus the limitations in the nature of implied rights to be discerned in the Constitution, due to the Court's reluctance to rely on the concept of representative democracy to develop an implied Bill of Rights, was influenced by a return to the primacy of the constitutional text. To this extent *McGinty* appears to mark, at least for the near future, a narrowing if not truncation of the Court's implied rights jurisprudence, an unwillingness to advance beyond the implied right of political communication.

These changes in direction were clearly visible in the Court's 1997 decision on political communication, *Lange*.[52] *Lange* is a milestone in the Court's political communication decisions because it was a unanimous judgment of the Court that consolidated its jurisprudence on implied rights. The case concerned a defamation action against the Australian Broadcasting Corporation, alleging that in a 1989 *Four Corners* television program the ABC had defamed the New Zealand Prime Minister David Lange by stating that he had abused his public office and was unfit to hold public office. At issue was the validity of the defences pleaded by the defendant, including a defence based on the Constitution.

The High Court held unanimously that freedom of communication on matters of government and politics is an indispensable incident of representative government, created in the Constitution. It accepted the argument in *McGinty* that 'the Constitution gives effect to the institution of "representative government" only to the extent that the text and structure of the Constitution establish it'. Therefore 'the relevant question is not, "What is required by representative and responsible government?" It is "What do the terms and structure of the Constitution prohibit, authorise or require?" '[53] The Court referred to sections 1, 7, 8, 13, 24, 25, 28 and 30 of the Constitution as establishing the fundamental features of representative government.[54] But, as these questions point out, in *Lange* the Court introduced a new concept into its implied rights constitutionalism – in an unprecedented development, the Court also held that the terms of the Constitution, especially sections 6, 49, 62, 64, 83 and 128, establish a 'system of *responsible* ministerial government'.[55] The constitutional recognition of the conventions of responsible government represents a major advance on the Court's freedom of communication decisions as it creates the possibility that these conventions may become justiciable.

In *Lange,* the High Court took the opportunity to outline the major features of the implied freedom of political communication. According to the Court, freedom of communication is not a personal right, similar to the First Amendment to the American Constitution; it is more of an immunity from legal control.[56] It is not confined to the election period, as the necessity for informed political choice by the people requires communication not only during election periods but also between elections. Importantly, the freedom is not absolute: 'It is limited to what is necessary for the effective operation of that system of representative and responsible government provided for by the Constitution'.[57] Accordingly, in *Lange* the Court devised a test to accommodate laws enacted to satisfy some other legitimate end, which will be upheld provided they satisfy two conditions:

> The first condition is that the object of the law is compatible with the maintenance of the constitutionally prescribed system of representative and responsible government or the procedure for submitting a proposed amendment to the Constitution to the informed decision of the people which the Constitution prescribes. The second is that the law is reasonably appropriate and adapted to achieving that legitimate object or end.[58]

Finally, the Court accepted the decisions in *Theophanous* and *Stephens* that common law rules of defamation must conform to the requirements of the Constitution. However, it distinguished between constitutional freedoms which do not confer private rights and common law defences. Therefore constitutional rights and freedoms influenced defamation proceedings by altering the common law and statutory enactments regarding the defamation, in this case the common law defence of qualified privilege, and not directly by being pleaded in defence to a defamation action.[59]

To see the direction of the Court's jurisprudence on rights, it is helpful to turn to two of its recent decisions, *Kruger* and *Levy*.[60] In 1997 the Human Rights and Equal Opportunity Commission Report titled *Bringing Them Home* was tabled in federal Parliament.[61] The report had investigated the policy of separating Aboriginal children from their parents and had recommended appropriate reparation and restitution. *Kruger* represented an attempt by Aborigines to seek such compensation, relying on the provisions of the Constitution. The plaintiffs in *Kruger* were Aborigines who claimed that between 1925 and 1960 they had been removed from their parents and families in the Northern Territory and kept in Aboriginal reserves or institutions by protectors appointed under the *Aboriginals Ordinance 1918* (NT). The law had been made by the Governor-General pursuant to the *Northern Territory (Administration) Act 1910* (Cth).[62] The plaintiffs challenged the validity of the Ordinance on a number of grounds, including that it was contrary to the implied constitutional principles of due process of the law, equality, freedom of movement and association.[63] They sought to recover damages from the Commonwealth, claiming that breach of these rights gave rise to a right of action against the Commonwealth distinct from an action in tort or contract.

The Court's decision is complicated by the fact that the case principally concerned section 122 of the Constitution, dealing with the territories power. Nevertheless, the majority of the Court rejected that the text or structure of the Constitution provided an implied right of substantive equality, due process, freedom of association and movement. In their minority judgments, Justices Toohey and Gaudron were prepared to accept that the Constitution secured an implied freedom of association. Justice Toohey went further by claiming that the Constitution provided equality of treatment.

The Court in *Kruger* was given the opportunity to outline an extensive implied rights jurisprudence that would go beyond the right of political communication to include due process, freedom of movement and association, and equality. Though a minority were prepared to elaborate a notion of freedom of association, the majority declined to do so.

Indeed, the Court went out of its way to deny such a possibility.[64] In doing so it confirmed its reluctance to expand the rights decisions beyond the immediate confines of freedom of communication. The textual foundation for implied rights as outlined in *McGinty* and *Lange*, including the concept of rights and freedoms as negative and residual rather than positive personal claims, as well as the framing of the problem in terms of the territories power, may have accounted for the Court's more limited reading in *Kruger*. It is also important to recall the hostile reception of the Court's recent *Wik* decision. A decision that discerned more rights in the Constitution at a time when the Court was being accused of unjustified activism, may have been politically imprudent. In any case, given the Court's rejection in *Lange* of constitutional rights as defences in defamation actions, it seemed unlikely that the Court would be prepared to formulate a constitutional personal right.[65]

Of course, the Court's reluctance to extend its implied rights decisions into new areas did not mean it would not do so in the future. Nor did it mean that its freedom of communication jurisprudence would remain unchanged. *Levy* concerned Laurence Levy, who was charged under the *Wildlife (Game) (Hunting Season) Regulations 1994* (Vic.) with entering a hunting area during prohibited times without holding an authority.[66] Levy argued that he had entered the prohibited places to protest against Victorian hunting laws by attracting media attention, especially television coverage. He claimed that the Victorian Regulations limited his implied constitutional freedom to speak publicly or protest by physical activity about legislation concerning hunting and the policy concerning the activities of game shooters. In *Levy*, the Court applied its *Lange* decision to uphold the validity of the Regulations. Though the Regulations may have limited freedom of expression, they were reasonably appropriate and adapted to the protection of individual or public safety. Thus *Levy* confirmed that implied rights would not necessarily override other social and public concerns, though balancing of interests would now be overseen by the judiciary. In one important respect *Levy* advanced the Court's jurisprudence on political communication. A majority of the Court held that the constitutional implied freedom of communication protected not only verbal communication but also non-verbal conduct intended to be expressive.[67] In this way *Levy* demonstrated the incremental nature of the advances in the Court's understanding of political communication.

Theoretical Foundations of Implied Rights

How are we to characterise the Court's implied rights jurisprudence? What emerges from the above review is the consistent attempt to source or ground such rights and freedoms in institutions. Initially, the favoured institution is representative democracy. *Lange* augments this notion, with responsible government. This theoretical foundation for freedom of communication means that it is not a personal right but a necessary consequence of entrenching representative and responsible government in the Constitution. Typically, the Court seeks to explain this by denying that it is an 'American' type of right, comparable to the First Amendment to the American Constitution. Implicit in such a formulation is the rejection of freedom of speech as a natural right or essential aspect of human dignity. This reliance on an institutional foundation for rights and freedoms is consistent with the common law notion of freedom as residual or negative, the area left uncontrolled by the law. It is also consistent with a constitutionalism that considered representative and responsible government as essential for human development and progress. Thus it is not accidental that Justice McHugh in *McGinty* describes this jurisprudence as Millian.

If we accept this argument, then the Court's rights jurisprudence appears to be consistent with the orthodox constitutionalism in Australia, bringing out and developing notions that are inherent in the idea of responsible government. In other words, these decisions are not as radical as suggested by some commentators. Nor are they novel – though the concepts are supported in previous decisions of Justices Murphy and Stephen, it is more accurate to trace the source of this jurisprudence to the early Canadian Supreme Court decision by Chief Justice Duff in the *Alberta Press* case where he held that there was a right of public discussion because 'the practice of this right of free public discussion of public affairs, notwithstanding its incidental mischiefs, is the breath of life for parliamentary institutions'.[68] That decision formed the basis of later Canadian implied rights decisions that preceded the enactment of the Canadian Bill of Rights in 1960.[69]

Why did the Australian implied rights jurisprudence confine itself to freedom of speech? A range of reasons account for the course the Court adopted in its rights decisions. Certainly, an initial difficulty was the way the Court formulated the theoretical foundation of such rights. By suggesting that representative democracy could be an extra-constitutional concept, the Court encountered difficulties in reconciling constitutional principles with the development of the common law, as well as appearing to allow itself an unlimited source for developing rights and exercising judicial review. The shift from representative democracy to the text of the Constitution that secured representative democracy established the Court's jurisprudence on more solid foundations, at the expense of limiting its scope. We should also remember that as it was developing this jurisprudence the Court was increasingly subjected to unprecedented attacks over its native title decisions. The public attacks on the Court over its decisions in *Mabo* and *Wik* go some way to explaining its reluctance to rely on *Kruger* to advance its implied rights jurisprudence. Finally, we should not discount the change in the Bench. The retirement of Chief Justice Mason and Justice Deane, and the appointment of Justice Brennan as Chief Justice, had a major effect on the direction taken by the Court.

Thus what initially appeared to be an attempt by the judiciary to elaborate an implied Bill of Rights was confined to the development of an implied freedom of communication. However, we should remember that the ground has been cleared for the future development of rights and freedoms. For example, in *Levy* the Court extended freedom of communication to non-verbal conduct. And if Justice Gaudron's suggestion in *Kruger* and *Levy* that the Constitution secures the right of movement is adopted, it is possible to imagine an expansion in rights to include not only freedom of association but also perhaps a larger notion of privacy.

Human Rights

It would appear, therefore, that the Court's implied rights jurisprudence, elaborating a regime of rights and freedoms implicit in the Constitution, was broadly in agreement with the orthodox Australian constitutionalism. It derived rights from representative and democratic institutions rather than from 'nature' or 'humanity'.

But a number of its recent decisions seem to show that the Court has moved beyond these Millian institutional moorings in developing a concept of rights and freedoms. In these cases the Court has been prepared to turn to, and rely upon, international conventions, treaties and evolving common law to shape Australian constitutionalism. In doing so the Court has implicitly, and inevitably, relied on legal concepts and regimes that are founded on traditions of natural and human rights, thereby introducing and gradually incorporating into Australian constitutionalism a human rights jurisprudence.[70]

Treaties and International Law

In Australia a Convention ratified by the executive does not become part of Australian law unless the provisions have been validly incorporated into municipal law by statute. In *Teoh* the High Court, arguing that mere ratification was an adequate foundation for a legitimate expectation that administrative decision-makers would act consistently with the Convention, appeared to undermine this principle.[71] *Teoh* concerned a Malaysian citizen, Ah Hin Teoh, who had come to Australia on a temporary entry permit. He married an Australian citizen who had four children from an earlier relationship. There were three children of the marriage.

Teoh applied for permanent entry but while the application was pending he was convicted of drug offences and was sentenced to six years imprisonment. He was subsequently informed that his application for a permanent entry permit was refused on the ground that his conviction showed that he was not of good character. An Immigration Review Panel accepted that Teoh's wife and family faced a bleak future if resident status was not granted, but compassionate claims were not compelling enough to waive the character requirement. Accordingly, the Minister of State for Immigration and Foreign Affairs made an order to deport Teoh. Teoh's application to the Federal Court was dismissed in the first instance, but allowed after an appeal to the Full Court. The Minister appealed to the High Court. The majority of the High Court held that, provided there were no statutory or executive indications to the contrary, ratification of a Convention, in this case the UN Convention on the Rights of the Child, gave rise to a legitimate expectation that the Minister would act in conformity with it and treat the best interests of the applicant's children as a primary consideration.[72] As the Minister had not treated the best interests of the children as a primary consideration and the applicant had been denied a fair opportunity to present a case against a decision that was inconsistent with legitimate expectations, the Minister's appeal was dismissed.

The *Teoh* decision was praised for overcoming Australia's 'split personality' regarding human rights, involving impressive international commitment to human rights issues but half-hearted and inadequate domestic implementation of multilateral human rights instruments.[73] The Keating Labor government saw it in a different light. The Minister for Foreign Affairs stated that *Teoh* was a 'plainly bad decision', creating 'a decision-making environment that is unworkable in practice' upsetting the balance between the executive, legislature and judiciary.[74] A joint statement was issued by the Minister for Foreign Affairs and Attorney-General on 10 May 1995, stating that an unincorporated treaty would not raise legitimate expectations that governmental decision-makers would act in accordance to the treaty nor would it form the basis for challenging administrative decisions. The government's legislative displacement of the legitimate expectations found by the Court in *Teoh* took the form of the Administrative Decision (Effect of International Instruments) Bill 1995, which lapsed when Parliament was dissolved for election.

Upon taking office, the Howard Coalition government revised the treaty-making procedures, providing greater roles to Parliament, the States, Territories and the community in the treaty-making process as well as establishing a Joint Parliamentary Committee on Treaties and a Treaty Council. A Joint Statement by the Minister for Foreign Affairs and the Attorney-General and Minister for Justice issued on 25 February 1997 confirmed that unincorporated treaties did not give rise to legitimate expectations in administrative law. The government also adopted the recommendation of the Senate Legal and Constitutional Legislation Committee to implement the Administrative Decision (Effect of International Instruments) Bill 1997, almost identical to the Labor Bill. Though the Bill had the support of the Labor Opposition in the House of Representatives, in September 1997 the Shadow Attorney-General announced that Labor would oppose it on the grounds that the *Teoh* decision did not cause the problems initially feared.

Leaving aside the merits of the argument regarding the administrative burden imposed by the *Teoh* principle, it is clear that the decision allows the Court to rely upon ratified Conventions and treaties to evaluate administrative decisions. As Australia is presently party to over 900 such Conventions and treaties, *Teoh* would seem to have subjected the Australian legal regime to the major human rights treaties as well as numerous related international instruments that form the fabric of international human rights laws. True, the executive or Parliament can exclude such a review. But to do so would appear inconsistent at best and hypocritical at worst, with significant political costs. Thus *Teoh* is much more far-reaching than the Court's implied rights jurisprudence and, in so far as many of these treaties and Conventions are based on natural rights and human rights, it introduces the potential for a fundamental shift in the character of liberal democracy in Australia.

International Law as a Common Law Benchmark

The Court's statements that it will rely on international Conventions and treaties to shape the common law of Australia highlights the other major means of introducing natural rights- and human rights-based constitutionalism into Australia. As we have seen, treaties are not part of the domestic law until implemented by legislation. Nevertheless the Court has recently accepted that treaties, and possibly even customary international law, may have a legitimate and important influence on the development of the common law.[75] Though an earlier formulation of this principle can be found in the judgments of Justice Murphy, the greatest supporter and advocate of the proposition before it was adopted by the High Court was Justice Kirby. The Bangalore Principles, as Justice Kirby referred to them, stated that international law is a source of law-making only when there is uncertainty, either a gap in the common law or obscurity or ambiguity in a statute. In such instances the judiciary could incorporate a rule into domestic law.[76]

The High Court in *Mabo (No 2)* accepted that international law, including international Conventions, could be used to influence the development of the common law. As Justice Brennan put it: 'The common law does not necessarily conform with international law, but international law is a legitimate and important influence on the development of the common law, especially when international law declares the existence of universal human rights'.[77] Subsequent decisions have confirmed this principle, though the Court has advised caution and circumspection where Parliament has not enacted the treaty obligations into law. The principle raises major questions regarding the authority of the judiciary in employing such methods of interpretation as a backdoor means of incorporating treaties not enacted into law.[78] This difficulty can be seen in the judicial uncertainty over whether an international instrument can justify a change in the common law, as distinct from resolving an ambiguity, uncertainty or gap.[79]

Though it is not clear how the judiciary will limit or constrain the exercise of judicial discretion in interpretation, it appears that the development of the common law in Australia will be significantly shaped by the increasingly influential international human rights regime, as interpreted and mediated by the judiciary. Indeed, if Justice Kirby's decision in *Newcrest Mining* is any indication of the future reach and direction of this jurisprudence, interpretation of the Constitution itself may also be subject to international legal developments.[80]

As noted above, this form of interpretation will have major implications for the theoretical foundations of the rights and freedoms discerned in the common law and the Constitution and thereby the nature of liberal democracy in Australia. Importantly, and in a larger sense (in so far as courts of final jurisdiction in common law countries are undertaking such a task), it would seem that the judiciary is one of the most important institutions in mediating and negotiating changes in international and domestic regimes. In relying on and contributing to the development of a new international common law, the judiciary is undertaking a significant role in meeting the challenges of globalisation and its perceived threat to national sovereignty.[81]

A New Regime of Human Rights

Responding to international and institutional changes which it confronted and in some cases facilitated, as well as a perceived need to protect rights and freedoms, the Court entered into an ambitious attempt to develop an implied Bill of Rights in Australia. In attempting to bridge the gap between an international rights regime and the domestic legal situation, the Court was conscious of the theoretical bases of its undertaking:

the rights would be based on the democratic institutions secured in the Constitution. The rights were not personal 'American' rights; they were negative, residual, derived from the efficient workings of institutions. To this extent the Court's implied rights jurisprudence was consistent with the orthodoxy in Australian constitutionalism. Yet for various reasons, including changes in the make-up of the Court, different theories of interpretation, differences between constitutional and public rights and entitlements and public reception of its decisions, the Court confined its jurisprudence to the implied right of political communication.

In contrast, decisions that have attempted to incorporate international law principles into the domestic regime incrementally, indirectly and administratively show the introduction of different notions of rights and freedoms into Australian constitutionalism. This aspect of the Court's jurisprudence, though subtle, is unprecedented and innovative. It represents perhaps the most important means for the Court to judge democracy in the future.

Notes

1 For an earlier presentation of some of the arguments developed in this chapter see Patapan, H. 1996, 'Rewriting Australian Liberalism: The High Court's Jurisprudence of Rights', *Australian Journal of Political Science*, 31, 2: 225; Patapan, H. 1997, 'The Liberal Politics of Rights: Changing Constitutionalism and the Bill of Rights Debate in Canada and Australia' (PhD, University of Toronto); Patapan, H. 1997, 'Competing Visions of Liberalism: Theoretical Underpinnings of the Bill of Rights Debate in Australia', *Melbourne University Law Review*, 21: 497.

2 See generally Williams, G. 1999, *Human Rights under the Australian Constitution*, Melbourne, Oxford University Press. Some argue that this list should include equal voting rights (ss 24, 25), the right to vote (s. 41), freedom of interstate trade (s. 92), non-discrimination regarding Commonwealth taxes and bounties (ss 51ii, 51iii, 86, 88 and 90), inconsistency provision (s. 109) and the full faith and credit requirement (s. 118): see, for example, Deane J in *Street v Queensland Bar Association* (1989) 168 CLR 461 at 521.

3 Windeyer, Sir Victor 1962, '"A Birthright and Inheritance": The Establishment of the Rule of Law in Australia', *Tasmanian Law Review*, 1: 635 at 636.

4 Subject to the rule against repugnancy and territorial limits, the colonial governments had plenary power to enact legislation and though subordinate to Imperial Parliament were not delegates of it. See the various colonial Constitutions in Lumb, R. 1991, *The Constitutions of the Australian States,* 5th edn, Brisbane, University of Queensland Press; *R v Burah* (1878) 3 App Cas 889; *Hodge v The Queen* (1883) 9 App Cas 117; *Powell v Apollo Candle Co* (1885) 10 App Cas 282.

5 Patapan, H. 1997, 'The Dead Hand of the Founders? Original Intent and the Constitutional Protection of Rights and Freedoms in Australia', *Federal Law Review* 25: 211.

6 Menzies, Sir Robert 1967, *Central Power in the Australian Commonwealth*, London, Cassell, 34.
7 Dixon, Sir Owen 1965, *Jesting Pilate and Other Papers and Addresses by Sir Owen Dixon*, Melbourne, Law Book Co., 53.
8 See generally Williams, *Human Rights under the Australian Constitution*; Galligan, B. 1990, 'Australia's Rejection of a Bill of Rights', *Journal of Commonwealth and Comparative Politics*, 28: 344; Charlesworth, H. 1993, 'The Australian Reluctance about Rights', *Osgoode Hall Law Journal*, 31: 195; Bailey, P. 1990, *Human Rights: Australia in an International Context*, Sydney: Butterworths.
9 See Commonwealth of Australia Parliamentary Debates, 1944, 1338ff.
10 For the complex range of issues and arguments advanced in the course of the campaign see Galligan B. & Nethercote, J. (eds) 1989, *The Constitutional Commission and the 1988 Referendums*, Canberra, Centre for Research on Federal Financial Relations/Royal Australian Institute of Public Administration.
11 Malleson, K. 1999, 'A British Bill of Rights: Incorporating the European Convention on Human Rights', *Choices*, 5, 1: 21.
12 Locke, John 1992, *Two Treatises on Government*, Book 2, Cambridge, Cambridge University Press, ch. ii.
13 ibid., ch. ix, s. 123, original emphasis.
14 ibid., ch. ix, s.131; ch. xix, ss 221–2.
15 Kant, Immanuel 1991, *Metaphysics of Morals*, Cambridge, Cambridge University Press, 124–9; Gregor, Mary 1988, 'Kant's Approach to Constitutionalism' in A. Rosenbaum (ed.), *Constitutionalism: The Philosophical Dimension*, New York, Greenwood Press.
16 Kant, *Metaphysics of Morals*, 63.
17 ibid., 117, 126.
18 The trend towards the recognition of a more diverse range of rights has, at its extreme, led to a rejection of 'right-talk' altogether. See especially Glendon, M. 1991, *Rights Talk: The Impoverishment of Political Discourse*, New York, Free Press; Sandel, M. 1982, *Liberalism and the Limits of Justice*, Cambridge, Cambridge University Press; Beiner, R. 1992, *What's the Matter with Liberalism?*, Berkeley, University of California Press.
19 See Patapan, 'Competing Visions of Liberalism', 503–4.
20 By 1994 Australia was or had been party to 2289 treaties: see Department of Foreign Affairs and Trade, *Australian Treaty List*; see generally Opeskin, B. & Rothwell, D.R. (eds) 1997, *International Law and Australian Federalism*, Melbourne, Melbourne University Press.
21 *Koowarta v Bjelke-Petersen* (1982) 153 CLR 168.
22 Charlesworth, H. 1995, 'Australia's Split Personality: Implementation of Human Rights Treaty Obligations in Australia' in P. Alston & M. Chiam (eds) 1995, *Treaty-making and Australia: Globalisation versus Sovereignty*, Sydney Federation Press, 129–40.
23 Tenbensel, T. 1996, 'International Human Rights Conventions and Australian Political Debates: Issues Raised by the "Toonen Case"', *Australian Journal of Political Science*, 31: 7; Charlesworth, H. 1991, 'Australia's Accession to the First Optional Protocol to the International Covenant on Civil and Political Rights', *Melbourne University Law Review*, 18: 428.
24 *Dietrich v R* (1992) 177 CLR 292 at 305.
25 See generally Patapan, 'Rewriting Australian Liberalism'.

26 Mason, Sir Anthony 1989, 'A Bill of Rights for Australia?', *Australian Bar Review* 5: 79 at 85–6.
27 ibid., 79.
28 ibid., 81.
29 Brennan, Sir Gerard 1992, 'The Impact of a Bill of Rights on the Role of the Judiciary: An Australian Response', paper delivered at a conference on Human Rights, University House, Canberra, 16 July, 9. See also his conditional agreement with Lord Hailsham that 'We live under an elective dictatorship, absolute in theory if hitherto thought tolerable in practice' in 'The Parliament, the Executive and the Courts: Roles and Immunities' presented at the School of Law, Bond University, 21 February 1998.
30 *Miller v TCN Channel Nine Pty Ltd* (1986) 161 CLR 556 (Murphy J dissenting).
31 *Union Steamship Co of Australia Pty Ltd v King* (1988) 166 CLR 1 at 8.
32 *Nationwide News Pty Ltd v Wills* (1992) 177 CLR 1; *Australian Capital Television Pty Ltd v Commonwealth* (1992) 177 CLR 106.
33 See Gruen, F. & Grattan, M. 1993, *Managing Government*, Melbourne, Longman Cheshire, 87.
34 *Australian Capital Television Pty Ltd v Commonwealth* (1992) 177 CLR 106 at 133.
35 ibid. at 169.
36 ibid. at 212, citations omitted.
37 ibid. at 161.
38 ibid. at 182.
39 *Theophanous v Herald & Weekly Times Ltd* (1994) 182 CLR 104; *Stephens v Western Australian Newspapers Ltd* (1994) 182 CLR 211.
40 *Theophanous v Herald & Weekly Times Ltd* (1994) 182 CLR 104 at 133.
41 ibid. at 65–7.
42 ibid at 71–6.
43 ibid. at 28–9.
44 *Cunliffe v Commonwealth* (1994) 182 CLR 272.
45 For McHugh, Dawson and Brennan JJ the relevant restrictions were not imposed on political discussion – debate about institutions of government or the exercise of governmental powers were not restricted by the relevant provisions.
46 See in general *Symposium on Constitutional Rights for Australia* 1994, *Sydney Law Review*, 16: 1; *Symposium on the High Court of Australia, 1960–1993* (1993) WALR 11; Goldsworthy, J. 1995, 'The High Court, Implied Rights and Constitutional Change', *Quadrant*, March, 46; Craven, G. 1999, 'The High Court of Australia: A Study in the Abuse of Power', *University of New South Wales Law Journal* 22, 1: 216–42.
47 *McGinty v Western Australia* (1996) 186 CLR 140.
48 ibid. at 183.
49 ibid. at 250.
50 ibid. at 288–9.
51 ibid. at 205.
52 *Lange v Australian Broadcasting Tribunal* (1997) 189 CLR 520.
53 ibid. at 566–7.
54 ibid. at 557.
55 ibid. at 558, emphasis added.
56 ibid. at 560; 563.

57 ibid. at 561.
58 ibid. at 562.
59 ibid. at 562–78.
60 *Kruger v Commonwealth* (1997) 190 CLR 1; *Levy v Victoria* (1997) 189 CLR 579.
61 HREOC 1997, *Bringing Them Home: Report of the National Inquiry into Separation of Aboriginal and Torres Strait Islander Children from their Families,* Sydney, HREOC.
62 One of the plaintiffs, Rosie Napangardi McClary, is a mother who claims that her child, Queenie Rose, was taken from her.
63 The plaintiffs also claimed that the provision purported to confer judicial power of the Commonwealth contrary to ch. III of the Constitution and that it prohibited the free exercise of religion contrary to s. 116 of the Constitution, and that they were subject to the implied right to freedom from crimes against humanity of genocide.
64 It could have followed the lead of Brennan CJ and declined to determine these questions.
65 For a general discussion of the question of reparation see Young, S. 1998, 'The Long Way Home: Reparation for the Removal of Aboriginal Children', *University of Queensland Law Review* 20, 1: 70.
66 *Levy v Victoria* (1997) 189 CLR 579.
67 ibid. per Brennan CJ, Toohey, McHugh, Gummow and Kirby JJ. Gaudron J restated her views in *Kruger* regarding freedom of movement.
68 *Reference re Alberta Statutes* [1938] SCR 110 at 133.
69 See *Saumer v City of Quebec and Attorney-General of Quebec* [1953] 2 SCR 299; *Switzman v Elbing and Attorney-General of Quebec* [1957] SCR 285.
70 See generally Opeskin & Rothwell, *International Law and Australian Federalism; Symposium: The Internationalisation of Australian Law* 1995, *Sydney Law Review* 17: 1.
71 *Minister of State for Immigration and Ethnic Affairs v Ah Hin Teoh* (1995) 183 CLR 273. For a discussion of the previous case law see Walker, K. 1996, 'Treaties and the Internationalization of Australian Law' in Saunders, C. (ed.) 1996, *Courts of Final Jurisdiction: The Mason Court in Australia,* Sydney, Federation Press, 204, 209–11.
72 Per Mason CJ, Deane, Toohey and Gaudron JJ; McHugh J dissenting.
73 Charlesworth, 'Australia's Split Personality'. See also Walker, 'Treaties and the Internationalization of Australian Law'; Mathew, P. 1995, 'International Law and the Protection of Human Rights in Australia: Recent Trends', *Sydney Law Review,* 17: 177.
74 Evans, G. 1996, 'The Impact of Internationalisation on Australian Law: A Commentary' in Saunders, *Courts of Final Jurisdiction,* 236–41. See also Lavarch, M. 1995, 'The Role of International Law-Making in the Globalisation Process' in Alston & Chiam, *Treaty-making and Australia,* 177–84.
75 Regarding customary international law see Shearer, I. 1995, 'The Implications of Non-treaty Law-making: Customary Law and its Implications' in Alston & Chiam, *Treaty-making and Australia,* 93–106.
76 See Kirby, M. 1995,. 'The Role of International Standards in Australian Courts' in Alston & Chiam, *Treaty-making and Australia,* 74–92; *Ago v District Court of New South Wales* (1988) 12 NSWLR 558 at 569.
77 *Mabo (No 2)* (1992) 175 CLR 1 at 42. Mason CJ and McHugh J agreed with Brennan J.
78 See *Teoh* (1995) 183 CLR 273 at 288.

79 See the discussion in Walker, 'Treaties and the Internationalization of Australian Law', 212–18, especially regarding *Dietrich v R* (1992) 177 CLR 292; *Western Australia v Commonwealth* (1995) 183 CLR 373; *Teoh* (1995) 183 CLR 273.

80 *Newcrest Mining (WA) Ltd v Commonwealth* (1997) 190 CLR 513 at 657–61 per Kirby J.

81 See for example Saunders, *Courts of Final Jurisdiction*, where the justices appear to favour and anticipate the possibility of such an international common law.

CHAPTER 4

Democracy and Citizenship

Because the nature and character of a regime are implicitly defined by its notion of citizenship, the often pressing practical question of who is a citizen yields a rich seam for theoretical examination and reflection. How the High Court approaches and engages the question of who is a citizen is therefore an important starting-point for examining the new politics of the High Court and its implications for Australian democracy.

As we have seen, the High Court's implied rights decisions were founded upon a notion of representative democracy secured in the Constitution, so that in discerning the rights and freedoms in the Constitution the Court was also defining and delineating the character of representative democracy in Australia. In its 1995 decision in *McGinty*, where major aspects of citizenship such as the nature of the franchise, the right to vote and one-vote–one-value were raised, the Court had an unparalleled opportunity to give greater content and meaning to its notion of Australian democracy. How it took up this opportunity, and the consequences for the Australian regime, are the themes explored in this chapter. Examining *McGinty* in depth and comparing it with the Court's previous judgment on one-vote–one-value, the *McKinlay* decision of 1975, allows us to evaluate the Court's understanding of citizenship and democracy and thereby the character of the new politics of the High Court. This comparison will provide an insight into the way the matter in dispute influences the development of the Court's jurisprudence, the limits imposed on the Court by theories of adjudication and, finally, the way political considerations frame and in some instances constrain the Court's decisions.

Citizenship and the Constitution

The Australian Constitution is curiously silent on the question of who is a citizen. Though there is a reference to 'a subject of the Queen' (sections 34, 117), citizenship is not mentioned in the Constitution. Perhaps this is not surprising since, prior to the enactment of the *Nationality and Citizenship Act 1948* (Cth), which defined an Australian citizen, Australians who were not aliens were considered British subjects, owing allegiance to the Crown.[1] It would appear, then, that the constitutional formulation that comes closest to citizenship is 'subject of the Queen'.[2] But this does not mean that the framers of the Constitution did not contemplate an Australian citizenship. Andrew Inglis Clark, Attorney-General of Tasmania, sought to include in the Constitution a federal citizenship based on the Fourteenth Amendment of the American Constitution. His proposal was rejected, not simply on the grounds that citizenship was a republican concept, but because such a provision would have impinged on States' rights to enact legislation based on race. The formula that was finally adopted in the Constitution (section 117) provided 'A subject of the Queen, resident in any State, shall not be subject in any other State to any disability or discrimination which would not be equally applicable to him if he were a subject of the Queen resident in such other State'. The Constitution confirmed the right of the States to determine their own citizenship criteria, subject to the specific powers given to the Commonwealth.[3]

From a different perspective, however, the constitutional silence regarding citizenship is deceptive. According to Aristotle, the question of who is a citizen is a crucial starting-point for ascertaining the nature of a regime.[4] However, it was not conventional notions of citizenship such as birthplace or parentage that revealed the nature of the regime to Aristotle, but citizenship understood as ruling and being ruled in turn. This theoretical orientation allows us to see the Constitution in a different light, directing our attention to its provisions on political rule and thereby the character of the regime as a whole.

Representative Democracy and the States

In examining the nature of rule secured by the Constitution it is important to keep in mind the federal nature of the constitutional settlement. An essential aspect of the Australian founding was the preservation, as far as possible, of the continuing independence of the former colonies. For this reason section 106 of the Constitution provides that

> The Constitution of each State of the Commonwealth shall, subject to this
> Constitution, continue as at the establishment of the Commonwealth, or
> as at the admission or establishment of the State, as the case may be, until
> altered in accordance with the Constitution of the State.

The Constitution of each colony, and thereby the provisions and legislation governing representative and responsible government, including
electoral boundaries, the franchise and qualifications for holding office
at the time of founding, were preserved by the Australian Constitution.

During the nineteenth century the colonial governments adopted
English democratic institutions, at first representative but later those of
responsible government. By 1859 all colonies had responsible parliamentary government, widely considered to be the most significant check
on executive dominance.[5] More complex, however, were the principles
underlying the concepts of representation evident in colonial legislation
concerning the franchise and electoral boundaries. There were three
contending views of representation, appropriated and altered from
English constitutionalism, which influenced the character of the franchise and electoral boundaries in the Australian colonies.[6] One of the
earliest was the concept of 'community representation', based on an
organic view of the nation. Parliament was a forum for informing the
monarch, who was responsible for the government of the country;
members of parliament represented the concerns and grievances of various communities within the nation. The nexus between community and
land, evident in shires or boroughs, meant that communal interests
could properly and adequately be represented through the land.

This view contrasts with the Whig belief in the representation of
interest. Parliament, not the monarch, was responsible for governing,
which meant that members should give expression to various opinions,
grievances and interests within society.[7] In doing so, however, members
looked to the general good; as Burke put it, Parliament was 'not a *congress
of ambassadors from different hostile interests*'. It was a representative
and deliberative body that sought the best interests of the nation as a
whole. The importance of interest in Whig representational theory
meant that communities and interests not directly represented in
Parliament could be 'virtually' represented by members for other parts of
the country which shared similar interests. Restricted franchise, corrupt
and rotten boroughs and extreme inequalities in the size of constituencies did not constitute a serious defect as long as communities and
interests were represented in parliament, either directly or virtually.[8]

These views of representation, based on communities, classes or
interests, soon gave way to the idea of individual representation. Though
the concept could be traced to the Levellers (who professed egalitarian-

ism), an influential source of the idea was the natural rights theories which provided theoretical support for the American and French Revolutions. Though modern natural rights theories played an important role in England, the Utilitarians had greater influence. Their teachings concerning individual self-interest and the 'greatest happiness principle' issued in the most far-reaching parliamentary reforms, evident in the *Reform Act 1832* and subsequent enactments. Assuming rational individualism, Utilitarians saw Parliament as a locus of conflicting opinions, a debating chamber in which principles could be resolved. Since members represented individual opinions, all individuals had to be represented: the franchise was to be expanded to include male suffrage initially and universal suffrage ultimately; voting was to be by secret ballot; territorial constituencies were to be equalised; plural voting by business proprietors and university graduates repealed.[9]

In many respects the Australian colonies led the shift from geographic and interest representation to individualism. Plural voting either never existed (South Australia) or was abolished in the colonies starting in the 1890s (abolished in the UK in 1948). Payment of members was introduced in the 1880s (1911 in the UK). By the mid 1850s most colonies had legislated for the secret ballot and male suffrage (1872 and 1918 respectively in the UK). By the time of federation South Australia and Western Australia had adult suffrage, by 1904 adult suffrage existed in all the States (1928 in the UK).[10] The theoretical foundations of this trend in the colonies could have been, as noted above, either natural rights theories or Utilitarianism. But given the influence of Utilitarians in the reform process in the UK, with their avowed rejection of the 'nonsense on stilts' of natural rights, and the influence of Chartists in Australia, who advocated radical democratic reform, it seems more likely that the notions of individual and popular sovereignty that animated such reforms in Australia derived from the Utilitarian stream, as modified by John Stuart Mill.

It should be noted, however, that representation of interests was retained in important respects. The Upper Houses maintained a more limited franchise in various forms. Though the franchise in the Lower Houses was based on individual representation, the existence of electoral boundaries recalled the importance of land in representing both community and interest. Moreover, zonal boundaries that took into account farming, mining and commercial interests still assumed a Burkean notion of communal representation. Indeed, the new federal settlement, to the extent that it designated the Senate a 'States' House', introduced geographic and community interests into the Australian Constitution. Thus the evolutionary character of change in Australian constitutionalism meant that innovations in the nature of the franchise – and thereby a theoretical change in the conception of citizenship, sovereignty and parliamentary rule – coexisted with older conceptions of representation and citizenship.

In one important respect, however, the founders were not prepared to implement a comprehensive notion of individualism. Influenced by racial theories, the American experience with slavery and economic and defence concerns, the colonies sought to limit or exclude 'coloured' races from Australia. Initially the colonies were concerned with the perceived threat posed by the Chinese in the furniture and mining industries, especially in Victoria. Use of Kanaka or Islander labour in the sugarcane industry in Queensland was seen by the southern colonies as a threat comparable to the use of slave labour in the cotton fields in the southern US. Finally, the Anglo-Japanese Treaty of Commerce and Navigation of 1894 and the Japanese defeat of China in 1895, combined with reports of Japan's increasing interest in trade and immigration to Australia, presented the colonies with the opportunity to legislate against all 'coloured' peoples. A 'White Australia' became part of the political platform of all parties at the time of the first national election.[11]

For Aborigines, the situation varied. Queensland and Western Australia had specific legislation preventing Aborigines from voting for either House, subject to freehold qualifications which were subsequently removed. Though there was no express statutory bar on voting in Victoria, New South Wales, South Australia and Tasmania, franchise legislation in effect gave the same result. For example, in New South Wales franchise legislation prevented people in receipt of charitable aid from voting. As Aborigines on missions and reserves were considered to be in receipt of charitable aid, they were excluded from the vote.[12]

Representative Democracy and the Commonwealth

The federal government provided for in the Constitution was characterised by a popular and representative democracy. Thus the first paragraph of section 24 provides 'The House of Representatives shall be composed of members directly chosen by the people of the Commonwealth, and the number of such members shall be, as nearly as practicable, twice the number of senators', and section 7 requires senators be 'directly chosen by the people of the State'. In choosing senators or members each elector can only vote once (sections 8, 30). Members of the House of Representatives have a maximum term of three years (section 28), senators are in office for a maximum of six years (sections 7, 13). There are provisions for casual vacancies in the Senate (section 15) and for disqualifying senators or members from holding office (sections 44, 45). There are also provisions for the election of President in the Senate and Speaker in the House, and general provisions regarding resignations,

quorums and voting for both the Senate and the House of Representatives (sections 17–23, 35–50).

As a transitional measure – until Parliament otherwise provided – the
Constitution relied on, and appropriated, State electoral regimes to elect
the first Parliament. Consequently, the qualifications of senators and
members (sections 16, 34), qualifications of electors (sections 8, 25, 30,
41), the electoral divisions (sections 7, 29) and the method for electing
(sections 9–11, 31) were based on State legislation. This presented
special difficulties for South Australia at the time of federation and
Western Australia by 1901, as they had introduced female suffrage. At the
Constitutional Convention Debates in Adelaide, Holder from South Australia advocated uniform adult suffrage in order to preserve the voting
rights of women in that State. Other States considered that an intrusion
into their jurisdiction, an attempt to introduce female suffrage into the
States by means of federation. The solution restricted the Commonwealth's power to disenfranchise anyone who had a right to vote at a
State election (section 41). But this meant that, until the Commonwealth
adopted uniform suffrage, the double number of electors in South Australia would have a disproportionate influence in referendums. For this
reason it was provided that in any State with adult suffrage only half the
votes would be counted in any referendum (section 128).[13]

The other major question concerned State franchise restrictions based
on race. According to the Constitution, until Parliament provided otherwise, the number of people of each State was to be used to determine the
number of members in the House of Representatives (section 24). But
in ascertaining the number of the people in the State or Commonwealth,
persons who had been disqualified from voting at State elections on the
basis of race would not be counted (section 25). Therefore, until the
Commonwealth enacted its own legislation, State provisions limiting
the franchise on the grounds of race were relied upon in determining
the number of members of the House of Representatives to be chosen in
each State. The Convention Debates are ambiguous on whether this provision was intended to refer to Aborigines, though the words by themselves do not clearly exclude such a reading.[14] It is true that Aborigines
were excluded from the census: until its repeal in 1967, section 127 provided that 'In reckoning the numbers of the people of the Commonwealth, or of a State or other part of the Commonwealth, aboriginal
natives shall not be counted'. The exclusion from the census was not
intended to deny the right to vote. Though such exclusion could not be
defended in principle, it was sanctioned by the framers on pragmatic
grounds that the numbers of Aborigines were too small to affect the
representational calculation and that such exclusion would financially
benefit some States.[15]

At federation, the States had responsibility for legislating for Aborigines, hence the Commonwealth's power to make special laws for 'people of any race' excluded the 'aboriginal race in any state' (section 51xxvi). Combined with section 41, which was enacted chiefly to protect female suffrage but also to guarantee the voting right for those who had the right under State laws, it seemed that the Constitution did not present a barrier to Aborigines' right to vote. But given the limited voting rights of Aborigines within the States, this provision did not greatly assist them.

The first elections for the Australian Parliament were conducted on 29–30 March 1901. The new Parliament met in Melbourne on 9 May 1901, and among its first legislation was the *Commonwealth Electoral Act 1902* and the *Franchise Act 1902*. The Electoral Act established Distribution Commissioners for each State, to distribute each State into electoral divisions. Parliament had the power to accept, with or without amendment, or reject the proposals of the Commissioners. In making any proposed distribution the Commissioners were required to give due consideration to a number of factors, including community and diversity of interests, means of communication, physical features, existing boundaries and State boundaries. The quota for distribution was not to vary by more than one-fifth. The Franchise Act established universal adult franchise, the age of majority being set at twenty-one. It continued, however, the exclusion of 'Aboriginal natives'.[16]

These Commonwealth enactments were consistent with and advanced the trend toward the representation of individual interests. Adult suffrage, secret ballot, payment of members – all emphasised the importance of individual representation. But older notions of representation persisted: a 20 per cent margin, electoral boundaries taking into account community and diversity of interests, and the Senate as a 'States' House' retained communal and territorial conceptions of representation. Importantly, the major colonial limitation on individual representation based on race remained, and was implemented at the federal level by the enactment of various provisions excluding aborigines of Australia, Asia, Africa and the Pacific Islands from the franchise.[17]

McKinlay's Case

This broad overview of the constitutional and legislative provisions regarding citizenship and representation suggests that the founders were prepared to impose minimal restrictions on the authority of Parliaments to define and alter the character of representative democracy in Australia. Apart from the transitional provisions that relied on State laws in respect of voting, and some minimal requirements as noted above, the question of who should have the right to vote, the nature of the electoral and voting system, and therefore the character of representative democracy in Australia appeared to be left to the determination of the Commonwealth and State Parliaments. The practical import of this for the High Court was that, until *McKinlay's* case, it did not have a major opportunity to articulate its understanding of the constitutional provisions and therefore its conception of representative democracy and citizenship in Australian constitutionalism.[18]

At issue in *McKinlay* was the validity of section 19 of the *Commonwealth Electoral Act 1918–1975* (Cth) and certain sections of the *Representation Act 1905–1974* (Cth). Section 19 of the *Commonwealth Electoral Act 1918–1975* (Cth) required that, in any proposed distribution of a State into electoral divisions for the election of the House of Representatives, the Distribution Commissioner should give consideration to the community of interests, the means of travel and communication, the trend of population changes, and the physical features within the division. Subject to this section, the Act required that variations in the number of electors in each division should not exceed one-tenth more or less than the quota for the State (ascertained by dividing the number of electors in the State by the number of members to be chosen for the State). The Act was challenged on the grounds that the requirement in section 24 of the Constitution that members be 'chosen by the people' meant that the State electoral divisions were required to have (as nearly as practicable) equal numbers of people. The Representation Act was challenged as contravening section 24 of the Constitution because it required a determination of the number of people in each State only when there was a census under the *Census and Statistics Act 1905–1973* (Cth), and because the requirement to refer to the census could indefinitely postpone the redistribution of electoral divisions. The plaintiffs applied for injunctions to restrain the chief electoral officer from holding an election for the House of Representatives on the basis of existing boundaries, and declarations that the provisions of the Representation Act were invalid. The Court held (by a majority) that section 24 of the Constitution did not require the number of people or the number of electors in electoral divisions to be equal. It did, however, hold that the provisions of the Representation Act were unconstitutional.

Legalism and Parliamentary Democracy

The dominant view of the Court is developed in clearest terms in the judgment of Chief Justice Barwick. According to him, the problem before the Court is a matter of legal construction of a legal document, namely, the Constitution as an Act of Imperial Parliament. 'The problem is not to be solved by resort to slogans or to political catch-cries or to vague and imprecise expressions of political philosophy.' One of the important reasons for adopting this method is 'stability':

> The only true guide and the only course which can produce stability in constitutional law is to read the language of the Constitution itself, no doubt generously and not pedantically, but as a whole: and to find its meaning by legal reasoning. I respectfully agree with Sir Owen Dixon's opinion that 'there is no other safe guide to judicial decisions in great conflicts than a strict and complete legalism'.[19]

What implication does this way of reading the Constitution have for section 24 and the requirement that members of the House of Representatives be 'directly chosen by the people of the Commonwealth'? According to Chief Justice Barwick:

> the expression 'directly chosen by the people' is merely emphatic of two factors: first, that the election of members should be direct and not indirect as, for example, through an electoral college and, secondly, that it shall be a popular election. It is not an indirect reference to any particular theory of government.[20]

This legal reading is based not only on the text of the Constitution but on the historical context of the founding. The two important matters in this regard are the character of franchise and electoral boundaries apparently endorsed by the Constitution. To the extent that the Constitution accepted – until the Commonwealth Parliament provided otherwise – State franchises and electoral boundaries for the election of members of the House, it implicitly endorsed such arrangements. A review of the State franchises at the time of the founding showed wide variation, with qualifications based on age, sex, residency and property. The conclusion is that the Constitution recognised a range of valid franchises and therefore did not prescribe adult suffrage, let alone equality of vote. Similarly, until Parliament provided otherwise, the Constitution adopted State boundaries for electing members for the House of Representatives (section 29). The Australian colonies in 1900 did not insist on practical equality of numbers of electors in the electoral divisions. For example, in New South Wales deviations from quota were allowed, taking into account 'community or diversity of interests, lines of communication and physical features'.[21] Therefore the Constitution allowed a range of electoral districts that took into account these historical and practical factors.[22]

What emerges from the 'natural' or 'legal' reading of the Constitution is a view of franchise, voting rights and thus citizenship that is not spelled out in the terms of the Constitution, an interpretation that relies fundamentally on 'history'. In fact, what becomes clear is that the natural reading presupposes an understanding not only of 'history' but also of 'politics', something it sought to avoid from the beginning. This can be seen in Chief Justice Barwick's analysis of precedents from the US Supreme Court. Those precedents that had interpreted 'directly chosen by the people' to imply equal voting rights are rejected by Chief Justice Barwick and the other justices because of the different historical found-ations of the two Constitutions.[23] However, Chief Justice Barwick goes further in articulating fundamental theoretical (and hence not simply 'legal') distinctions between the two Constitutions. The crucial differ-ence may be summed up as a 'denial of complete confidence in any single arm of government' in the American model, while 'the Australian Constitution is built upon confidence in a system of Parliamentary Government and ministerial responsibility'. Thus Chief Justice Barwick's legalism – his rejection of 'political philosophy' as necessary for inter-preting the Constitution – presupposes a political view of the Constit-ution as an enactment that entrenches plenary power in Parliament.[24]

Not only does Chief Justice Barwick rely on this implicit notion for interpreting the Constitution, but he considers that this political arrange-ment is superior. In canvassing the practical limitations to equality of votes, he observes that mere equality of numbers is likely to produce inequality of voting power. Long parliamentary experience, taking into account various considerations, 'represents a practical endeavour to solve the problem and does represent a scheme designed to produce equality of voting value'. While conceding that such equality is the proper goal of the present Parliament, Chief Justice Barwick denies that written or enacted solutions – formulas – will achieve a result superior to the outcome achieved by parliamentary process and experience. Similar views are expressed by Justice Gibbs, who rejects the American preced-ents because they rely on the particular needs of the US or because they reflect the view that 'every major social ill . . . can find its cure in some constitutional "principle"'.[25]

These judgments apparently give extensive authority to Parliament. Only Justice Mason raises the possibility that, if variations in numbers of electors are 'grossly disproportionate', a question may be raised whether an election held on boundaries so drawn would produce a House of Representatives directly chosen by the people. Yet it is not clear how 'gross disproportion' is to be evaluated if not on the basis of equality or reasonable 'proportion', or where this principle is to be located if not in section 24 of the Constitution.

The overall character of this form of judicial review can be discerned in the enactments that are held invalid by the majority. Sections 3 and 4 of the Representation Act are held invalid because they require determ-ination of the number of members only when there is a census. Section 12 of that Act is invalid because redistribution of electoral divisions could be indefinitely postponed. The Court will exercise oversight over the broad structure and ground-rules of the electoral process. Beyond this, however, Parliament has extensive and significant discretion. This view should be contrasted with the contending views on the Bench, the judgments of Justice Stephen, Justices McTiernan and Jacobs, and Justice Murphy.

Representative Democracy

What is notable about Justice Stephen's judgment is that he is prepared to interpret the meaning of section 24 in terms of 'principles', apparently rejecting the legalism and literalism of the orthodoxy:

> Three great principles, representative democracy (by which I mean that the legislators are chosen by the people), direct popular election, and the national character of the lower House, may each be discerned in the opening words of s. 24. Nothing however is said as to the composition of electoral divisions.[26]

According to Justice Stephen, representative democracy predicates the enfranchisement of electors, the existence of an electoral system with representatives and the bestowal of legislative functions upon the selected representatives, but the 'particular quality and character of the content of each of these three ingredients of representative democracy, and there may well be others, is not fixed and precise'. For Justice Stephen:

> representative democracy is descriptive of a whole spectrum of political institutions, each differing in countless respects yet answering to that generic description. The spectrum has finite limits and in a particular instance there may be absent some quality which is regarded as so essential to representative democracy as to place that instance outside those limits altogether; but at no one point within the range of the spectrum does there exist any single requirement so essential as to be determinative of the existence of representative democracy.[27]

To deny a 'spectrum' of possible institutions is to ignore the 'long chapters in the evolution of democratic institutions both in this country and overseas'. Yet Justice Stephen concedes that there is a 'pure form' of representative democracy which he appears to equate with 'individual representation':

> It is no doubt true that something approaching numerical equality of electors within electorates is an important factor, together with much else,

in the attainment of what many will regard as representative democracy in its purest form, just as adult suffrage, free of discrimination on the grounds of race, sex, property or educational qualification will likewise aid in its attainment.[28]

It is not clear whether his view of a 'pure' form can coexist with the notion of a 'spectrum': doesn't a pure form suggest a hierarchy and hence a means of ranking forms of representative democracy? If evolution has determined the pure form, isn't it proper for the judiciary to reject what has obviously been left in the past? The difficulty faced by Justice Stephen is that, having introduced a theoretical and evolutionary standard in evaluating the Constitution, he is not prepared to employ it to restrict parliamentary discretion – he returns to literalism to defend judicial deference. Thus the Constitution does not necessarily import a specific form of representative democracy as a mode of government for the nation. It leaves the legislatures to determine the appropriate model of representative democracy and therefore 'it is not for the Court to intervene so long as what is enacted is consistent with the existence of representative democracy as the chosen mode of government and within the power conferred by s. 51(xxxvi)'.[29] Judicial restraint is justified by his political and theoretical understanding of what the Constitution prescribes. Justice Stephen's approach is a curious amalgam of a theoretical and contextual reading of the Constitution, limited by a form of literalism.

Common Understanding of the Time

Justices McTiernan and Jacobs face a similar problem in attempting to give meaning to the phrase 'chosen by the people'. They reject the argument that section 24 provides an equal number of people per electoral division – in their view, the section could not be given such an exact content. To them, 'chosen by the people' did not mean chosen by the enfranchised electors since that could include the most limited franchise and therefore justify an oligarchy:

> The words 'chosen by the people of the Commonwealth' fall to be applied to different circumstances at different times and at any particular time the facts and circumstances may show that some or all members are not, or would not in the event of an election, be chosen by the people within the meaning of these words in s. 24.[30]

How is this variable meaning to be ascertained? According to Justices McTiernan and Jacobs:

It is a question of degree. It cannot be determined in the abstract. It depends in part upon the common understanding of the time of those who must be eligible to vote before a member can be described as chosen by the people of the Commonwealth. For instance, the long-established universal adult suffrage may now be recognised as a fact and as a result it is doubtful whether, subject to the particular provision of s. 30, anything less than this could now be described as a choice by the people.[31]

To Justices McTiernan and Jacobs, the franchise is a historically variable concept that may be defined as universal adult suffrage. Yet the notion of equality inherent in this current view does not extend to the equality of numbers of people in every electoral district. For this reason, though they concede that the inequalities in the number of people in State electoral divisions are serious, 'they are not in any State so great that an election conducted by those divisions would not be a choosing of members by the people'. Justices McTiernan and Jacobs accept that there are minimal standards, as well as evolving notions of the franchise and one-vote–one-value; like Justice Stephen they confront the difficulty of evolving and 'pure' forms. However, they choose to resolve this difficulty by assuming a form of progress: the latest or current form, and the form that shows longevity, represents the ideal. In adopting this standard they cannot extend it to the principle of one-vote–one-value, which has not demonstrated such a pedigree.

Silent Operation of Constitutional Principles

The tension between a historically determined pure form and a spectrum of options also emerges in the judgment of Justice Murphy. Justice Murphy relies extensively on American authorities, both the decisions of the US Supreme Court and the views of America's founding fathers, such as Jefferson. He does so because he claims that American history is part of Australia's cultural heritage. In contrast, his Australian references are principally journal articles and Harrison Moore's *Constitution of the Commonwealth of Australia*; there are few references to Australian founders or the Federation debates. Justice Murphy's extensive use of, and references to, American constitutionalism may have been due to his view that there was insufficient Australian material to support his arguments. As Attorney-General in the Whitlam Labor government Murphy had claimed that the Constitution did not provide for one-vote–one-value. His proposal to amend the Constitution to entrench such a measure was unsuccessful at the 1974 referendum. In this light it seemed that Murphy, appointed to the Bench in early 1975, was undertaking as a judge what he had been unable to achieve as a politician.[32]

Justice Murphy interprets section 24 in terms of the political and philosophical view that it entrenches and preserves a democratic sharing of power: it 'expresses the most basic right of the people and commands that there shall be equal representation, an equal sharing of power in the election in each State for the House of Representatives'.[33] But what of those provisions in State laws that seemed to contradict the principle of equal sharing and appeared to be endorsed by the Constitution? Justice Murphy resolves this difficulty by arguing that as a practical matter at Federation such laws were permitted under sections 29 and 30 and not made subject to the Constitution. Once Federation was established, section 24 rather than section 26 became operative.[34] Thus he dismisses the argument that the character of State laws at the time of Federation could be used to give meaning and content to section 24. If this argument is adopted, there is still the problem of the meaning to be given to the phrase 'chosen by the people'. Justice Murphy's response relies on the 'silent operation of constitutional principles':

> It may have been accepted in 1900 that 'chosen by the people' could exclude women and people without certain property. Women were then deprived of the vote in certain States and this was referred to obliquely in s. 128 of the Constitution. Because of the silent operation of constitutional principles, this is no longer so. In 1975, any law of the Parliament which deprived persons of a right of representation or to vote on the ground of sex or lack of property would be incompatible with the command that the House of Representatives be 'directly chosen by the people'. It would contravene s. 24 and be thus unconstitutional.[35]

But if these principles are 'silent', how do they articulate or manifest themselves? Are they to be discerned by the character of parliamentary enactments? Apparently not, since enactments may sometimes be incompatible with such principles. Are they 'contemporary standards', as suggested by Justice Stephen and Justices McTiernan and Jacobs? If so, Justice Murphy appears to be outlining a changing notion of the franchise and what it means to be 'chosen by the people'. Moreover, the pregnant phrase 'silent operation of constitutional principles' hints at a hidden source of development, influencing, guiding and in some sense unfolding the proper or true meaning of 'democratic equality'. This progressive notion of human development appears at odds with the Declaration of Independence that speaks of inalienable rights and inherent equality. It is not clear how such natural rights are consistent with evolving, and therefore fundamentally historically determined, rights.

However, Justice Murphy also has a powerful practical argument in favour of judicial review that raises profound questions concerning the efficacy of responsible government. His claim is that it is 'hollow' to

argue that if Parliament fails, the remedy is with the people. 'If the legislature fails to ensure fairness, and there is no constitutional right en-
forceable in the courts, where is the remedy?'[36] The judiciary is required
to correct the potential deficiencies of representative democracy, especially concerning the franchise and equality of voting rights. As Justice
Murphy notes, since the case was heard on 3 and 5 November 1975 and
judgment reserved, both Houses of Parliament had been dissolved and a
general election was to be held on 13 December 1975. Enrolments and
nominations for the existing divisions, based on divisions made in 1968
and 1969, were closed:

> The result of glaring inequalities between the electoral divisions in each of
> the States, in my opinion, is that in those States, the election proposed to
> be held on the 13th December next will not be one in which the members
> will be 'chosen by the people' as the Constitution requires.[37]

In effect, Justice Murphy was declaring that the next election based on
the current electoral divisions would be unconstitutional. This reference
to the 1975 election is an important reminder that it is not possible to
appreciate the significance of *McKinlay* unless it is placed within the
larger political context.

1975 Whitlam Dismissal

The Whitlam Labor government that took office in 1972 did not control
the Senate. This presented considerable difficulties for the passage of
its extensive and ambitious legislative agenda. After six Bills, one of
which was the Commonwealth Electoral Bill ensuring one-vote–one-
value, were twice rejected by the Senate, Whitlam advised the Governor-
General to dissolve both the Senate and House of Representatives. The
double dissolution election of 1974 returned Labor to power although
the four referendum proposals submitted to electors during the election,
one of which was for 'democratic elections', were defeated. Significantly,
the election did not deliver Labor control of the Senate. As a result, an
unprecedented joint sitting of the Senate and the House of Representatives was convened by the Governor-General. The calling of the
double dissolution and the validity of the Bills passed at the joint sitting
resulted in a number of appeals to the High Court, one of which was
McKinlay.[38]

Argument in *McKinlay* was heard on 3 and 5 November 1975, but
before judgment was handed down Australia had experienced a series of
constitutional crises. On 11 November 1975 Governor-General Sir John
Kerr, after seeking advice from Chief Justice Barwick concerning his

authority to act, dismissed Prime Minister Gough Whitlam from office and asked Malcolm Fraser, Leader of the Opposition, to form a caretaker government on condition he advised dissolution of both Houses of Parliament. A double dissolution was proclaimed that day, with elections set for 13 December 1975.[39] Thus the swiftness of the judgment in *McKinlay*, handed down on 1 December 1975, reflected the urgency of the issues and the importance of the decision for the validity of the forthcoming elections.

Importantly, the political context appeared to impose a number of theoretical and practical constraints on the outcome of the case. Chief Justice Barwick's intervention in the dismissal of the Whitlam government embroiled him in political controversy. At issue were the propriety of the Chief Justice of the High Court advising the Governor-General and the merit of that advice. Inevitably, the sustained political criticism had major implications for the legitimacy of the Court. A decision that would have necessitated an electoral redistribution for the coming elections risked being seen as another High Court political intervention in the constitutional crisis – not simply a decision about electoral boundaries but a judicial intrusion that sought to shape the outcome of the election. This explains Chief Justice Barwick's insistence in *McKinlay* that the Court was undertaking a 'legal' task in deciding the case. It also accounts for a majority decision that effectively declined any further involvement in the constitutional and political crisis that was going to unfold. The Court's decision upholding the electoral boundaries but striking down the provisions of the Representation Act seemed to provide an apparently neutral and non-partisan response to a contentious and politically volatile issue.

In contrast, Justice Murphy's decision appeared to be a judicial attempt at securing what was rejected in the 1974 referendum, a decision that would improve Labor's prospects in the election. His position was fraught with theoretical difficulties. Though the declarations sought by the plaintiffs regarding the validity of the Electoral Acts and Representation Acts were prospective – they concerned the constitutionality of future elections – it was not clear how earlier elections based on these unequal divisions could be protected from invalidity. What was the status of the 1972 and 1974 elections based on those divisions?[40] Justice Murphy's judgment potentially cast doubt on the Whitlam Labor government's, and thereby his own, legislative achievements. Never before had such a wholesale exercise of judicial striking down of parliamentary enactments been contemplated in Australia. It was also unclear how the ensuing gaps in legitimacy and authority could be repaired. Practically, and in terms of institutional legitimacy, there were strong arguments that suggested finding against the plaintiffs.

Democracy and Citizenship in McKinlay

In deciding the constitutional status of one-vote–one-value, the judges in *McKinlay* reflected on a range of crucial questions, such as how to undertake the judicial task of interpreting the Constitution, the nature of representative democracy secured by it, and the definition of citizenship implicit in the notions of representation, voting and the franchise. To Chief Justice Barwick and Justice Gibbs, a natural legal reading of the Constitution did not require articulation of any political concepts such as representative democracy. Accordingly, the Constitution was silent regarding the limits to franchise and one-vote–one-value. However, this perspective presupposed a regime where a parliamentary responsible government exercised plenary power. In general Justice Mason agreed with this view, though he was prepared to acknowledge that a system of democratic representative government was provided by the Constitution, placing limits on grossly disproportionate electorates.

The other judges were prepared to rely on the idea of representative democracy, with the evolutionary nature of democracy proving crucial for determining its character. To Justice Stephen, although the concept of representative democracy had limits, it accommodated a spectrum of meanings that included a restrictive notion of franchise as well as variations in electoral sizes. To Justices McTiernan and Jacobs, representative democracy was an evolving concept to be determined by contemporary standards. This meant that universal adult suffrage was now the standard. However, it did not entail one-vote–one-value. Only Justice Murphy was prepared to define the terms of the franchise and voting entitlements on the grounds that the dominant feature of the Constitution is the prevalence of democratic principles.

Taking the case as a whole, the practical consequence of *McKinlay* was that the judiciary would exercise minimal oversight of electoral boundaries or the franchise. Whether a provision was constitutional depended upon the circumstances of the case. The Australian Constitution did entrench a system of representative democracy, but its precise scope and character were subject to change, determined principally by Parliament. The Court would merely guard the boundaries of the political process or, at best, acknowledge current practice.

McGinty: A New Citizenship?

The Legislative Assembly of Western Australia consists of fifty-seven members, elected from districts established by the Electoral Distribution Commissioners and divided between the metropolitan area and the remainder of the State. The Commissioners are required to fix the boundaries of the districts in each area to comprise an equal quota of enrolled electors plus or minus 15 per cent. In 1987, when changes were made to the *Electoral Distribution Act 1947* (WA), there were approximately 669 292 voters enrolled in the metropolitan area to select thirty-four members and 240 081 voters enrolled in the remainder of the State to elect twenty-three members of the Assembly. By the 1993 elections, shifts in population and the consequence of the 15 per cent tolerance from the average quota had produced large divergences in the number of voters. For example, the quota for a metropolitan electorate was 21 988 and Wanneroo, the most populous electorate, had 26 580 enrolled voters, while the quota for a non-metropolitan electorate was 11 702. Ashburton, the least populous electorate, had 9135 enrolled voters. There was a 291 per cent difference between the number of voters in Wanneroo and Ashburton.

Similar divergences were evident in the election of Councillors to the Legislative Council, the Western Australian Upper House. The Legislative Council consists of thirty-four members returned from six electoral regions as determined by the Electoral Distribution Commissioners. At the 1993 elections the three metropolitan regions had comparable quotas: North Metropolitan 34 161 returning seven members; South Metropolitan 33 876 returning five members; and East Metropolitan 32 822 returning five members. In contrast, the Mining and Pastoral Region remote from the capital had a quota of 9097 and returned five members; the Agricultural Region (south and west of the Mining and Pastoral Region) had a quota of 13 161 returning five members; and the South West Region (the remainder of the State), had a quota of 13 721, returning seven members. The number of voters in the quota for the North Metropolitan Region was 376 per cent of the number in the Mining and Pastoral Region.[41]

James McGinty and Geoffrey Gallop, Labor members of the Legislative Assembly of Western Australia, and Stanley Halden, a Labor member of the Legislative Council, challenged the constitutionality of the Western Australian laws governing the distribution of electorates for both the Assembly and the Council. The challenge was made on the grounds that the significant disparity in voting power in metropolitan and non-metro-politan districts was inconsistent with the principle of representative democracy as that principle is currently understood.[42] According to them, this understanding requires a wide franchise where every legally capable adult has the vote and each person's vote is equal to the vote of every other person. The principle of representative democracy was implied in the Western Australian Constitution itself or applicable to it from the implication of representative democracy in the Australian Constitution.

In challenging the Western Australian legislation, the plaintiffs were no doubt encouraged by the recent jurisprudence of the High Court that relied on the concept of representative government to impose limits on States and the Commonwealth. As we have seen, in recent decisions the High Court had used the notion of representative democracy secured in the Constitution as the theoretical basis for discerning an implied freedom of political communication. This allowed it to invalidate legislation limiting criticism of industrial court justices,[43] as well as federal legislation that attempted to limit political advertising.[44] Subsequently, the concept of representative democracy and the implied freedom of communication were held by the Court to be a suitable defence in defamation proceedings. The implied freedom of communication could shape the common law and State defamation laws in Australia.[45] Importantly, the Court held that either because of the intimate links between the different levels of government or because representative government was secured in the State Constitutions, the implied freedom of communication limited the States as well as the Commonwealth.[46] The Court's use of the concept of representative government, and its extension and application to State and Commonwealth governments, appeared to provide a promising precedent for reintroducing a comparable democratic notion – the principle of one-vote–one-value – into Australian constitutionalism.[47]

There were obstacles in the path of such an attempt. Though *McGinty* primarily concerned State electoral boundaries, the challenge raised questions concerning the Court's previous decision in *McKinlay* rejecting one-vote–one-value in the Commonwealth Constitution. In fact the plaintiffs in *McGinty* did not want to confront *McKinlay* directly. They attempted to argue that there were positive and negative holdings in *McKinlay*: the positive holding was that normative or prescriptive limits could be implied in the words 'chosen by the people' in section 24; the negative was that the phrase did not guarantee near or practical equality of the value of each vote. Because of the principle of representative democracy recognised in recent judicial decisions, the plaintiffs argued that the negative holding in *McKinlay* should be overruled – without rational justification, variations in the value of an individual's vote infringed the principle of representative democracy in both State and Commonwealth Constitutions.

If the Court's recent decisions seemed promising to the plaintiffs in *McGinty*, the case in turn presented the Court with an invaluable opportunity to advance its jurisprudence founded upon the concept of representative government beyond the field of political communication to the related, and equally important, notion of political equality. To the extent that *McGinty* concerned electoral boundaries, one-vote–one-value and, implicitly, the character of the franchise, it seemed to offer the Court a chance to move beyond the supervision and maintenance of the broad contours and institutional structure of Australian democracy toward a more fundamental and substantial definition of representative democracy and citizenship in Australia.[48]

But the Court in *McGinty* did not take that step. Indeed, in upholding its previous decision in *McKinlay* and rejecting the principle of one-vote–one-value in State Constitutions it went further, moving away from its jurisprudence based on the concept of representative democracy. Why did the Court check the development of its implied rights jurisprudence in *McGinty*? What conception of representative government and citizenship in the Australian polity did it outline and settle in that case? To explore these important and related questions, we must consider the judgments in *McGinty* in some detail.

Constitutional Interpretation

The majority of judges in *McGinty* who reject the argument of one-vote–one-value in the Australian Constitution do so by reconsidering the Court's recent decisions on representative government.[49] To them, *McGinty* provides the opportunity to restate their understanding of the proper way to interpret the Constitution. What emerges from this re-assessment is the view that constitutional adjudication requires an interpretation of the words or structure of the document; to go beyond the words or necessary implications is to undertake what is not permissible, either in terms of the Constitution or the Court's previous decisions. As Chief Justice Brennan observes, the 'principle of "representative democracy" can be given the status of a constitutional imperative, but only in so far as the meaning and content of that principle are implied in the text and structure of the Constitution'. Thus it is the text and not the concept that is decisive: 'The constitutional question is whether there is inconsistency with the text and structure of the Constitution'.[50]

The need to shift from an interpretation that relies on a free-standing concept such as representative government to one based on the text and structure of the Constitution is put most forcefully by Justice McHugh. According to him, the meaning of the Constitution must be determined by 'ordinary techniques of statutory interpretation and by no other means'. This requires the text to be the starting-point. Implications may be derived only from the text or structure of the Constitution, and only when they are logically or practically necessary. It is not permissible, as the Court has attempted to do in recent cases, to turn to underlying or overarching constitutional doctrines in order to explain or illuminate the text. This way of proceeding is contrary to the *Engineers* case, and in effect inserts a new free-standing principle of representative democracy in the Constitution. For this reason, he is particularly critical of the Court's decisions in *Theophanous* and *Stephens.* Justice McHugh summarises his position in these terms:

> as much as I admire the noble vision of those justices who have found, contrary to what the overwhelming majority of lawyers had always thought, that the Constitution contains a free-standing principle of representative democracy, the principles of constitutional interpretation compel me to reject their reasoning.[51]

To decide cases on this principle is to 'give the Court a jurisdiction which the Constitution does not contemplate and which the Australian people have never authorised'. Political decisions should be left to the people. Accordingly, Justice McHugh evaluates the text of the Constitution, the history of electoral equality before Federation and the history of franchise at Federation, concluding that equality of voting power is not a fundamental feature of the Constitution.

Contours of Representative Democracy

What implication does the majority emphasis on the primacy of the text and structure of the Constitution have for representative democracy? The question is important in *McGinty* because if the principle of one-vote–one-value is established for the Commonwealth, it may be possible to extend it, in terms similar to *Stephens* case, to the Western Australian Constitution.

The majority accept that the Commonwealth Constitution secures representative democracy. However, their argument is that the Constitution attempts to accommodate a variable notion of representative democracy. Justice Dawson agrees with the judgment of Justice Stephen in *McKinlay* that the quality and character of representative democracy are not fixed and precise. The Constitution provides minimum requirements but does not purport to go significantly further:

> Thus, it may be seen that the form of representative government, including the type of electoral system, the adoption and size of electoral divisions, and the franchise are all left to parliament by the Constitution.[52]

Subject to a number of restrictions (in sections 7, 8, 9, 13, 15, 29, 30, 41, 44, 47), the Constitution leaves it to Parliament 'to determine questions of a political nature about which opinions may vary considerably'.

Justice McHugh argues that it is not established in Australia that one-vote–one-value is a tenet of representative democracy. It is a controversial question. He cites the *Final Report of the Constitutional Commission* (1988), the failed referendums in 1974 and 1988 that attempted to entrench such a provision in the Constitution, Canadian precedents and Justice Stephen's judgment in *McKinlay* to argue for judicial deference:

> Notwithstanding the views of eminent political scientists and the Constitutional Commission, a very substantial number of Australian electors, perhaps a majority, do not see equal representation for equal numbers as indispensable to representative government or democracy in Australia. When such a division of opinion occurs about what is essentially a political question, this Court should be slow to substitute its views for that of the Parliaments as to what representative democracy requires.[53]

Justice Gummow examines the Constitutional Convention debates and the founders' views to argue that the founding was characterised by advanced ideas in political representation: the new Constitution was seen at the time as extremely democratic. But the founders provided the minimum requirements of representative democracy and were prepared to leave as much discretion as possible for Parliament to facilitate and encourage the dynamic and evolutionary nature of democracy. A number of matters were not included in the Constitution simply because there was trust in Parliament. Others were fixed as minimum requirements, for example single-member constituencies, adult franchise and the rejection of plural voting. Equality of votes was not included. On this basis Justice Gummow argues that single-member districts may be so disproportionate as to deny ultimate control by popular election. He accepts the judgments of Justice Mason and Justices McTiernan and Jacobs in *McKinlay* that 'such a question is to be determined by reference to the particular stage which then has been reached in the evolution of representative government'. Examples of such evolutionary change include the minimum age for voting and universal adult suffrage. These measures:

> could not be abrogated by reversion to the system which operated in one or more colonies at the time of Federation. In my opinion, this is so notwithstanding that ss 8 and 30 of the Constitution, subject to the prevention of plural voting, permitted the qualification of electors to be ascertained in that way, until federal Parliament otherwise provided.[54]

Justice Gummow states that Australian constitutionalism can be characterised as a Millian evolutionary and progressive liberal democracy, and on this basis he is prepared to give the Constitution a new evolutionary meaning. This meaning is to be derived from the principle of longevity: long-established practice, especially in legislated form, will determine the advancing frontiers. The same principle cannot be applied to relative parity in voting numbers because, though it is a dominant principle, it is subject to historical, geographical and communal considerations that are better weighed by the legislative branch than by the legal. Whether a matter is open to judicial review (because of gross disproportion) depends on the circumstances of that case.[55]

Chief Justice Brennan declines to decide the question of whether the Constitution implicitly precludes electoral distributions that produce disparities of voting power on the grounds that, even if it did, the Commonwealth Constitution contains no implication affecting disparities of voting power among franchise holders for the election of members of a State Parliament.[56]

State Constitution and Representative Government

If the Australian Constitution does not mandate one-vote–one-value, the next question to be addressed in *McGinty* is whether such a requirement can be discerned in the Western Australian Constitution. According to Chief Justice Brennan, though he had accepted in *Stephens* that 'directly chosen by the people' implied a general freedom to discuss political matters, it did not extend to equality of voting power. Rather, the context and circumstances of the provisions suggested that the Western Australian Constitution had historically preserved the impugned electoral divisions. Thus the Western Australian Parliament was free to enact measures consistent with the constitutional history of the State.[57] Justice Dawson agrees with the views of Chief Justice Brennan that the system of representative government prescribed in the federal Constitution is confined to the Commonwealth Parliament and is not intended as a prescription to the States. He also accepts that the Western Australian Constitution does not contain any implication of electoral equality.[58] Similarly, Justice McHugh rejects the view in *Theophanous* and *Stephens* that the free-standing principle of representative democracy applies generally to the Constitution and therefore could require equality of electoral divisions for State elections. State Constitutions must be evaluated on their own terms. Such an analysis, based on the ordinary and natural meaning of the provisions and the history of the enactments, shows that equality of vote is not a principle in the Western Australian Constitution. The entrenched provisions made the discussions concerning representative democracy irrelevant. Justice Gummow agrees with Justice McHugh that there is no necessary connection between the type of representative democracy in the Commonwealth and the States: 'there is nothing in the Constitution to bind the States to any particular subsequent stage of evolution in the system of responsible government'. The States have extensive authority to determine the character of representative democracy, provided elections take place by direct vote rather than by other indirect methods.[59]

Dissenting Views

In contrast to the views of the majority, the minority judgments of Justice Toohey and Justice Gaudron reveal the alternative direction of the Court's jurisprudence based on representative democracy, expanding beyond the implied freedom of political communication to introduce a principle of one-vote–one-value. Justice Toohey attempts to answer the question by first considering the character of the federal Constitution. He acknowledges that the Court's recent decisions have varied on the meaning to be given to the phrase. Though the Constitution does not use the expression 'representative democracy', once it is conceded that it established a system of representative democracy 'it is apparent that more is involved than freedom of political communication'. He rejects giving meaning to the phrase by referring to the historical circumstances of the founding. Democracy is dynamic and the Constitution must be construed as a living force. Therefore, the Court must take into account political, social and economic developments since Federation.[60] Alternatively, although the connotation of the words in the Constitution remains fixed, their denotation may vary over time.

He relies on *Cheatle*, where a unanimous High Court held that the qualifications for jurors had changed since Federation so that by 1993 representative juries under section 80 of the Constitution required women and unpropertied persons be eligible jurors.[61] By parity of reasoning, Justice Toohey cites Justices McTiernan and Jacobs as well as Justice Murphy in *McKinlay* to argue that 'according to today's standards, a system which denied universal adult franchise would fall short of a basic requirement of representative democracy'. Likewise, he states that one-vote–one-value is now a minimal requirement of representative democracy.[62] There are, however, some limitations to this requirement. He denies that the concept requires absolute parity, as a matter of practicality and principle. He adopts the views of Justice McLachlin from the Supreme Court of Canada:

> Factors like geography, community history, community interests and minority representation may need to be taken into account to ensure that our legislative assemblies effectively represent the diversity of our social mosaic.[63]

Having stated the principle and accepted the requirement for practical equality as well as a range of historical and political exigencies, Justice Toohey is reluctant to state a precise rule for the proper standard to be adopted – except to suggest that the legislative means chosen to facilitate representation must be proportionate to the aim. The 'courts must exercise restraint in this area', because there may be 'room for disagreement as to whether a particular system offends the principle of electoral equality demanded by representative democracy'.[64]

Having decided that equality of voting power is an aspect of the Constitution, Justice Toohey attempts to determine its relevance for the Western Australian Constitution. Rejecting a series of arguments based on sections of the federal Constitution as well as the indivisible nature of government in Australia, he accepts the argument of the majority in *Stephens* that representative democracy was contained in the Western Australian Constitution for the same reasons it was contained in the Australian Constitution. Accordingly, the arguments with respect to the franchise and electoral boundaries apply with equal force in Western Australia. As a result, Justice Toohey is prepared to hold that relevant provisions of the *Constitution Act 1899* and the *Electoral Distribution Act 1947* are invalid. The consequences of this decision are not made clear except for the indication that forthcoming elections would be unconstitutional.

Justice Gaudron agrees in general with the opinion of Justice Toohey. She agrees that although a system of representative democracy is inherent in the text and structure of the federal Constitution, this is not sufficient to determine the character of State Constitutions. An analysis of the State Constitution is needed. In considering the State Constitution, Justice Gaudron argues that the expression 'chosen directly by the people' which appears there is to be given the same meaning that it has in the federal document. Consequently, the State Constitution can be said to require a system of representative democracy.

Justice Gaudron presents in the clearest terms the view that the Constitution should be read in terms of progressive standards. The test is to be 'current democratic standards' as revealed in the electoral laws of the Commonwealth and the other Australian States. The words 'chosen by the people':

> are to be approached on the basis that, although their general essential meaning is unchanged, 'their full import and true meaning can often only be appreciated when considered, as the years go on, in relation to the vicissitudes of fact which from time to time emerge'. They must be interpreted bearing in mind that democracy was not a perfectly developed concept at the time of Federation and, perhaps, is not yet so. These considerations necessitate that the content and application of the words

'chosen by the people' be determined in the light of developments in democratic standards and not by reference to circumstances as they existed at Federation, with the consequence, as McTiernan and Jacobs JJ acknowledged in *McKinlay*, that what was permitted by s. 24 at one time may not be permitted at another.[65]

This evolutionary standard means that 'chosen by the people' now requires a franchise that cannot exclude women and racial minorities. It cannot be based on property or educational qualifications and it rejects significant disparity in the number of electors in electorates.[66] Justice Gaudron agrees with Justice Toohey that the electoral laws in Western Australia reveal a maldistribution not consistent with Commonwealth and State standards, and that they are arbitrary, inflexible, inappropriate and not adapted to the dispersed nature of the State population.

In terms of remedies, however, Justice Gaudron goes further. If laws are evolutionary, do they gradually become invalid, as the plaintiffs argue? Justice Gaudron is not convinced that analogies drawn from defence power are appropriate to election laws. She holds that if elections were to be held the elected members would not be chosen by the people under the Constitution. It is not clear how the issue is confined to prospective elections; would prior elections held under the same arrangements be free of unconstitutionality?[67]

McGinty and Representative Democracy

McGinty appeared to return the Court to a form of legalism evident in the judgment of Chief Justice Barwick in *McKinlay*. In doing so it reintroduced the notion of the 'legal' and the 'political'. A legal activity that the judiciary is qualified to undertake consists of interpretation that starts from the words, text and structure of the Constitution. Reading the Constitution in terms of underlying or overarching concepts, such as representative democracy, is inherently political, loosening the judicial activity from the firm moorings of the text and judicial method, ultimately usurping the authority of the people or the Constitution.

But as we have seen from Chief Justice Barwick's judgment, the distinction between legal and political could not be, and was not, politically neutral; it presupposed a political foundation and arrangement that gave meaning and substance to the very character of the judicial activity and such concepts as representative democracy. The majority in *McGinty* justify this political view by referring to Australia's founding. The Constitutional Convention debates, the history of electoral distributions and the writings and comments of contemporary scholars suggest that the judiciary is to exercise only the very broadest oversight over the structures of representative democracy. Because representative democracy is a dynamic evolving entity that requires room to develop, Parliament and indirectly the people should provide the source and substance of this change.

This political insight is intended to justify the strictly legal, or natural and ordinary, reading of the Constitution. As the substance and character of representative democracy are changing, and therefore contested, it is improper for the judiciary to fix any one version of such an arrangement in the Constitution. That is not its role, nor is it competent to do so. The proper judicial response is to defer to the Parliaments of the Commonwealth and the States. In this light, the questions of who is entitled to vote and the value that vote should have, are precisely the sorts of contested and contestable political ideas that should be left in the hands of the people's representatives as there is no inherently correct answer.

This view of the judicial role presupposes and anticipates a political settlement. The strict demarcation of the legal and the political results in a multiple if not fragmented Australian citizenship, within the States and nationally. Moreover, in declining to adjudicate between different concepts of representation this view is not prepared to accept that sovereignty of the people now justifies franchise laws and electoral boundaries that secure individual representation. Therefore such a neutral and natural reading of the text assumes a political and theoretical conception of parliamentary and progressive democracy.

However, if the Constitution (which has 128 sections) does not have a section 129 on representative democracy, as Justice McHugh put it bluntly, neither does it have a section 129 on a dynamic and evolving representative democracy. If progress is implied in the text of the Constitution then it seems that the majority in *McGinty* has not applied it fully, for once progress is assumed and the general structure that facilitated progress is secured constitutionally and by means of judicial review, there would seem to be no reason why the judiciary should not also secure the fruits of progress, the 'advancing frontiers of public thought', understood as individualism.[68] Why did the Court have to look to Australia's founding and the past in order to determine the nature of historically evolving and improving standards? The judiciary was required by this very argument to look to the present for guidance. Originalism was important for justifying progress but not for limiting it. On this basis, the Court has a responsibility to acknowledge the ever-expanding boundaries of social innovation, as it did in *Cheatle* with respect to who could be a juror. Thus it seemed that the majority accepts only half of the founders' vision – the importance of dynamic change – without adopting the other, which assumed that change was progressive and salutary. It was not a question of 'freezing' the Constitution, it was more a matter of reckoning and capitalising on the gains that had been made through parliamentary experimentation.

This, in a way, is the argument of the minority. Both Justice Toohey and Justice Gaudron argue that the standard to be adopted is that of the present, rather than the past. Democracy and citizenship are changing concepts, but their present formulation is preferable to their historical predecessors. Thus the idea of representative democracy has evolved to such an extent that it now includes a form of one-vote–one-value. There are clear echoes here of the minority judgments in *McKinlay*. But Justice Toohey and Justice Gaudron are aware of the limitations of the absolute equality required by the American jurisprudence. Instead they draw upon Canadian decisions, where the test for equality is less strict and takes into account the give and take of history, politics and community – in short, context. It is in the tradition of English, Canadian and presumably Australian evolutionary pragmatism that the standards for the Commonwealth will gradually but inevitably apply to the States.

Justice Toohey is more consistent, arguing that the Constitution is a skeletal structure that will sustain a growing and evolving body politic and therefore allows the judiciary to evaluate it in terms of progress. That is, the choice provided and allowed to Parliament by the Constitution is to allow it to grow, to expand the boundaries of thought. It is not meant to facilitate regression. But the foremost practical difficulty with this position concerns the problem of discerning the forefront of evolutionary development or the outer boundaries of thought. From where does Justice Toohey derive the current notion of the franchise or the idea of equality of voting power? After all, if parliamentary provisions do not reflect this, what does? His response is that both the Constitutional Commission and federal Parliament have acknowledged it. But he is vulnerable to the claims made by Justice McHugh that such a measure was rejected at two referendums. Superficially, it would seem that the judiciary is ill-suited to the role of boundary markers of progress. Would it not be tempting for the judiciary to act, in good faith, as the *avant-garde*? Can it do so without jeopardising its most important but vulnerable asset, its authority?

This difficulty can be clearly seen in the judgment of Justice Gaudron. Her view is that 'current democratic standards' are to be determined by what is enacted by the States and the Commonwealth. Yet this standard would by definition make all parliamentary provisions 'progressive' and therefore beyond judicial review. For example, it would have made it difficult to determine at Federation whether South Australian legislation that secured the franchise for women represented a salutary development, or whether it was regressive and therefore unacceptable because it was contrary to the majority position. From this perspective, federation as an institutional arrangement that will encourage social experimentation and therefore progress becomes questionable. How is one to tell between a foolhardy measure and an inspired experiment? J.S. Mill's rhetoric in *On Liberty* denies the possibility of discerning the difference at that time. It may well be, of course, that the reference to progress implicitly adopts a different standard. For example, Justice Gaudron's judgment seems to suggest that, rather than acknowledge standards not of her own choosing, she does in fact have a view of what is properly progressive, namely, the notion of unconstrained egalitarianism: the more inclusive the franchise and therefore the more democratic the electoral boundaries the more progressive it is, by definition. Does this mean that progress is to be simply equated with increased equality?

One possible answer to the problem of determining the frontiers of public thought is suggested by Justice Gummow, who is in the majority regarding the validity of the Western Australian provisions but agrees with the minority when it comes to the federal Constitution. He relies on Mill and the views of the founders to argue that there is an evolving conception of representative government and the franchise. His observations on the minimum age for voting and the requirement of universal adult suffrage indicate the proper bases for establishing an evolutionary standard: the minimum age requirement has been so for more than twenty years for both State and Commonwealth elections; universal adult suffrage is 'long-established'. The longevity of a measure, as well as its general acceptance at both State and Commonwealth levels, is an important indicator of its evolutionary development. Where there is uncertainty regarding the validity of a measure the decision should be left to the legislative branches.

These practical considerations highlight the profound questions concerning the notion of progress presupposed by both the majority and minority judgments. Is it entrenched in the Constitution, as a necessary structural implication (if not textual provision)? What assures its 'progressive' character? Though both the majority and the minority presuppose such a notion, they result in a different view of the role of judicial review. This is because the majority is not prepared to accept the complete notion of progress: it is not prepared to judge the 'progressiveness' of laws. Therefore the majority is influenced significantly by the problem of evaluation. It solves this difficulty by distinguishing between the legal and the political: the question of progress is consigned to the non-judicial, or political. It does not acknowledge that such a demarcation is also inherently 'political'.

But perhaps there is a greater concern among the majority about undertaking a 'progressive' judicial review. The notion of progress seems to fundamentally question the role of precedent and therefore judicial authority. If all judgments are radically historically contingent there is little room left for precedent and *stare decisis*. This historicising tendency undermines judicial judgments as they are announced – there can be no transhistorical claims about a judgment, it is essentially rooted to the facts and context of the case. Judging is a contingent and limited activity that cannot make grander claims. This poses formidable questions concerning the authority of judicial review. Without a larger vision of directed progress or an immemorial and unfolding common law, this view of judging makes it almost an act of will, removed from the demands of justice.

Limits to Jurisprudence

Justice Toohey in *McGinty* states that the Court should take opportunities such as that case to outline the principles that animate the Constitution. His claim, in other words, is that constitutional decisions of this sort have crucial implications for shaping the character of the regime, either in articulating what is already present or, in a more ambitious sense, noting the paths that should be followed in the future. What is remarkable about *McGinty* is that the Court declines to perform either task. It defines its role as simply that of maintaining the broad structures of the political activity, an umpire in its largest signification. However, in defining its responsibilities that way it inevitably defines a version of representative government and citizenship. According to the majority, representative government in Australia is a contentious and variable concept, with many forms. The precise contours of representative democracy, because contentious, are difficult to define and therefore the Court will only reluctantly do so. Only the most extreme instances warrant such intervention, though what those are is not made clear. Similarly, the franchise and one-vote–one-value, essential aspects of citizenship, are regarded as variable concepts, to be determined by Parliament. To the majority of the High Court, taking its bearings from the founding, the Australian regime does not have a fixed notion of democracy or citizenship. This view contrasts with the minority position, which either attempts to fix a definite view (based on the notion of equality derived from the terms of the Constitution, as per Justice Murphy), or marks out provisional yet definitive understandings of representative democracy and citizenship. According to the minority, Australia is a democracy where everyone is equal, where one vote is equal to another, where all who are of legal age and of sound mind are citizens. What is notable about the minority view is that although it gives content to the meaning of citizenship, it does so by prescribing the widest definition of citizen: it is more concerned with not excluding from citizenship than defining the character of citizenship. It almost seems that the most inclusive definition of citizen becomes a *de facto* definition of citizenship. In this case, it is not clear whether the minority's definition is any more precise than that of the majority. This may be because the minority refuse to be limited by history: definitions are historically contingent and the proper content of citizenship will evolve over time.

The consequence of the majority's deference to Parliament is that, generally speaking, Parliament has wide discretion over the range of laws it may pass on electoral boundaries, the franchise and, broadly, representative democracy. This discretion is even more extensive for State Parliaments. A striking consequence is that the majority view leaves Parliament free to devise electoral boundaries and perhaps define the franchise in order to advance the interests of certain groups that have for historical, social or political reasons been improperly burdened or discriminated against. The minority judgments of the Court in *McGinty*, in so far as they elevate one-vote–one-value and adult universal suffrage as a dominant constitutive principle, would be less likely to accept such redefinitions of electoral boundaries or the franchise.

The practical implications of the Court's position in *McGinty* could be seen in its decision in *Hill's* case, which concerned the election of Heather Hill, a member of the One Nation Party, as a senator for the State of Queensland.[69] It was claimed that at the time of nomination Hill was a British subject or citizen. She was therefore a citizen of a foreign power within the meaning of section 44 of the Constitution and constitutionally incapable of being chosen or sitting as a senator. The majority of the High Court agreed, holding that Hill could not be elected a senator.

Consistent with its view in *McGinty*, *Hill* reveals a Court that has assumed the responsibilities of adjudicating and reinforcing the broad framework of democratic governance. Though a minority of judges was prepared to accept Hill's claim that the qualifications of senators should be left to the determination of Parliament, the Court in *Hill* held that it had the jurisdiction to hear and determine the case. But in assuming a form of representation-reinforcing jurisdiction, the Court is presented with some difficulties.

The Court's decision that the UK is now a foreign power reveals the difficulty of a progressive interpretation. The Court takes judicial notice of the changes in constitutionalism in the two countries, and holds that since 1986 and the enactment of the Australia Acts Australia has been a legally sovereign and independent nation. But as Justice Callinan observes, such an evolutionary view gives rise to doubts over people's rights, status and obligations since the nature and extent of change can be determined only by the Court's pronouncement.

Importantly, the strict legalistic interpretation that accompanies this evolutionary method results in anomalous consequences for citizenship as it would appear that, though eligible to vote, all Australians who have not formally renounced their British ties would be ineligible for office. Thus the Court's decision reinforced a varied Australian citizenship, with different classes that could participate in varying degrees in the essential aspect of citizenship – ruling and being ruled.

'Political Thicket' and International Precedents

The majority in *McGinty* deny the judiciary the authority to give content to, or define in any but the most general and minimal way, representative democracy and citizenship.[70] Greater flexibility and authority are given to State Parliaments in defining the terms of electoral participation and voting. To the extent that this perspective is generally consistent with the Court's previous decision in *McKinlay*, it is possible to say that *McGinty* represented a fundamental restatement of the status quo rather than an innovation in the Court's jurisprudence.

But why did the majority in *McGinty* decline the opportunity to pursue its previous jurisprudence on representative government and thereby formulate a conception of citizenship that included an expanded notion of the franchise and one-vote–one-value? I suggest that the factual circumstances in *McGinty* presented a range of jurisprudential and practical difficulties to the application of the Court's representative government jurisprudence. These difficulties limited the High Court's jurisprudence and therefore its ability to reshape the nature of representative democracy in Australia. Doctrinal and political considerations influenced the Court's articulation of the character of the Australian regime and citizenship, and thereby the nature of judicial review.

By the time *McGinty* reached the Court, Chief Justice Mason and Justice Deane, who had strongly favoured the Court's representative government jurisprudence, had left the Bench.[71] Also, the Court's latest decisions in *Theophanous* and *Stephens* had raised questions regarding the Court's representative democracy jurisprudence. Therefore, *McGinty* became a case about the way to proceed with the representative democracy arguments as a whole, as much as a case about one-vote–one-value.

In what Chief Justice Earl Warren considered its most significant accomplishment during his tenure, the US Supreme Court overcame its reluctance to enter the 'political thicket' and enunciated in two 1964 cases the one-person–one-vote principle.[72] Since those decisions the Supreme Court had insisted on a standard of precise mathematical equality in apportionment, applying the one-person–one-vote command of equal representation with an unprecedented degree of exactitude.[73] Although the decisions resulted in districts that had equal representation

in terms of numbers, they did not address the compactness of the
electoral boundaries – it was possible to draw electoral boundaries in
such a way that though the districts were identical in population, their
irregular shapes made it possible to exclude groups and communities,
entrenching political gerrymander. The American experience suggested
that this form of judicial review did not adequately address the underlying problem of political gerrymander. This was because gerrymandering or vote dilution could take a number of forms, ranging from
the creation of districts with vastly different populations, to the creation
of multi-member districts or at-large representation and the creation of
districts which underrepresented identifiable groups of voters, either by
concentrating their votes (the 'excess votes' method) or by diluting their
votes ('wasted votes' method).[74] Indeed, the Canadian Supreme Court,
in interpreting the provisions of the Charter of Rights and Freedoms
guaranteeing the right to vote, declined to follow the American precedents, justifying some departures from equality based on geographical and
historical considerations.[75] Finally, as Justices Gummow and McHugh
noted in *McGinty*, the question of equality of voters did not address the
reality of party politics in Australia. Party affiliation rather than parity of
numbers in districts was a more decisive consideration in Australia.[76] The
judicial experience in other jurisdictions indicated that in entering the
political thicket the Court would not significantly advance democratic
governance yet would expose itself to major theoretical and practical
difficulties.

Constitutional Invalidity

There were also, as noted in examining Justice Murphy's judgment in
McKinlay, theoretical obstacles in the way of the Court holding electoral
divisions unconstitutional. The High Court has held that in striking
down a provision as unconstitutional the 'pretended law made in excess
of power is not and never has been a law at all'.[77] The *void ab initio*
doctrine, as it is known, assumes that judges do not make the law, they
declare it and that it is the Constitution and not the judiciary that
invalidates the provision. The retrospective aspect of the *void ab initio*
doctrine reveals its debt to the common law declaratory theory where
judges are the 'oracle' of the law, interpreting and applying rather than
making the law. Arguably it is an appropriation of the common law,
transposed to constitutional judicial review. In contrast, where judges are
seen to be law-makers, and therefore the invalidity of the purported law
springs from the judicial decision at hand, there is no necessary requirement for invalidity to be retrospective. Indeed, the potential for inequity
and injustice in the retrospective invalidation of laws would suggest that

the judiciary should in certain cases exercise discretion, declaring laws to be prospectively invalid.[78] The High Court has rejected such a view, on the grounds that the 'adjudication of existing rights and obligations as distinct from the creation of rights and obligations distinguishes the judicial power from non-judicial power'.[79]

The Court's rejection of prospective overruling imposes serious limits on the exercise of judicial review.[80] In the case of judicial review of the validity of electoral laws, where the status of Parliament itself becomes questionable, the difficulty of retrospectivity becomes acute, as all the laws enacted by that Parliament are implicitly also invalidated. Both Justice Toohey and Justice Gaudron in *McGinty* give prospective orders: future elections based on such boundaries were unconstitutional. But if the 1993 elections had been based on those boundaries, what would prevent that election being unconstitutional? And if unconstitutional, does this not make the current government illegal and all the legislation passed since then invalid? Indeed, if one were to claim that from Federation the principle of one-vote–one-value has been a constitutional mandate, does not this make all Western Australian legislation since Federation invalid?[81] A possible response to these objections is the comments made by Chief Justice Barwick and Justice Gibbs in *McKinlay* to the effect that federal parliamentary elections which are conducted otherwise than in accordance with constitutional requirements are not thereby rendered void.[82] In other words, it is possible to argue that irregularly constituted legislatures may be an exception to the *void ab initio* doctrine.[83]

The plaintiffs in *McGinty* proposed other solutions to this difficulty. One, noted and rejected by Justice Gaudron, is the view that 'at some unspecified time, the provisions became invalid and remain so, in the same way, presumably, as laws with respect to defence power may cease to be laws with respect to defence and become void when hostilities have ceased'. The changing aspects of a state of war seemed far removed from the evolutionary developments on representation and franchise, and the idea of electoral laws gradually becoming unconstitutional clearly poses insurmountable problems for democratic representation and the rule of law.

The other proposal by the plaintiffs was that the Court declare the laws invalid but defer the effect of the declaration to give the government of Western Australia the opportunity to take remedial action. In support of this proposition the plaintiffs referred to the Canadian case of *Re Manitoba Language Rights*.[84] In that case a provision in the Constitution of the Province, the *Manitoba Act 1870*, provided that Manitoba statutes were to be enacted in both English and French. In 1890, Manitoba enacted the Official Language Act, which provided that Manitoba statutes need only be enacted in the English language. The Supreme Court held that failure to comply with the constitutional requirement meant that all of Manitoba's statute law, except laws enacted in both languages, was invalid. In order to overcome the legal vacuum created by this decision, the Court held that the Acts enacted only in English were to be 'deemed to have temporary force and effect for the minimum period necessary for their translation, re-enactment, printing and publication'. The temporary validation was justified on the basis that it upheld the principle of rule of law, which states that law and order is an indispensable element of civilised life.[85]

This decision has been criticised as an unjustified exercise of legal authority.[86] In the Australian context it seems very unlikely that the Court would follow such a precedent. The proposed solution – holding laws valid until remedied by Parliament – was simply inapplicable in *McGinty* because, unlike the Manitoba problem where subsequent actions by Parliament would remedy the invalidity, the only way to correct the invalidity in Western Australia was to hold new elections which would in turn result in new enactments. There was no easy way of upholding the validity of the legislation except by some extreme claim for necessity, a difficult claim in the circumstances.[87] Moreover, such an exercise of judicial review is inevitably contentious, and in this instance politically inconceivable. The Premier of Western Australia, Richard Court, had been a vehement critic of the High Court's decision in *Mabo*, and his legislative response to the Commonwealth's native title legislation had been rejected by the High Court in the 1995 *Native Title* case.[88] A decision that implicitly questioned his legitimacy as a representative of Western Australia would have been construed as a direct attack on him, especially since the action was started by his political opponents Gallop and McGinty. Thus there were theoretical and political reasons – reasons that went to the heart of the Court's legitimacy – that would have inclined the High Court not to overturn its decision on one-vote–one-value in *McKinlay*.

Citizenship and the High Court

The High Court's jurisprudence based on representative democracy appeared to be undertaking a comprehensive statement on the nature of Australian constitutionalism. It had indicated one aspect of Australian democracy by its decisions on the implied right of political communication. In *McGinty* it seemed that the Court would develop its understanding of Australian citizenship by deciding the constitutive principles regarding the franchise and equality of vote. In fact it was not prepared to decide these questions. Moreover, it attempted to limit its representative government jurisprudence by returning to a literal and legal reading of the Constitution. The main reason for this is that the juris-prudence of representative democracy, developed in the context of an implied right of political discussion, posed innumerable difficulties for the resolution of the case. These difficulties were not novel – they had been acknowledged in the earlier decision of *McKinlay*. However, and ironically, the Court's other decisions on native title and implied rights made the situation even more difficult.

The application of the idea of representative democracy and therefore one-vote–one-value in *McGinty* would have posed intractable theoretical problems regarding judicial review and the legitimacy of the rule of law. It would also have resulted in significant practical and political dif-ficulties for the Court. Consequently, the principle had to be confined and limited. The Court did this by restating the way it interprets the Constitution and the meaning to be given to such super-constitutional concepts. In attempting to meet these theoretical and political chal-lenges, the Court felt compelled to limit its definition of Australian democracy and citizenship. In other words, the requirements of legal adjudication and the need to secure the institutional legitimacy of the Court encouraged the retention of the Court's previous view of the Australian regime. In this way, *McGinty* reveals most clearly how the aspirations of the judiciary are hedged by institutional constraints.

Notes

1 See generally Pryles, M. 1981, *Australian Citizenship Law*, Sydney, Law Book Co.
2 Section 34 states that members of the Australian Parliament must be 'a subject of the Queen'. Section 117 provides that a 'Subject of the Queen, resident in any State, shall not be subject in any other State to any disability or discrimination which would not be equally applicable to him if he were a subject of the Queen resident in such other State'. Note that citizenship of a foreign power disqualifies a person for membership of the Australian Parliament under s. 44(i) of the Constitution.
3 See generally Williams, J. 1996, 'Race, Citizenship and the Formation of the Australian Constitution: Andrew Inglis Clark and the "14th Amendment"', *Australian Journal of Politics and History*, 42, 1: 11; Rubenstein, K. 1995, 'Citizenship in Australia: Unscrambling its Meaning', *Melbourne University Law Review*, 20: 503; Winterton, G. 1986, 'Extra-constitutional Notions in Aus-tralian Constitutional Law', *Federal Law Review*, 16: 223; Irving, H. 1997, *To Constitute a Nation: A Cultural History of Australia's Constitution*, Cambridge: Cambridge University Press.
4 Aristotle, *Politics* (trans. Carnes Lord), Chicago, University of Chicago Press, Bks I and III.
5 See Uhr, J. 1998, *Deliberative Democracy in Australia: The Changing Place of Parliament*, Melbourne, Cambridge University Press.

6 See Birch, A.H. 1964, *Representative and Responsible Government: An Essay on the British Constitution*, London: Unwin University Books; Pitkin, H.F. 1967, *The Concept of Representation*, Berkeley, University of California Press.

7 See Birch's terminology of Tory and Whig in *Representative and Responsible Government*, 26–7.

8 See Pitkin, *The Concept of Representation*, ch. 8.

9 Birch, *Representative and Responsible Government*, 70.

10 In contrast, male suffrage was introduced in the UK in 1918; adult suffrage in 1928. See generally Crisp, L.F. 1983, *Australian National Government*, Melbourne, Longman Cheshire, 137.

11 See Bennett, S. 1971, *The Making of the Commonwealth*, Melbourne, Cassell Australia, ch. 4.

12 Chesterman, J. & Galligan, B. 1997, *Citizens without Rights*, Melbourne, Cambridge University Press, ch. 3.

13 Mullins, A. 1994, 'Women and the Text of the Australian Constitution', *Constitutional Centenary*, March, 18–22; Irving, *To Constitute a Nation*, ch. 10.

14 Chesterman & Galligan, *Citizens without Rights*.

15 ibid.

16 ibid., 84–120.

17 ibid., 89.

18 *Attorney-General (Cth); Ex rel McKinlay v Commonwealth* (1975) 135 CLR 1. See, however, the early decision concerning the right to vote in *King v Jones* (1972) 128 CLR 221 and the subsequent decision in *R v Pearson; Ex parte Sipka* (1983) 152 CLR 254 where the Court in effect reduced the force of s. 41 of the Constitution.

19 *Attorney-General (Cth); Ex rel McKinlay v Commonwealth* (1975) 135 CLR 1 at 17. Gibbs J expresses a similar view when he states that the words of s. 24 should be read 'in their natural sense, without seeking for implications or hidden meanings'(at 43). Mason J adopts a similar position, though he is also prepared to accept that the Constitution provides for a system of democratic government (at 61).

20 ibid. at 21. These minimal restrictions on parliament are accepted by Gibbs J (at 43) and Mason J (at 61).

21 ibid. per Barwick CJ at 20.

22 ibid. per Barwick CJ at 18–21, per Gibbs J at 43–5, per Mason J at 61–3.

23 ibid. per Barwick CJ at 23, per Gibbs J at 45, per Mason J at 62–3.

24 ibid. at 24.

25 ibid. at 25, 47.

26 ibid. at 56.

27 ibid. at 56, 57.

28 ibid. at 57.

29 ibid. at 57–8.

30 ibid. at 36.

31 ibid. at 36.

32 See Goldsworthy, J. 1997, 'Commentary' in M. Coper & G. Williams (eds), *Justice Lionel Murphy: Influential or Merely Prescient?*, Sydney, Federation Press, 268–71.

33 *Attorney-General (Cth); Ex rel McKinlay v Commonwealth* (1975) 135 CLR 1 at 73.

34 When Parliament made laws pursuant to ss 29 and 30 it did so pursuant to s. 51 which is subject to the Constitution and therefore to s. 24.

35 *Attorney-General (Cth); Ex rel McKinlay v Commonwealth* (1975) 135 CLR 1 at 69.

36 ibid. at 71.
37 ibid. at 79.
38 For an extensive discussion see Whitlam, E.G. 1985, *The Whitlam Government 1972–1975*, Melbourne, Penguin, ch. 17.
39 For differing views and justifications of these events see Whitlam, G. 1979, *The Truth of the Matter,* Melbourne, Penguin; Barwick, Sir Garfield 1983, *Sir John did His Duty,* Sydney, Serendip Publications; Barwick, Sir Garfield 1995, *A Radical Tory: Garfield Barwick's Reflections and Recollections,* Sydney, Federation Press; Kerr, Sir John 1978, *Matters for Judgment,* Melbourne, Macmillan.
40 See Barwick CJ's summary of the plaintiff's claims in *Attorney-General (Cth); Ex rel McKinlay v Commonwealth* (1975) 135 CLR 1 at 14.
41 These figures are taken from the judgment of Brennan CJ in *McGinty v Western Australia* (1996) 186 CLR 140.
42 ibid.
43 *Nationwide News Pty Ltd v Wills* (1992) 177 CLR 1. See especially the decision by Deane and Toohey JJ that 'the general effect of the Constitution is, at least since the adoption of full adult suffrage by all the States, that all citizens of the Commonwealth who are not under some special disability are entitled to share equally in the exercise of those ultimate powers of governmental control' (at 72).
44 *Australian Capital Television Pty Ltd v Commonwealth* (1992) 177 CLR 106.
45 *Theophanous v Herald & Weekly Times Ltd* (1994) 182 CLR 104.
46 *Stephens v Western Australian Newspapers Ltd* (1994) 182 CLR 211. See, however, *Cunliffe v Commonwealth* (1994) 182 CLR 272.
47 See Kirk, J. 1995, 'Constitutional Implications from Representative Democracy', *Federal Law Review,* 23: 37; Creighton, P. 1994, 'Apportioning Electoral Districts in a Representative Democracy', *Western Australia Law Review* 24: 78.
48 Cf Ely, J.H. 1980, *Democracy and Distrust: A Theory of Judicial Review,* Cambridge, Harvard University Press.
49 Brennan CJ, Dawson J, McHugh J and Gummow J.
50 *McGinty v Western Australia* (1996) 186 CLR 140 at 170, notes omitted.
51 ibid. at 236.
52 ibid. at 183.
53 ibid. at 250.
54 ibid. at 287.
55 ibid. at 288–9.
56 ibid. at 175.
57 ibid. at 178.
58 ibid. at 189–90.
59 ibid. at 293, 300.
60 ibid. at 200, 204.
61 *Cheatle v R* (1993) 177 CLR 541.
62 In doing so he attempts to distinguish rather than overrule *McKinlay*. The argument that *McKinlay* only considered the meaning of s. 24 and did not address the question of representative democracy, and therefore can be distinguished, is rather strained (at 205, cf his reading of s. 24 at 203).
63 *McGinty v Western Australia* (1996) 186 CLR 140 at 204; McLachlin J in *Reference re Electoral Boundaries Commission Act* [1991] 2 SCR 158 at 184.
64 *McGinty v Western Australia* (1996) 186 CLR 140 at 213.
65 ibid. at 221, references omitted.

66 ibid. at 222. Gaudron J distinguishes *McKinlay,* arguing that it only decided that s. 24 does not require absolute or as near as practicable equality between electorates. It is not authority that justifies significant malapportionment (at 219).

67 ibid. at 224.

68 See Brennan CJ's reference in *McGinty* at 167, note 145, to the observation of Isaacs J in *Commonwealth v Kreglinger & Fernau Ltd and Bardsley* (1926) 37 CLR 393 at 412–13.

69 *Sue v Hill* (1999) 163 ALR 648.

70 See, however, the judgment of Brennan CJ who declined to discuss this, and Gummow J who was prepared to hold that adult suffrage was now the standard (see below).

71 Six judges sat on the case, with Brennan as Chief Justice and Gummow J appointed in March 1995. The appointment of Kirby J in February 1996 brought the Court to its full complement.

72 *Reynolds v Sims* 377 US 533 (1964); *Wesberry v Sanders* 376 US 1 (1964). See Bagger, R. 1985, 'The Supreme Court and Congressional Apportionment: Slippery Slope to Equal Representation Gerrymandering', *Rutgers Law Review* 38: 109 at 111.

73 As Bagger, 'The Supreme Court and Congressional Apportionment' notes (118–28), in *Karcher v Dagget* 462 US 725 (1983) the congressional reapportionment plan that was struck down had an average deviation of 0.14 per cent and a maximum deviation of 0.70 per cent.

74 See Bagger, 'The Supreme Court and Congressional Apportionment', 110.

75 *Reference re Electoral Boundaries Commission Act* (1991) 81 DLR (4th) 16.

76 *McGinty v Western Australia* (1996) 186 CLR 140 per Gummow J at 258–9, per McHugh J at 248–50.

77 Latham CJ in *South Australia v Commonwealth* (1942) 65 CLR 373 at 409. See also *Victoria v Commonwealth* (1975) 134 CLR 338; Campbell, E. 1994, 'Unconstitutionality and its Consequences' in G. Lindell (ed.), *Future Directions in Australian Constitutional Law*, Sydney, Federation Press, especially regarding the American jurisprudence on prospective unconstitutionality.

78 Mason, K. 1989, 'Prospective Overruling', *Australian Law Journal* 63: 526.

79 *Ha v New South Wales* (1997) 189 CLR 465 per Brennan CJ, McHugh, Gummow and Kirby JJ at 503–4, reference omitted.

80 Mason, 'Prospective Overruling', 530–1. Consider, for example, the problems with retrospectivity regarding native title in *Mabo* and *Wik*.

81 See Brennan CJ's discussion at 178.

82 Campbell, 'Unconstitutionality and its Consequences', 92.

83 See Campbell, 'Unconstitutionality and its Consequences', 92–4, especially the discussion of *Victoria v Commonwealth* (1975) 134 CLR 81.

84 *Re Manitoba Language Rights* [1985] 1 SCR 721.

85 ibid. at 749, 782. For similar cases see *R v Mercure* [1988] 1 SCR 234 (Saskatchewan); *R v Paquette* [1990] 2 SCR 1103 (Alberta); *Sinclair v Quebec* [1992] 1 SCR 579.

86 See Mandel, M. 1989, *The Charter of Rights and the Legalisation of Politics in Canada*, Toronto, Wall & Thompson.

87 Hogg, P. 1992, *Constitutional Law of Canada*, Scarborough, Ont., Carswell, 1250–60.

88 *Western Australia v Commonwealth* (1995) 181 CLR 373.

CHAPTER 5

Native Title and the High Court

Two days before Christmas, on 23 December 1996, the High Court handed down its *Wik* decision. Overjoyed, Wik elder Gladys Tybingoompa celebrated the outcome by dancing in the forecourt of the High Court building. The powerful images of the jubilant traditional dance appeared in the evening television bulletins and on the front pages of newspapers the next morning. Here was the public face of the new politics of the High Court – the Court as patron and protector of the weak, dispensing true justice. Before long, however, this image would contend with another, that of an activist judiciary that was making the law as it saw fit, a legal body that was improperly intruding into the political. This conflict of images highlighted the contentious nature of the High Court's native title jurisprudence and the significant obstacles to public debate and deliberation regarding the Court's decisions.

It is difficult to deny the ground-breaking nature of the Court's decisions in *Mabo* and *Wik*.[1] Though litigated within the legal context of property and land law, the decisions clearly reached more fundamental issues concerning indigenous rights, civilisation and culture, history and justice, and the nature of the Australian polity. Because of the importance of these two decisions in directing and shaping Australian democracy, this chapter will examine them in some detail. It looks at the sophisticated and subtle interplay between law and politics evident in the development of native title in Australia to discern, within the Court, the differing views of the nature of the common law, the role of the judiciary within the regime and the character of Australian constitutionalism.

Native Title in Australia

Until the High Court's decision in *Mabo*, it was generally accepted that native title did not exist in Australia. Though the High Court itself had

not decided the question, there was significant English authority supporting that view.[2] The issue had been addressed directly by the Australian courts only once, in the Supreme Court of the Northern Territory
in the *Gove Land Rights* case.[3] In the late 1960s Nabalco, a consortium of
Swiss and Australian mining companies, sought to mine bauxite in the
Gove Peninsula in the north-east of the Northern Territory. The Yolngu
people from Yirrkala on the Gove Peninsula petitioned the Commonwealth government not to allow leases until there had been appropriate
consultation. Unsuccessful in their attempts to appoint a House of
Representatives Committee to hear their claims, the Yolngu decided to
sue the miners and the Commonwealth government on the grounds that
they enjoyed sovereign and native title rights over their land. After a
lengthy hearing, Justice Blackburn decided against the plaintiffs on the
basis that there was insufficient evidence of a continuing link with the
land. Relying on a Canadian decision, Justice Blackburn also held that
the common law did not recognise communal or group interests in land
and, irrespective of the individual or communal nature of the claim, the
British assertion of sovereignty over Australia extinguished all such
claims.[4]

Though the *Gove Land Rights* case was extensively criticised – there
were even suggestions by the High Court that the existence of native title
at common law required reconsideration – the election of the Whitlam
Labor government in 1972 shifted the land rights focus from the judicial
to the political forum.[5] The 1967 referendum had removed the constitutional provision that had excluded 'aboriginal natives' from the census
(section 127), and allowed the Commonwealth to legislate for people of
any race, including Aborigines (section 51xxvi). The Whitlam government, relying on these developments, began to implement a broad
range of measures to advance Aboriginal interests in Australia. A federal
Department of Aboriginal Affairs and a representative body, the National
Aboriginal Consultative Committee, were established to develop a
national approach to Aboriginal assistance. A Royal Commission headed
by Justice Woodward was set up to inquire into the granting of land to
Aborigines in the Northern Territory, which resulted in the enactment
of land rights legislation.[6] Importantly, the government ratified the 1965
International Convention on the Elimination of All Forms of Racial Discrimination, enacting the Commonwealth *Racial Discrimination Act 1975*.

The legal status of indigenous land rights in Australia at the time
contrasted sharply with increasing international recognition of the rights
of indigenous peoples and, more specifically, with the jurisprudence in
America, Canada and New Zealand.[7] Congress and the US Supreme
Court had consistently acknowledged Indian tribes as political bodies
with powers of self-government, with sovereignty over their members and

territories. They had done so because, since the beginning of white settlement, numerous treaties had been concluded between US governments and Indian nations, and the Constitution itself granted Congress power to regulate commerce with Indian tribes. In Canada the Royal Proclamation of 1763 had recognised Indian ownership of lands, resulting in treaties between the Crown and Aboriginal people. In 1973 the Supreme Court of Canada decided in *Calder* that native title continued to exist in a settled colony, three judges criticising the propositions of law outlined by Justice Blackburn in the *Gove Land Rights* case as 'wholly wrong'.[8] Further significant judicial pronouncements, including *Guerin* in 1984 which recognised a fiduciary duty owed by the Crown to the first nations, followed the greater recognition of Aboriginal treaty rights in the constitutional settlement of 1982 when the Canadian Constitution was repatriated and the Charter of Rights and Freedoms entrenched.[9] Similar developments were taking place in New Zealand. The sovereignty of the Maoris had been acknowledged in the Treaty of Waitangi, which was signed in 1840. In 1975 the Treaty was implemented in part by the Treaty of Waitangi Act, which also established the Waitangi Tribunal with powers to make recommendations to the government on the application of Treaty principles to claims brought before it. In 1985, the jurisdiction of the Tribunal was extended to claims arising from events which had occurred in or after 1840. Significantly, since the 1987 landmark case of *New Zealand Maori Council* the courts applied Treaty principles in the interpretation of legislation.[10]

Mabo (No 2)

It was in the light of these legal, political and jurisprudential developments, and an evolving international consensus regarding the rights of indigenous peoples, that Australia's High Court confronted the question of native title in *Mabo*. In 1982 a group of Torres Strait Islanders, including Eddie Mabo, commenced legal action on behalf of the Meriam people against the State of Queensland, asking the courts to declare that the Meriam people held native title to the islands of Mer, Dauar and Waier, constituting the Murray Islands. The statement of claim acknowledged that the islands came under the sovereignty of the Crown in 1879, as part of the colony of Queensland, but subject to the rights to lands according to local custom, native title or actual possession. In 1985 Queensland enacted legislation designed to extinguish any native title rights which may otherwise exist. The intention of the *Queensland Coast Islands Declaratory Act 1985* (Qld) was to declare, retrospectively, that the Queensland legislature's intention in 1879 was not only to acquire sovereignty over the islands but also to extinguish the land rights of those who, by annexation, became British subjects. The issue before the Court in *Mabo (No 1)* was whether the 1985 Queensland Act was inconsistent with the *Racial Discrimination Act 1975* (Cth). If it was, the question of whether the law recognises pre-existing indigenous title could be addressed. In *Mabo (No 1)* the High Court held that Queensland's attempt to extinguish traditional land rights by means of its Queensland Coast Islands Declaratory Act was inconsistent with the Racial Discrimination Act and was therefore invalid.[11] The decision allowed the litigation to proceed, and the determination of facts was remitted to the Supreme Court of Queensland where it was assigned to Justice Moynihan.

On 16 November 1990 Justice Moynihan delivered the Supreme Court's determination on the issues of fact raised in the pleadings. Argument was heard by the High Court in May 1991, and the Court handed down its judgment on 3 June 1992. By a six to one majority, the Court upheld the plaintiffs' claim to native title. Chief Justice Mason and Justice McHugh agreed with Justice Brennan's reasons for judgment; Justices Deane and Gaudron and Justice Toohey gave separate judgments. With the exception of Justice Dawson, who dissented, all agreed that the common law of Australia recognises a form of native title. Regarding the question of extinguishment of native title, a differently constituted majority comprising Justice Brennan (with whom Chief Justice Mason and Justice McHugh agreed) and Justice Dawson held that extinguishment by inconsistent grant is not wrongful and does not give rise to compensatory damages.

Because *Mabo* was the ground-breaking decision that defined and shaped the development of native title in Australia, implicitly involving fundamental questions regarding culture, civilisation and the nature of democracy in Australia, it is important to consider in detail the different arguments and reasons for judgment advanced in the case.

Civilisation and Culture

It is appropriate to start with the judgment of Justice Brennan, because it was significant for the outcome of the case – it had the greatest support within the Court – and because, with the judgment of Justice Dawson, it was decisive in determining the question of compensation. Justice Brennan starts with a general description of the Murray Islands and the Meriam people, who are Melanesian and who occupied the Murray Islands before first European contact.[12] Justice Brennan quotes extensively from the finding of fact by Justice Moynihan, which showed a society regulated more by custom than by law. The people lived in groups of huts that were organised as villages. Significantly, land and gardening were of profound importance to the Meriam people. Gardening provided subsistence as well as produce for exchange, especially for rituals such as marriage and adoption:

> Prestige depended on gardening prowess both in terms of the production of sufficient surplus for the social purposes of such as those to which I have referred and to be manifest in the show gardens and the cultivation of yams to a huge size. Considerable ritual was associated with gardening and gardening techniques were passed on and preserved by these rituals.[13]

Justice Brennan's extensive references to gardening at the start of his judgment are meant to show that the Murray Islanders' use of property, by building and cultivation, clearly fitted the European notions of proper use of land. Indeed, it appears that the Islanders held a definite idea of private property. Justice Brennan quotes Captain Pennefather, who visited the islands and noted that:

> The natives are very tenacious of their ownership of the land and the island is divided into small properties which have been handed down from father to son from generation to generation, they absolutely refuse to sell their land at any price, but rent small portions to the beche-de-mer men and others. These natives, though lazy like all Polynesians on their islands, build good houses and cultivate gardens, they are a powerful intelligent race and a white man is safe if not safer residing amongst them, as in Brisbane.[14]

After presenting the history of the Murray Islands and the way they were annexed to Queensland, Justice Brennan turns to the legal consequences of these events.

The legal argument concerns the implication of the act of annexation. Did annexation vest in the Crown absolute legal ownership, legal possession and exclusive power to confer title to all land in the Murray Islands? A number of judgments apparently supported the view that where a colony was settled, the law of England so far as applicable became the law of the colony and, by that law, the Crown acquired the absolute beneficial ownership of all land in the territory.[15] Justice Brennan is prepared to examine this notion critically because 'Judged by any civilised standard, such a law is unjust and its claim to be part of the common law to be applied in contemporary Australia must be questioned'.[16]

In examining the legal theories relating to the acquisition of sovereignty and the introduction of the common law, Justice Brennan starts with the proposition that the act of acquisition by a state cannot be challenged in the courts of that state. He notes, however, that international law permitted the acquisition of territory otherwise inhabited where the indigenous inhabitants 'were not organised in a society that was united permanently for political action'. This expanded notion of *terra nullius* was justified on the grounds of the benefits of Christianity and European civilisation, and that the land was otherwise uncultivated. But since the Meriam people were devoted gardeners, Justice Brennan questions whether the Murray Islands could be said to be properly annexed under international law.

At any rate, the municipal courts have jurisdiction to determine the body of law in force in the new territory. The common law distinguished between methods of acquiring sovereignty. On acquisition of uninhabited territory by occupation or 'settlement', to the extent that it was applicable to the new colony English law would become the law of the new settlement. In conquered or ceded countries that already had laws of their own, the laws of the country continued until they were altered by the sovereign. The difficulty arose in cases where the territory was not 'desert uninhabited' but it was claimed that the indigenous inhabitants had no laws, were without sovereignty and were primitive in their social organisation. In such cases the common law did not distinguish between uninhabited and 'barbarous' country, deeming both to have been 'settled colony'.

On what grounds were these notions of an 'absence of law' or 'barbarian theory' (as Justice Brennan calls them) justified? Justice Brennan quotes Lord Sumner, speaking for the Privy Council in *In re Southern Rhodesia*, to explain the premises underlying this notion:

> The estimation of the rights of aboriginal tribes is always inherently difficult. Some tribes are so low in the scale of social organisation that their usages and conceptions of rights and duties are not to be reconciled with the institutions or the legal ideas of civilised society. Such a gulf cannot be bridged. It would be idle to impute to such people some shadow of the rights known to our law and then to transmute it into the substance of transferable rights of property as we know them.[17]

Having outlined the theoretical bases for the common law position, Justice Brennan presents the choices open to the Court:

> The theory that the indigenous inhabitants of a 'settled' colony had no proprietary interest in the land thus depended on a discriminatory denigration of indigenous inhabitants, their social organisation and customs. As the basis of the theory is false in fact and unacceptable in our society, there is a choice of legal principle to be made in the present case. *This Court can either apply the existing authorities and proceed to inquire whether the Meriam people are higher 'in the scale of social organisation' than the Australian Aborigines where claims were 'utterly disregarded' by the existing authorities or the Court can overrule the existing authorities, discarding the distinction between inhabited colonies that were terra nullius and those which were not.*[18]

Given the 'scale of social organisation' of the Meriam people as outlined by Justice Brennan, it is clear that in applying the existing authorities the Meriam people would succeed in their claim. Overruling the authorities would also favour the claims of the Meriam people. Either option, then, will decide the case for the Meriam people. Yet as Justice Brennan presents it, the choice between distinguishing the previous cases and overruling them marks a crucial point in the Court's jurisprudence; it indicates the character of the problem as conceived by the Court and represents a major intersection in the way the common law acknowledges the demands of indigenous Australians. Accordingly, it is appropriate to attempt to understand the theoretical sources of each path.

The 'barbarian theory', as Justice Brennan terms it, assumed a hierarchy of social organisations and therefore was implicitly based on a notion of 'civilisation' which originated in the eighteenth century and was associated with the early modern doctrines of natural rights and human equality, of scientific and technological progress. It conveyed the idea of universal human progress and advancement, culminating in the modern liberal state.[19] However, by the late eighteenth and early nineteenth centuries, the idea of civilisation became linked with notions of human hybridity and race.[20] Although Christian and Enlightenment humanitarian ideals of universality and equality prevailed, by the mid nineteenth century new racial theories in America, Britain and France, based on comparative anatomy and craniometry, endorsed the 'polygenetic' view that there were different species of human beings. The idea of racial 'types' persisted even though undermined by Darwinian theory.[21] The prevailing notions of social Darwinism, craniology and phrenology dominated English thought and thereby helped shape the attitudes of early explorers, officials and military officers in the Australian colonies.[22] They also provided the theoretical defence of what came to be known as the 'White Australia' policy.[23] Therefore the universalist humanitarian notion of civilisation was, during the settlement of Australia, linked to racial theories.[24] This is the view Justice Brennan recognises as a formative influence on the common law, and is prepared to reject.

But if 'civilisation' is rejected, what is the theoretical foundation of Justice Brennan's decision in *Mabo*? It appears to be 'universal human rights'.[25] In this instance, however, rather than providing a standard that transcends the vagaries of different societies, 'humanity' guarantees the legitimacy, and to some extent the incommensurability, of different 'civilisations'. 'Humanity' rather than 'civilisation' becomes the new measure and therefore allows a more inclusive, non-racist, non-European notion of society. An important element of the new standard is that society is not to be judged by the level of its technological achievements, nor (more fundamentally) by its use of property. Humanity makes possible a more spiritual and hence nobler understanding of land.

Though Justice Brennan does not employ the term, he is suggesting the alternative of 'culture', which acquired its modern meanings in the writings of eighteenth-century German thinkers who were developing Rousseau's critique of modern liberalism and the Enlightenment.[26] Though culture originally assumed a movement away from barbarism towards perfection, it subsequently came to mean the entirety of social life.[27] In the works of Herder, however, culture is not simply an overcoming of nature – nature provides the standard for original wholeness and therefore is an expression of original and pre-rational nature.[28] In this way the folk community, with mythic and poetic origins, takes precedence over rational and deliberative politics. Herder was responsible for the modern emphasis on diverse and fundamentally equal though incommensurable cultures as expressions of native folk spirit.[29]

It appears, therefore, that Justice Brennan's judgment is a legal re-enactment of the choice between 'civilisation' and 'culture'. The choice is to accept the theory of 'civilisation' and distinguish *Mabo (No 2)* on the basis that the Meriam people had a well-developed social and legal system that relied on the cultivation of land, or to reject it altogether. Justice Brennan chooses to reject the standard. Though the positions are not simply antithetical, Justice Brennan's preference for 'humanity', with its implicit rejection of hegemonic Western materialism and science and, in the Australian instance racism, supports a pluralist understanding of culture. Difference, however incommensurable or inaccessible, is to be recognised and accepted by the common law.

The first ground on which Justice Brennan makes this choice is international law, which no longer commands this expanded notion of *terra nullius*. From Justice Brennan's reference to the decision of Judge Ammoun in the International Court of Justice decision in *Advisory Opinion on Western Sahara*, it would appear that the change in international law is based upon a change in the notion of property that underlies the concept of civilisation. Judge Ammoun distinguishes between a 'materialistic concept of *terra nullius*' and a 'spiritual' notion. On this basis land cannot be appropriated by someone other than the person born there. The 'Western norm' which had a different idea of property was the foundation of European civilisation and public law. If the common law is to keep step with international law, then it is arguable that Justice Brennan implicitly introduces into Australian law this 'spiritual', non-Western notion of property, abandoning the previous notion of 'civilisation'.

The second reason for rejecting the common law of 'civilisation' is that 'an unjust and discriminatory doctrine of that kind can no longer be accepted'. It is contrary to the 'contemporary values of the Australian people'. It is not clear from which source Justice Brennan discerns the 'contemporary values of the Australian people'. Perhaps this is a matter of judicial notice, or he may be referring to the enactment of the Racial Discrimination Act. If so, Justice Brennan is suggesting that the idea of 'civilisation' is inherently racist – hence his remark that the common law should 'neither be nor be seen to be frozen in an age of racial discrimination'.[30]

Return to Civilisation?

From this perspective, Justice Brennan's discussion at the start of his judgment of the villages and huts and the customary legal system of the Meriam people, of their gardening skills, is irrelevant. Its purpose is rhetorical, directed at those who subscribe to the 'barbarian' theory in an attempt to demonstrate to them that, 'Judged by any civilised stand-ard', depriving indigenous inhabitants of their right to occupy traditional lands, exposing them 'to deprivation of the religious, cultural and economic sustenance which the land provides' is unjust.[31]

What are the consequences of choosing 'culture' over 'civilisation', for the claims made in *Mabo*? As noted, irrespective of the choice the Meriam people would have succeeded in their claims. Therefore it is necessary to determine the implications of the choice of culture, for both indigenous Australians and the common law. However, in the rest of the judgment it becomes clear that, far from choosing culture, Justice Brennan returns to a notion of civilisation in giving content and sub-stance to the notion of native title. This can be seen when we consider the character, limits and extinguishment of native title.

In discussing the nature and incidents of native title, Justice Brennan directly confronts the problem of accommodating the differing concep-tions of law, custom and land. His characterisation of native title there-fore becomes a crucial test for evaluating the extent to which he favours the 'cultural' approach. His starting-point is the acknowledgment of fundamental differences between native title and the common law:

> Native title has its origin in and is given its content by the traditional laws acknowledged by and the traditional customs observed by the indigenous inhabitants of a territory. The nature and incidents of native title must be ascertained as a matter of fact by reference to those laws and customs.[32]

Though these are matters of fact, Justice Brennan is prepared to state some general propositions about native title without reference to evidence. It is helpful to draw out some of the themes in the three propositions he outlines.

According to Justice Brennan, native title is not an institution of the common law although it is recognised by the common law. Consequently, native title is not alienable at common law, there being no machinery that can enforce the rights of the alienee. The effect is that rights and interests possessed as native title can only be transferred to other indigenous people consistent with laws and customs of the people; a non-indigenous person who does not acknowledge and observe their laws and customs cannot acquire such rights or interests. This attempt to accommodate the unique nature of native title limits its character so that indigenous peoples cannot dispose of native rights and interests to anyone other than the Crown.

Moreover, customary title recognised by the common law must be consistent with the common law. Justice Brennan notes that at one stage the common law was too rigid to admit the recognition of native title. He cites the custom of tanistry (where the most vigorous adult relative was elected to succeed a Celtic chief), part of the Brehon law of Ireland that was held to be void because it was founded on violence.[33] The example is intended to show that the common law now favours traditional native title, but it is not clear to what extent differences between native title and the common law are tolerated. Legal or equitable remedies are available to protect particular rights and interests, but they will inevitably be forced into the legal categories of 'proprietary', 'personal' and 'usufructuary'. In any case, there are some matters that will not be acknowledged:

> The incidents of a particular native title relating to inheritance, the transmission or acquisition of rights and interests on death and marriage, the transfer of rights and interests in land and the grouping of persons to possess rights and interests in land are matters to be determined by the laws and customs of indigenous inhabitants, *provided those laws and customs are not so repugnant to natural justice, equity and good conscience that judicial sanctions under the new regime must be withheld.*[34]

The laws and customs of indigenous inhabitants must be evaluated before gaining judicial sanction. Though the suggestion is that a version of tanistry, and therefore ritual or customary violence of some form, may now be tolerated, the boundaries of the permissible are unclear. What is clear is that native laws and customs will be acknowledged on the terms established by the new regime.

Perhaps the most important aspect of native title as presented by Justice Brennan concerns the need for a 'real acknowledgment of traditional law' and 'real observance of traditional customs'. Where these do not exist, native title disappears. The reference to law and custom supports the view that native title centres on a more 'spiritual' conception of the land. In fact the judgment confirms that real acknowledgment and observance are not possible without physical connection with the land. Without such a connection, irrespective of the way customs and laws are observed, native title is extinguished:

> Where a clan or group has continued to acknowledge that law (so far as practicable) to observe the customs based on the traditions of that clan or group, whereby their traditional connexion with the land has been substantially maintained, the traditional community title of that clan or group can be said to remain in existence.[35]

Therefore, at the core of native title is land use. Land, and its use by indigenous peoples, becomes the decisive factor in determining the existence of native title. But this view of land owes more to the tradition that relies on land use as a means of identifying 'culture', where land as a source of civilisation is given priority over customs and laws. It would seem therefore that native title in *Mabo* is ultimately determined on the basis of gardening and the 'productive' use of land.

A consideration of the problem of native title and extinguishment supports this observation. In Australia, municipal constitutional law determines the scope of authority to exercise sovereign power. When validly made, a grant of interest in land binds the Crown and the sovereign's successors and such an interest cannot be extinguished without statutory authority. Furthermore:

> As the Crown is not competent to derogate from a grant once made, a statute which confers a power on the Crown will be presumed (so far as consistent with the purpose for which the power is conferred) to stop short of authorising any impairment of an interest in land granted by the Crown or dependent on a Crown grant. But, as native title is not granted by the Crown, there is no comparable presumption affecting the conferring of any executive power on the Crown the exercise of which is apt to extinguish native title.[36]

Native title is not even protected by the presumption that protects interests in land. A Crown grant that vests an interest in land inconsistent with the right to enjoy native title, extinguishes native title. The only limit is that 'the exercise of a power to extinguish native title must reveal a clear and plain intention to do so, whether the action be taken by the Legislature or the Executive'.

That the executive or Parliament can extinguish native title, provided it is done in clear and unambiguous terms, and need not compensate for it, may represent acknowledgment of the harsh reality of dispossession that cannot be undone in any meaningful sense. It also represents a clear preference for Western notions of property in *Mabo* where there is a conflict between uses of property. It is true that there are restrictions imposed by the Constitution and the valid laws of the Commonwealth, for example the Racial Discrimination Act imposes limits on the extinguishment of native title. To this extent it may be argued that the Racial Discrimination Act itself entrenches the 'cultural' claim by making the indigenous notion of property identical to that of the 'civilised' view. Yet by securing non-discrimination the Act in effect claims there is no difference between the two concepts, or by utilising civilised standards for compensation the Act effectively adopts and implements such a concept.

Thus, in looking at the way native title is defined, the way its recognition is limited by prevailing notions of good conscience and property, and the way its extinguishment is justified on the grounds that it is not of the common law, it would appear that, far from putting the priority on culture, Justice Brennan favours the non-indigenous use of land. By preferring Western notions of property and giving them precedence over the spiritual, Justice Brennan implicitly favours the idea of scientific and social progress, as well as a universal liberal-democratic regime; he implicitly favours civilisation over culture. This is because the Western, Lockean notion of property – property that is made valuable by human labour, property that is a commodity – is the foundation of a theoretical perspective that favours civilisation.[37]

What are we to make of the crucial choice Justice Brennan declares he faced in deciding *Mabo*? Perhaps the choice is no more than a rhetorical device to satisfy those who prefer culture, just as the facts about gardening are meant to silence those who argue for civilisation. What cannot be ignored, however, is the fact that the reinstituted civilisation is more open to the claims of culture even though it will take precedence at decisive moments. Importantly, civilisation has been rid of its racist fellow-traveller: Justice Brennan's judgment cleanses the notion of progress and civilisation, refounding it on a new, non-racial foundation. *Mabo* is a decision that takes seriously the consequences of the Racial Discrimination Act and attempts to weave its principles through Australian constitutionalism. Far from being a radical decision, in this light *Mabo* represents a sophisticated defence of liberal democracy.

High Court and the Rule of Law

On another level, however, it seems to represent no more than a defence of the common law and the judiciary. According to Justice Brennan, the problem posed in *Mabo* – whether the exercise of sovereignty by the Crown made it the universal and absolute beneficial owner of all the land therein – is subject to critical evaluation principally because of its implications for the common law:

> According to the cases, the common law itself took from indigenous inhabitants any right to occupy their traditional land, exposed them to deprivation of the religious, cultural and economic sustenance which the land provides, vested the land effectively in the control of the Imperial authorities without any right to compensation and made the indigenous inhabitants intruders in their own homes and mendicants for a place to live. Judged by any civilised standard, such a law is unjust and its claim to be part of the common law to be applied in contemporary Australia must be questioned. This Court must now determine whether, *by the common law of this country*, the rights and interests of the Meriam people of today are to be determined on the footing that their ancestors lost their traditional rights and interests in the land of the Murray Islands on 1 August 1879.[38]

From this perspective, *Mabo* is concerned with the question of the culpability of the common law. This suspicion is confirmed by the statements Justice Brennan makes towards the end of his judgment:

> Does it make any difference whether native title failed to survive British colonisation or was subsequently extinguished by government action? In this case, the difference is critical: except for certain transactions next to be mentioned, nothing has been done to extinguish native title in the Murray Islands. There, the Crown has alienated only part of the land and has not acquired for itself the beneficial ownership of any substantial area. And there may be other areas of Australia where native title has not been extinguished and where an Aboriginal people, maintaining their identity and customs, are entitled to enjoy their native title. *Even if there be no such areas, it is appropriate to identify the events which resulted in the dispossession of indigenous inhabitants of Australia, in order to dispel the misconception that it is the common law rather than the action of governments which made many of the indigenous people of this country trespassers on their own land.*[39]

The decision in *Mabo* is important for its litigants, and it may have implications for others. But a crucial aspect of the case is the opportunity it affords the High Court to 'dispel the misconception' that the common law rather than governments dispossessed indigenous Australians. As Justice Brennan notes:

> Aboriginal rights and interests were not stripped away by operation of the common law on first settlement by British colonists, but by the exercise of a sovereign authority over land exercised recurrently by governments. To treat the dispossession of the Australian Aborigines as the working out of the Crown's acquisition of ownership of all land on first settlement is contrary to history. Aborigines were dispossessed of their land parcel by parcel, to make way for expanding colonial settlement. Their dispossession underwrote the development of the nation.[40]

Why does Justice Brennan think *Mabo* is the appropriate time to provide a correct historical account of Aboriginal dispossession? His judgment implies two related reasons for setting the record straight.

The first concerns the 'contemporary values of the Australian people'. Justice Brennan is aware that unjust discrimination is no longer accepted by the Australian people and therefore the legitimacy of the common law will become a matter of concern in the future. The role of the Court as the final arbiter of the common law is an important consideration:

> It is not immaterial to the resolution of the present problem that, since the Australia Act 1986 (Cth) came into operation, the law of this country is entirely free of Imperial control. The law which governs Australia is Australian law. The Privy Council itself held that the common law of this country might legitimately develop independently of English precedent. Increasingly since 1968, the common law of Australia has been substantially in the hands of this Court. Here rests the ultimate responsibility of declaring the law of the nation.[41]

The argument is that the deficiencies of the common law can be attributed to the control exercised by Imperial authorities: Australia's common law has been a victim of colonisation. But if Australian law now governs Australia, it is crucial to correct errors and set the law on its proper foundations. The Australian High Court is now able to set right the common law on indigenous rights.

The second reason for giving a correct historical account of Aboriginal dispossession concerns the 'expectations of international community [which] accord in this respect with the contemporary values of the Australian people'. International law is a 'legitimate and important influence on the development of the common law, especially when international law declares the existence of human rights'. Thus Justice Brennan argues that international standards are important for the development of Australian law. One major reason for this concerns the new remedies available to Australian citizens:

> The opening up of international remedies to individuals pursuant to Australia's accession to the Optional Protocol to the International Covenant on Civil and Political Rights brings to bear on the common law the powerful influence of the Covenant and the international standards it imports.[42]

The 'influence' was a potentially unfavourable determination by the Human Rights Committee. Justice Brennan was concerned that proceedings regarding the discriminatory character of the common law might be commenced by Aborigines, risking the reputation and therefore the legitimacy and authority of the Court.[43]

From this aspect the decision of the Court appears to be self-interested; it is attempting to protect its standing by reinterpreting the common law to fit into current Australian and international opinion. The decision does not reflect Aboriginal entitlements as much as the endeavours of a political institution to pre-empt anticipated problems. But this assessment of the Court's motives neglects the important role of the judiciary in the Australian polity. In securing the integrity of the highest legal body in the regime the Court was not self-interested in a narrow sense – it arguably looked to the welfare of the whole, based on the view that the 'peace and order of Australian society is built on the legal system'.[44] The Court always had the opportunity, as demonstrated in the judgment of Justice Dawson, to deny that it had the authority to decide 'political' decisions, and resolve not to change the common law. Its decision to do so, exposing the Court and individual justices to virulent criticism, argues against such simple calculations of institutional standing.

What is the Common Law?

It is not clear from Justice Brennan's judgment what he means when he personifies the common law as 'taking', 'exposing' and so on. When Justice Brennan states that the duty of the High Court is to 'declare the common law of Australia' it would seem that he is referring to a declaratory theory of the common law, the common law as the 'ancient constitution', declared but never made by the judiciary. This impression is strengthened by his references to the 'skeleton' of the common law. This organic model of the law harks back to other metaphors that have been employed to describe the common law, such as 'tree' or 'river', even the 'body' of the common law. That the common law has 'fundamental values', that it is just, supports the view of the common law as the unchanging yet variable foundation of the 'peace and order of Australian society'.[45] Therefore, Justice Brennan's attempt to overrule the previous decisions to accord with international and Australian standards could be seen as a correction of the previously misconceived common law, declaring the true and just basis of the common law. It represents, in other words, a return to the true common law.

No doubt the declaratory theory of the common law is a significant theoretical and rhetorical source for Justice Brennan. However, there are a number of other statements that seem to suggest that his view of the common law is not wholly within that tradition. He states that in declaring the common law of Australia, 'this Court is not free to adopt rules that accord with contemporary notions of justice and human rights if their adoption would fracture the skeleton of principle which give the body of our law its shape and internal consistency'. It would appear that the principle of the common law may be at tension with 'contemporary notions of justice' and human rights. Whether a rule should be kept or maintained is a matter for judicial assessment, based on an evaluation of the rule as an essential doctrine of the legal system, and a prudential evaluation of whether 'the disturbance to be apprehended would be disproportionate to the benefit flowing from the overturning'.[46]

This view of the common law – of law as a 'prisoner of its history' that needs to be remedied or corrected by the Court to keep it up to date, of the common law as a product of 'theories' that are no longer tenable – sees it as the haphazard and primitive work of the 'dead hand of the past'. Rational and clear-sighted judges may alter, renovate and improve it while not disturbing the foundations of the entire edifice. It is difficult to decide whether Justice Brennan wholly favours one view. It may not be necessary for the judgment to decide clearly between the two – or perhaps it is no longer possible to do so. What is evident is that both notions of the common law require a judicial return to the correct path.

Contrition and Restitution

Having explored in some detail the main judgment in *Mabo*, we must consider the alternative views that challenged the majority's theoretical and practical resolution of the dispute. It is evident from the start of the joint judgment delivered by Justices Deane and Gaudron that their concerns are not those of Justice Brennan. According to Justices Deane and Gaudron, the common law always recognised native title rights and therefore, at least in theory, the native inhabitants were entitled to invoke the protection of the common law in a local court or (in some cases) English courts. However, to the extent that they probably knew nothing of their common law rights, they were essentially helpless. Even if native inhabitants in the eighteenth century did institute proceedings against the Crown, they would have failed because of Crown immunity from curial proceedings. This did not mean that common law recognition of native title was unimportant. Such personal rights could be asserted as a defence in both criminal and civil proceedings and this recognition imposed some restraint upon the actions of the Crown. Not only did the common law recognise native title, it demanded compensation for wrongful extinguishment or infringement although Crown immunity prevented the recovery of compensation. The judgment of Justices Deane and Gaudron goes beyond Justice Brennan by recognising that the common law allows compensation for wrongful infringement. The

initial impression is that the common law is free from the 'shame' of dispossession. To them, the dispossession of the original inhabitants was a:

> conflagration of oppression and conflict which was, over the following
> century, to spread across the continent to dispossess, degrade and
> devastate the Aboriginal peoples and leave a national legacy of unutterable
> shame.[47]

It would seem that these shameful acts were committed not by the common law, as Justice Brennan held, but by Australians. Indeed, in presenting and thereby implicitly contrasting the different views regarding
indigenous inhabitants, Justices Deane and Gaudron place greater blame
on the shoulders of the free settlers and recent Australians than on
Imperial authority. Cook's observations, the instructions to Phillip on his
second commission, the observations of Governor King and the opinions
of the eminent jurist Dr Lushington disclose attempts to acknowledge
the rights of Australia's native inhabitants.[48] Justices Deane and Gaudron, quoting Wharton's comments on Cook's logbook, stress that 'the
statement that the "coarser order of colonists" treated the Aborigines "as
wild beasts to be extirpated" was written in 1893 and was obviously a
reference to free settlers and not to transported convicts'.[49] Even the
framers of the Australian Constitution are implicated in the acts of
oppression and obliteration. In apportioning shame as they do, Justices
Deane and Gaudron attempt to preserve and enhance the noble position
of the common law and therefore of the judiciary.

But towards the middle of their judgment they state:

> Inevitably, one is compelled to acknowledge the role played, in the
> dispossession and oppression of the Aborigines, by the two propositions
> that the territory of New South Wales was, in 1788, *terra nullius* in the sense
> of unoccupied or uninhabited for legal purposes and that full legal and
> beneficial ownership of all lands of the Colony vested in the Crown,
> unaffected by any claims of the Aboriginal inhabitants. Those propositions
> provided a legal basis for and justification for dispossession. They
> constituted the legal context of the acts done to enforce it and, while
> accepted, rendered unlawful acts done by the Aboriginal inhabitants to
> protect traditional occupation or use.[50]

The endorsement of these principles by administrators and the courts
'provided the environment in which the Aboriginal people of the contin-
ent came to be treated as a different and lower form of life whose very
existence could be ignored for the purpose of determining the legal
right to occupy and use their traditional lands'. What appeared to be an
accusation against the Australian people becomes an admission of guilt

by the Australian common law: the courts too have been complicit in the dispossession of Aborigines. This confession serves a number of purposes. It is meant to show the extent to which all of Australia – people, administrators and law – is responsible for injustice. It is a lesson to those who feel far removed from these acts and therefore not responsible for them – there is a need to acknowledge that benefits have been gained at a price of injustice. Finally, the admission is meant to reveal the proper response to that injustice: primarily a feeling of shame, and therefore of the need to atone. That *Mabo* has limited legal import is conceded by Justices Deane and Gaudron: the practical effect of the decision will be confined to lands that remain under Aboriginal occupation or use. However, *Mabo* is no ordinary case. It is unique because:

> The acts and events by which that dispossession in legal theory was carried into practical effect constitute the darkest aspect of the history of the nation. The nation as a whole must remain diminished unless and until there is an acknowledgment of, and retreat from, those past injustices.[51]

To Justices Deane and Gaudron, their judgment represents an act of contrition that is essential for the national health of Australia; it is a moral refounding of not only the common law but of Australia. The common law is to be the scapegoat for the sins of the past. The effect of the judgment is to renew Australia by acts of contrition and restitution. For this reason the compensation that Justices Deane and Gaudron make possible is more significant than that of Justice Brennan. Nevertheless, though giving greater room to native title, their characterisation of native title is not far removed from that of Justice Brennan – use of land, or connection to the land, remains an essential aspect.

Common Law, Equity and the Powerless

The judgment of Justice Toohey, unlike those of Justice Brennan and Justices Deane and Gaudron, reads like a conventional legal decision. There is no evidence of hard choices, of overruling decisions that have facilitated dispossession; there is no 'dark history' or 'unutterable shame'. Drawing upon cases from a range of jurisdictions, he decides that the common law does recognise native title which is not extinguished by annexation. Though native title may be extinguished by clear and plain legislation or by executive act authorised by such legislation, 'such extinguishment would involve a breach of a fiduciary obligation owed by the Crown to the Meriam people'.[52]

What of those decisions that appear to deny the existence of native title? Justice Toohey negotiates these obstacles by broadening the common law tradition to include decisions from England, Canada and America, allowing him to note that competing lines of authority in the common law justify his decision. He rejects the expanded notion of *terra nullius* as 'unacceptable in law as well as in fact'. The Australian decisions that were regarded as formidable authority to the contrary by Justices Deane and Gaudron are referred to in a footnote and dismissed as *dicta*. A line of authority that held that existing aboriginal interests in ancestral lands continue after annexation only if they are recognised by positive executive or legislative acts, is rejected in favour of a more persuasive 'doctrine of continuity' which presumes that the conqueror has respected private property rights. According to Justice Toohey, the common law at annexation did not make all indigenous inhabitants trespassers on the land where they and their ancestors had lived.

Justice Toohey addresses the 'scale of organisation' argument developed in *In re Southern Rhodesia* and confronted by Justice Brennan in terms of 'civilisation' and 'culture' by favouring the decisions of the North American courts over the English and Australian decisions that required proprietary title and a system of rules to establish the existence of native title. Consequently, he distinguishes between a threshold question of the existence of native title and the related question of the content of the interests protected. By adopting this division, inquiries into the nature of traditional title become 'essentially irrelevant':

> an inquiry into the kind of society from which rights and duties emanate is irrelevant to the existence of title, because it is inconceivable that indigenous inhabitants in occupation of land did *not* have a system by which land was utilised in a way determined by society.[53]

It is not necessary to inquire into the kind of society; the existence of a society sufficiently organised to create and sustain rights and duties is sufficient: 'Thus traditional title is rooted in physical presence. That the use of land was meaningful must be proved but it is to be understood from the point of view of the members of the society'.[54]

To this extent Justice Toohey's judgment appears to be the furthest-reaching in attempting to accommodate native title within the common law. For example, he is prepared to expand the notion of occupancy to include 'nomadic lifestyles', he undermines arguments based on period of occupancy and is prepared to accept that occupation may be non-exclusive. He is even prepared to question the claim that native title is inalienable.[55] In fact, he argues that although there is authority that assumes a power in the Crown to unilaterally extinguish traditional title, there is support for the proposition that consent is required. Having outlined the different arguments, he concludes that 'traditional title may not be extinguished by legislation that does no more than provide in general terms for the alienation of the waste lands of the colony or Crown land'.

But it is only when we turn to the most innovative aspect of Justice Toohey's judgment that we understand his treatment of the common law and the claims of indigenous Australians. Justice Toohey extends the notion of fiduciary obligation found in the common law, to the case of native title. He does so because 'a policy of "protection" by government emerges from the legislation'. Also, the 'fiduciary relationship arises, therefore, out of the *power* of the Crown to extinguish traditional title by alienating the land otherwise; it does not depend on the exercise of that power'. The consequence of establishing such a relationship is that there is a Crown obligation 'to ensure that traditional title is not impaired or destroyed without the consent of or otherwise contrary to the interests of the titleholders'. The Crown's power to destroy or impair a people's interests 'is extraordinary and is sufficient to attract regulation by Equity to ensure that the position is not abused'.

This is the heart of Justice Toohey's judgment: by means of its equitable jurisdiction the Court will become the protector of indigenous Australians. Relying on the doctrine of fiduciary duty, he appropriates to the Court the mantle of protector and patron. Implicit in this view is the belief that the interests of indigenous Australians will be better secured by the judiciary than by the Crown or Parliament. This is why Justice Toohey is not prepared to accept that the common law has taken any part in the oppression of indigenous Australians. As he presents it, the common law has always protected their interests and will do so in the future. He need not 'cleanse' the common law, nor does he wish to show the nation how to feel contrition. His response is much more immediate and (he would say) valuable: irrespective of future political developments, the common law will look to the welfare of native Australians. Justice Toohey is least sanguine about the future political prospects of indigenous Australians. He does not expect a national reassessment; nor does he expect great advances through parliamentary legislation. For these reasons he will do what he can to protect the dispossessed.[56]

Law and Politics

Given the majority concerns with the status of the common law, the welfare of indigenous Australians and the need to acknowledge the injustices committed against the indigenous population, it is necessary to determine why Justice Dawson, the only judge to dissent in the case, declines to take action.

To Justice Dawson, the principles concerning native title are clear and cannot be questioned. What is at issue is their application, an analysis of the relevant facts to ascertain the application of the law. These accepted principles are that 'the annexation of land does not bring to an end those rights which the Crown chooses, in the exercise of sovereignty, to recognise'. Such recognition is a question of fact, which can only be determined by reference to surrounding circumstances. Where there is no recognition, the rights are extinguished at the time sovereignty is assumed. The Crown is not legally bound to pay compensation for the compulsory acquisition of land or any interests in it by the exercise of sovereign rights.[57] What Justice Dawson rejects is the plaintiffs' claim that aboriginal title may be extinguished only by express legislation.

The extinction of aboriginal title does not, therefore, require specific legislation. No doubt the intention of the Crown must be plain, but there is no reason in principle or logic why it should not be inferred from the course taken by the Crown in exercise of its powers, whether in administering statute law or otherwise.[58]

Therefore, the major part of his judgment consists of a detailed historical account of the way land was disposed in Australia upon annexation. According to Justice Dawson:

> Upon any account, the policy which was implemented and the laws which were passed in New South Wales make it plain that, from the inception of the colony, the Crown treated all land in the colony as unoccupied and afforded no recognition to any form of native interest in the land. It simply treated the land as its own to dispose of without regard to such interests as the natives might have had prior to the assumption of sovereignty. What was done was quite inconsistent with the recognition, by acquiescence or otherwise, of native title. Indeed, it is apparent that those in authority at the time did not consider any recognisable form of native title existed.[59]

The policy of Imperial government upon settlement was that 'whilst aboriginal inhabitants were not to be ill-treated, settlement was not to be impeded by any claim which those inhabitants might seek to exert over land'. This could be seen in the governors' decisions and in legislation governing the alienation of land, including Crown lands legislation. There was a 'consciousness that the occupation of the land by white men was a deprivation of the Aborigines, but that nevertheless no attempt was made to solve this problem by way of creation or application of title to land which the Aborigines could invoke'.[60]

Justice Dawson argues that the very concept of waste lands indicates the Crown proceeded and was required to proceed in disregard of any notion of native title. The power to reserve waste lands for the use or benefit of aboriginal inhabitants confirmed this view. Aborigines were removed from their traditional lands and placed in reserves where the land was owned by the Crown. The location and size of reserves was largely dictated by the suitability of the land for white settlement. With the Murray Islands, the creation of a reserve is a 'clear indication that the Crown was proceeding upon a basis other than that of preserving any native rights in respect of land'.[61]

Therefore, in applying the accepted principles to the facts, Justice Dawson concludes that:

> assuming the native inhabitants of the Murray Islands to have held some sort of rights in land immediately before the annexation of those islands, the Crown in right of the colony of Queensland, on their annexation, exerted to the full its rights in the land inconsistently with and to the exclusion of any native or aboriginal rights. It did so under the law which it brought with it. It did so from the start by acting upon the assumption (which was also the assumption lying behind the relevant legislation) that there was no such thing as native title and the Crown was exclusively entitled to all lands which had not been alienated by it: lands which were designated as Crown lands.[62]

Why does Justice Dawson see this decision as a relatively straight-forward application of precedent while the other justices regard it as unique, a case that compels reassessment of the relevant principles? Justice Dawson justifies his decision by distinguishing between the legal and the political:

> There may not be a great deal to be proud of in this history of events. But a dispassionate appraisal of what occurred is essential to the determination of the legal consequences, notwithstanding the degree of condemnation which is nowadays apt to accompany any account. The policy which lay behind the legal regime was determined politically and, however insensitive the politics may now seem to have been, a change in view does not of itself mean a change in law. It requires the implementation of a new policy to do that and that is a matter for government rather than the courts. In the meantime it would be wrong to attempt to revise history or to fail to recognise its legal impact, however unpalatable it may now seem. To do so would be to impugn the foundations of the very legal system under which this case must be decided.[63]

Justice Dawson's judgment presupposes a hierarchy of the legal and the political, where the 'legal regime' is determined politically. Law is a reflection of politics and puts politics into effect; it is derived from, and subject to, the political. The political, on the other hand, is variable; what was once considered proper and appropriate can later be seen as 'in-sensitive' and 'unpalatable', even shameful. As the arena for contending views of justice and the good, political changes are not immediately reflected in the nature of law. Only strongly held and persistent views will achieve that, and the only way to discern such views is by accepting policies that are implemented. Government decisions are the conclusive indicator of an authoritative policy choice.

For various reasons it may be tempting for the judiciary to take the initiative in this process, but Justice Dawson sees dangers in doing so. It is difficult to be dispassionate about justice, and easy to confuse one's own sentiments with the prevailing political mood. Also, politics entertains many disparate opinions, making it difficult to evaluate the dominant policy. Finally, any such attempt, according to Justice Dawson, undermines the entire regime to the extent that it impugns the foundations of the legal system. Justice Dawson means that judicial attempts to change the law may follow two paths. One path is to 'revise history': in doing so it may be possible to alter the application of the law. But the legal task requires a dispassionate assessment of historical facts to determine their legal consequences. Thus this attempt to achieve justice undermines unbiased assessment of the facts – a chief aspect of the judicial task. The other path is to be dispassionate about facts and history yet 'fail to recognise its legal impact' – to reinterpret the legal meaning to accord with the newly desired outcome. This option is also contrary to the judicial office to the extent that it applies a new law based not on different circumstances – by distinguishing – but simply because it is warranted.

Justice Dawson's implicit critique of the majority judgments is that their attempts to alter the law are essentially at odds with the rule of law, which is fundamental to the legal system they are attempting to protect and use in pursuing justice. Does this mean that Justice Dawson is not concerned with questions of justice? The last sentence of his judgment reads: 'Accordingly, if traditional land rights (or at least rights akin to them) are to be afforded to the inhabitants of the Murray Islands, the responsibility, both legal and moral, lies with the legislature and not with the courts'.[64] Justice Dawson does not deny the moral dimension of the problem. His claim is that, to the extent that it makes the laws, Parliament should be held accountable for any perceived deficiencies in the nature of the regime. He too is prepared to absolve the common law of the moral responsibility of aboriginal dispossession. His strategy, however, is to strip the common law of any independent legal or moral status – perhaps a high price to pay for 'clean hands'.

Mabo and the Court

The Court engages a number of profound issues in *Mabo*. Foremost is the way indigenous Australians have been treated, historically and now – their dispossession and the continuing non-recognition of their claims. The Court uses various means in attempting to remedy these injustices.

The majority recognise native title but let Parliament and the people (as result of the *Racial Discrimination Act 1975*) decide the terms of compensation. To the other justices, whose judgments reveal a fundamental distrust of Parliament and the people, compensation is to be determined by the common law – the judiciary assumes the burden of protecting indigenous people as well as the responsibility of apportioning compensation for past injustices. Justice Dawson is prepared to leave all responsibility and therefore all determination of liability to the people: his stance appears to be most deferential to Parliament.

The other important theme in *Mabo* concerns the complicity of the common law or (what appears to be the same issue) the defence of the High Court as an institution. To the majority, *Mabo* is a necessary proof of the Court's non-racist credentials. Justice Brennan's judgment clearly shows the direction the Court takes in abandoning the path of racism and thereby cleansing the common law of previously improper decisions. The judgment of Justices Deane and Gaudron is an approximation of an apology from the common law for acts of shameful complicity: it means to remedy the law and therefore the High Court as an institution by means of contrition. In doing so it also attempts to set the precedent for the rest of Australia. On the other hand, Justice Toohey does not appear to even acknowledge the role of the common law in the dispossession. His position is that at its first opportunity in deciding native title the High Court has taken the just decision, untainted by previous (foreign) judgments. He makes the common law the patron and guardian of all Australians, in particular those who may be unjustly discriminated against because of their race. Justice Dawson also denies that the common law is to blame. He does so by making it the instrument of Parliament; it is in itself morally and legally neutral. Hence the judiciary need not feel any shame, nor should they feel compelled to protect the institution of the law by means other than enforcing the rule of law.

Politics of Native Title

If *Mabo* was more than a case about property, if it confronted fundamental or constitutive questions concerning Australian constitutionalism, it also disclosed the great limitations of posing such questions as legal problems. Though the case established a vital moral and legal foundation for the claims of indigenous Australians, it did so within the legal framework of property and a language that constricted the terms of debate and consequently the reach of any future settlement. It was a case that could have benefited from public deliberation and compromise rather than legal adjudication.

But perhaps this was what the Court sought to initiate in handing down its decision, for, as Chief Justice Mason observed, native title was one of those controversial questions that the political community was happy to defer to the judiciary.[65] Though the immediate effect of the decision was clear with respect to the litigants, its implications for land use in Australia were far from certain. Indigenous people entitled to native title would have to use the courts to justify their claims. The validity of land dealings since 1975 was in question. The States, mining and pastoral groups argued that the decision created uncertainty. In short, the decision made a judicial solution to the problem impractical and therefore unlikely. Though the High Court's decision and even the Court itself was criticised, it is undeniable that the case allowed a political resolution that would not have been possible otherwise.[66]

Native Title Act 1993

The political resolution, a result of extensive, complex and unpredictable negotiations and compromise, exacerbated by diversity of interests, federalism and the problem of representation in indigenous communities, took the form of the Native Title Act 1993 (Cth). The events that led up to the drafting and enactment of the Native Title Act have been detailed elsewhere.[67] For our purposes, it is sufficient to note the major steps in the negotiations.

Five months after the Mabo decision the Keating Labor government announced a process of consultation with State and Territory governments and representatives from all interest groups. In his Redfern address in December 1992, Keating acknowledged the Mabo decision as a historic turning-point in the relations between indigenous and non-Aboriginal Australians. With the tacit consent of Hewson, the Leader of the Opposition, Mabo was effectively kept out of the federal electoral campaign of March 1993 which returned Keating to power. In office, Keating had to fulfil his promise to implement the Mabo decision in national legislation.

One response from the indigenous community took the form of the Aboriginal Peace Plan, a proposal drafted in April 1993 by leaders of Aboriginal land councils and legal services to address the concerns of indigenous Australians. The Peace Plan was followed in June by the federal government's 33-point Plan, setting out the principles of the proposed legislation. The Council of Australian Governments meeting that followed the release of the federal government's plan ended without agreement, most State Premiers demanding legislation to dismantle native title rights, even at the cost of amending the Racial Discrimination Act. In response to the government's proposed legislation, the Council for Aboriginal Reconciliation helped organise a national meeting of over 500 Aborigines and Torres Strait Islanders leaders at Eva Valley Station. The Eva Valley group, which claimed to represent a broader constituency than the Aboriginal Peace Plan group, issued a statement in August 1993 rejecting the government's proposed legislation.

In September 1993 the government released *Mabo: Outline of Proposed Legislation,* which made important concessions to the State and Territory leaders and to mining demands. The low point of the negotiations for Aborigines and Torres Strait Islanders was reached on 'Black Friday', 8 October 1993, when it seemed that the federal government was prepared to amend the Racial Discrimination Act to validate property titles at the expense of native title. But by 'Ruby Tuesday', 19 October 1993, indigenous negotiators and their advisers negotiated a new deal with the Prime Minister.[68] However, the proposed legislation had to pass the Senate and get the support of the Greens, the Democrats and the Tasmanian Independent Brian Harradine, who held the balance of power. The Aboriginal negotiators who had dealt with the government, the 'A Team', now gave way to a 'B Team', which included the Aboriginal provisional government, the New South Wales Land Council and Western Australian Aborigines, who sought to extract as much as possible from the minor parties in the Senate. After a number of changes, the Native Title Act was passed on 22 December 1993 and became law on 1 January 1994.

The *Native Title Act 1993*, a complex and not always clear enactment, addressed a number of important issues. The Act confirmed the existence of native title in Australia. It established a Native Title Registrar who would maintain a Register of Native Title Claims, and a National Native Title Tribunal for determining native title claims, which may be subject to negotiation, mediation and finally hearings before the Federal Court. The Act validated all Commonwealth legislation before 1 January 1994. It provided that native title could not be extinguished contrary to the Native Title Act and, depending on the nature of the past Acts extinguishing native title, compensation would be payable. The Act provided for future actions affecting native title, with a right to negotiate provisions in the case of miners seeking access to native title land. Given the importance to indigenous Australians of not amending the Racial Discrimination Act, the Native Title Act was said to be consistent with the Racial Discrimination Act as a 'special measure' for the advancement and protection of Aboriginal peoples and Torres Strait Islanders. Complementary State and Territory legislation was authorised by the Act. In addition to the Native Title Act, the Keating Labor government promised a social justice package of assistance to indigenous Australians and a Land Act which would provide assistance to groups that were no longer able to claim native title.

Judicial Interlude

It appeared that the Native Title Act, as a political settlement of the *Mabo* decision, had moved the question of native title from the legal to the political arena. In fact, having decided *Mabo*, the High Court had in effect accepted a new and continuing commitment to the elaboration and articulation of native title and indigenous rights in Australia. Its decisions soon after *Mabo* demonstrated the Court's crucial role in the formulation and development of indigenous rights.

Soon after *Mabo* the Court had the opportunity to extend the principle of native title to include the notion of Aboriginal sovereignty. The *Wiradjuri Claim* case concerned the validity of a statement of claim made by Isabel Coe on behalf of the Wiradjuri people concerning land that encompassed southern and central New South Wales.[69] The action, commenced at the height of the *Mabo* political negotiations and partly intended to contribute to the political debates, included the claim of Wiradjuri sovereignty. Though the question of Aboriginal sovereignty had not been addressed directly and therefore not determined conclusively by the High Court, there were statements in a number of cases rejecting the proposition. In a 1979 decision the Court had rejected the application of an American notion of 'domestic dependent nation' to Aboriginal people.[70] In *Mabo* itself there were statements rejecting the possibility of challenging Crown sovereignty in Australian municipal courts.[71] In the *Wiradjuri Claim* case Chief Justice Mason struck out the statement of claim on the grounds that the wider notion of Aboriginal sovereignty, and the more limited residual sovereignty subordinate to Australian sovereignty identified in the American jurisprudence as domestic dependent nation, were entirely at odds with the Court's previous decisions, especially the *Mabo* case.[72]

In a subsequent case, *Walker*, it was claimed that just as native title was recognised in *Mabo*, customary Aboriginal criminal law was recognised by the common law and continues to this day.[73] Chief Justice Mason rejected the proposition on the basis that different criminal sanctions applying to different persons for the same conduct offended the principle that all should be equal before the law. He held that even if customary criminal law did survive British settlement, it was extinguished by the passage of criminal statutes of general application. There was no analogy between native title and criminal law: 'English criminal law did not, and Australian criminal law does not, accommodate an alternative body of law operating alongside it'.[74]

These decisions indicated that, at that stage, the Court was not prepared to follow Canadian and American precedents and alter the common law to recognise Aboriginal sovereignty. The continuing criticism of *Mabo* and the delicate state of the political negotiations would no doubt have influenced the rejection of the argument for sovereignty. Also, in *Mabo* the Court had decided upon native title rather than sovereignty as the more appropriate judicial path.

It was not surprising, therefore, that in the *Native Title Act* case the Court upheld the validity of the political settlement effected by the *Native Title Act 1993*. After the Native Title Bill was introduced into the Commonwealth Parliament in November 1993, the Western Australian government enacted the *Land (Titles and Traditional Usage) Act 1993* which purported to extinguish native title throughout the State and replace it with a statutory 'rights of traditional land usage'. Those statutory rights would be subordinate to all other interests and there were limited compensation rights. Upon the enactment of the *Native Title Act 1993* Western Australia initiated proceedings challenging its validity. Two Western Australian groups in turn challenged the validity of the Western Australian Act. The three actions were heard together as the *Native Title Act* case.[75] In the *Native Title Act* case the High Court held that native title existed in Western Australia and that the Western Australian Act was inconsistent with the federal Racial Discrimination Act. The Court upheld the *Native Title Act 1993* as a valid exercise of the races power in section 51(xxvi) of the Constitution. As the Commonwealth Act covered the field, the Western Australian Act was invalid.

The Native Title Act was made possible by the Courts, implemented by Parliament and finally endorsed by the judiciary, a complex interplay of the legal and political. It represented a new settlement for indigenous Australians and a transformation in Australian constitutionalism. To what extent was it conclusive? Whether the judiciary could consistently take the lead in formulating native title and rely on Parliament to support and follow its initiatives became crucial questions when the Court handed down its decision in the *Wik* case.[76]

Wik Case

Did pastoral leases necessarily extinguish native title? Put in such legal terms, the question obscured the profound practical import of the problem: if pastoral leases did not necessarily extinguish native title then 42 per cent of Australia (more than 3 million square kilometres of Crown leasehold land) could be subject to native title claims. In most views, the question had already been answered. In *Mabo* Justice Brennan had held that 'If a lease be granted, the lessee acquires possession and the Crown acquires the reversion expectant on the expiry of the term. The Crown's title is thus expanded from the mere radical title and, on the expiry of the term, becomes a *plenum dominium*'.[77] Justices Deane and Gaudron in *Mabo* appeared to agree, stating that the personal rights conferred by native title 'are extinguished by an unqualified grant of an inconsistent estate in the land by the Crown, such as a grant in fee or a lease conferring the right to exclusive possession'.[78] Prime Minister Keating also seemed to have endorsed that view in his Second Reading Speech on the Native Title Bill made to the House of Representatives in November 1993.[79] The preamble to the *Native Title Act 1993* and the *Native Title (South Australia) Act 1994* assumed that native title was extinguished by pastoral leases.

In June 1993, prior to the operation of the Native Title Act, the Wik people commenced proceedings in the Federal Court of Australia against the State of Queensland, the Commonwealth and others, claiming native title and possessory title rights over an area of land and waters in far north Queensland. The Thayorre people later joined as respondents, seeking similar relief in respect of lands that partly overlap those that were claimed by the Wik people. The lands claimed included parcels of land subject to leases, in particular the Holroyd River holding lease granted under the Queensland *Land Act 1910* and *Land Act 1962*, and the Michellton pastoral holding lease granted under the 1910 Act.

The Wik people made a claim under the *Native Title Act 1993* when it came into force but procedural rulings were made by Justice Drummond for the hearing and determination of issues in the Federal Court proceedings. It was thought that these might resolve the Federal Court proceedings as well as the claim under the Native Title Act. Without deciding the existence of native title, Justice Drummond held that the relevant lease was not subject to a reservation in favour of the Wik or the Thayorre people, that each lease gave the grantee rights to exclusive possession, that those rights were wholly inconsistent with the concurrent and continuing exercise of rights and interests which might compromise Aboriginal or possessory title, and that the grant of leases necessarily extinguished all incidents of Aboriginal title or possessory title by the Wik and the Thayorre peoples in respect of the relevant land. The Wik and the Thayorre peoples appealed the decision and the matter was removed to the High Court.[80]

The High Court in *Wik* divided on the question. The majority held that the grant of pastoral leases under the 1910 and 1962 Acts did not necessarily extinguish native title rights. However, to the extent native title was inconsistent with the particular rights and interests asserted with respect to the leasehold interests, leasehold interests would prevail over native title.[81] To the minority, as the lessees of the Michellton and Holroyd River leases had exclusive possession and that right was inconsistent with native title, native title cannot coexist with leasehold estate and is thereby extinguished.[82]

Though separate judgments are handed down by the justices in the majority, it is possible to discern some common themes. Perhaps the

most important is the need to interpret the State Acts and leases in the
light of the rule in *Mabo* that general legislation with respect to waste
lands or Crown land is not to be construed, in the absence of clear and
unambiguous words, as intended to apply in a way which will extinguish
or diminish rights under common law native title. A detailed examination of the leases and Acts does not disclose any such intention. Relying
on historical research into leasehold interests in Australia by legal
academics and historians Fry and Reynolds, the majority distinguish the
judgment in *Mabo* and a number of other cases on the grounds that
Crown lands legislation introduced into Australia new statutory interests
in land that displaced common law rules regarding leases and the
fictions of the doctrine of estates and tenures. Accordingly, the majority
reject the reversion principle enunciated by Justice Brennan in *Mabo*.
They conclude that the grants are not necessarily inconsistent with the
continued existence of any of the incidents of native title which would
have been subsisting at the time of the grants.

The minority position is outlined in the judgment of Chief Justice
Brennan (Justices Dawson and McHugh concurring). Chief Justice Brennan agrees with the majority view that the nature and effect of a lease
must be ascertained by reference to the language used in the relevant Act
and in the lease instrument. However, he refers to extensive authority in
favour of interpreting Crown lands legislation in light of the common
law, that it must be assumed that in enacting the relevant statutory
provisions Parliament anticipated the interests and language at common
law.[83] Interpreting the Act and leases according to these principles, Chief
Justice Brennan sees no reason to deny leases under the 1910 and 1962
Acts the right of exclusive possession characteristic of a leasehold estate
at common law. As such, they are inconsistent with the right of holders of
native title to enjoy that title.

Chief Justice Brennan accepts that adopting such a principle of
interpretation reveals 'a significant moral shortcoming in the principles
by which native title is recognised'. His response is that the shortcomings
cannot be remedied by denying the true legal effect of the Acts and
leases. As a matter of history, he considers it impossible to interpret the
1910 and 1962 Acts as though Parliament had native title in mind in
enacting them: native title was not recognised by the Australian courts
until 1992. To regard leasehold interests as merely a 'bundle of statutory
rights conferred on the lessees' would mean that a grant in fee simple
could be regarded as a larger bundle of statutory rights. But that would
lead to the conclusion that the underlying or residual title would subsist
in the holders of native title, a theory inconsistent with the fundamental
doctrines of the common law. Therefore, to Chief Justice Brennan the
majority view undermines the fundamental doctrines of tenure and

estates, the 'skeleton' and foundation of land law in Australia. To develop a new theory of land law, as attempted by the majority, would throw the whole structure of land titles based on Crown grants into confusion and would lead to uncertainty.

Wik, Justice and the Common Law

It is tempting to explain the *Wik* decision simply in terms of numbers: by the time the *Wik* case was heard, Chief Justice Mason and Justice Deane had been replaced by Justice Gummow and Justice Kirby. The new judges, aware of the Court's role in facilitating the enactment of the Native Title Act, were prepared to repeat the exercise and go beyond *Mabo* to expand the rights of native title holders. On one level this simple assessment is accurate – the decision in *Wik* was a bare four–three majority. But on another level *Wik* indicates the relative unimportance of the individual authority of judges: *Wik* shows how the Court's decisions are appropriated and reinterpreted by judges in subsequent cases. The opinions of the judges who sat on *Mabo*, as to the reach of the decision, had no greater standing in *Wik* than the opinions of those who would newly interpret its meaning. Thus the Court's decisions are protean and slippery, each in a sense consuming and rewriting all that went before. Indeed, the evaluation based on jurimetrics – numbers and who is appointed – tends to obscure not only this reinterpretation and the rewriting, but also the more fundamental bases upon which such rejuvenation takes place – the vying considerations of justice, doctrine and the common law.

Perhaps what is most remarkable about *Wik* is that both the majority and minority judges claim that they are resolving the case on the grounds of conventional statutory interpretation, almost a return to traditional 'legal' interpretation. How can such conventional readings produce such different outcomes? The differences between the majority and minority views seem to turn on what *Mabo* decided and the extent to which its principles can be applied to the past. According to the majority in *Wik*, the question of pastoral leases was not decided in *Mabo*. This starting-point allows the majority to evaluate the question in the light of the substantive holding in *Mabo* on native title. As a result the majority is able to construe the silence on native title in the relevant Acts as an intention not to extinguish native title. It also allows the majority to reject the doctrines of estates and tenures to the extent that they are fictions that will extinguish native title. In short, it justifies the majority's redefinition of the law of Crown lands in Australia.

But isn't there something unreal, even fictitious, in such a re-evaluation of the past? If the 'common law tends to abhor unreality, even when it is presented as legal doctrine', as Justice Kirby claims in *Wik*, how are we to understand his oracular claim that 'In this case the present must revisit the past to produce a result, wholly unexpected at the time, which will not cause undue collision and strife in the future'?[84] It would seem that the difference between the majority and the minority in *Wik* turns not on formal rules of statutory interpretation, but on the more philosophical question of the way the past is to be interpreted – the way the Court deals with 'history'. But in retelling history, the majority is in fact applying the declaratory theory of the common law that rejects prospective judgments and claims that the Court's judgment in *Mabo* should be interpreted from the beginning of Australian settlement. In *Wik* only Justice Gummow confronts and addresses in detail the theoretical and practical difficulties raised by such a theory.

Justice Gummow states that there have been few recent adherents to an absolute form of declaratory theory, because equity did not accept it and because it was argued that law had an evolutionary and functional nature. It would appear that, to Justice Gummow, the primary reason for not adopting a declaratory theory is the 'movement' in the common law. The movement may be gradual or radical, a consequence of changes in social or economic conditions or changes in legal system. *Mabo*, according to Justice Gummow, was such a shift in the foundation of the common law based on a changed concept of historical fact.[85] To Justice Gummow this means that the common law becomes a question of 'history' and the movement of the law subject to the uses of history. But the adversarial processes of the common law trial may, due to imperfections or absence of evidence, limit the historical method, not leading to the whole truth. The implication Justice Gummow seems to draw from this observation is that instead of pursuing history, which aims at an 'independent truth', the Court must do justice between parties. In other words, instead of history, the 'better guide must be the "time honoured methodology of the common law" whereby principle is developed from the issues in one case to those which arise in the next'.[86]

Thus Justice Gummow returns to and defends the declaratory theory of the common law on the grounds that it is consistent in procedure, metes justice in each case and avoids the problem of independent truth and 'history'. But what of the problems in statutory interpretation this entails, especially in construing statutes enacted at times when the state of the law was perceived as the opposite of that which has since been held? Justice Gummow indicates that the problem is resolved by a common law statutory method of interpretation which requires that in abrogating rights the legislature must clearly and distinctly authorise such abrogation. His excursions into the philosophical limitations of the declaratory theory appear to endorse the theory, on the grounds that there is no better method.

The above discussion seems to support the view that the minority in *Wik* do not in fact rely on declaratory theory. But as we have seen, in so far as Chief Justice Brennan endorses and adopts it in his judgment in *Mabo* he does employ a retrospective declaratory theory. It appears, therefore, that the main difference between the majority and the minority concerns the limits to the retrospectivity demanded by *Mabo*, the extent to which the reinterpretation required by *Mabo* is constrained by the skeleton of the doctrine of tenures and estates. For reasons of certainty and clarity, Chief Justice Brennan advises against reformulating the concept of leaseholds. By hedging the claims for justice and change within limits prescribed by *Mabo*, he claims to favour certainty while avoiding the theoretical problems the majority confront in *Wik*. On the other hand, to the majority the demands of certainty and the problems of 'history' are not sufficiently compelling to stop them from reinterpreting, consistent with the principles of *Mabo*, the doctrines of land law. Thus the difference between the majority and minority views in *Wik* is ultimately based on their perceived duty to be just. *Wik* is evidence of the power and reach of the desire to correct injustice, inevitably straining at limitations and thereby depicting them as unjust.

10-Point Plan

The majority decision to implement justice had serious political consequences.[87] Though the Court's decision was celebrated by indigenous Australians, it received a different reception elsewhere. It was attacked by graziers, farmers and miners as leading to uncertainty and a decline in the value of pastoral properties. Peak pastoral bodies such as the National Farmers Federation regarded it as undermining Aboriginal reconciliation. The Queensland government refused to issue further leasehold and mining tenements and placed restrictions on further development work on pastoral properties.[88] The High Court came under extraordinary and serious political attack, Queensland Premier Rob Borbidge describing it as 'an embarrassment'.[89] Prime Minister John Howard entered the debate by rejecting a law-making role for the judiciary, while Deputy Prime Minister Tim Fischer criticised the judgment as an example of judicial activism.[90]

The Howard government's response to *Wik*, after discussions with Premiers and chief ministers, pastoralists, mining and resource groups and the National Indigenous Working Group, was its '10-Point Plan' proposal to amend the Native Title Act. The government's Bill was opposed by the Labor Party on the grounds that only legislation benefiting Aborigines was valid. The National Indigenous Working Group on Native Title, comprising representatives of the Aboriginal and Torres Strait

Islander Commission, native title representative bodies and other key indigenous organisations, prepared a position paper, *Coexistence: Negotiation and Certainty*, outlining its reasons for rejecting the Bill.[91] Though the *Wik* Bill was passed in the House of Representatives it was opposed in the Senate by Labor, the Democrats, the Greens and the Independent from Tasmania, Brian Harradine. The Bill was returned to the Senate a second time and a number of amendments were agreed upon, such as a new registration test for native title applicants. But on four contentious matters, 'sticking-points' as Howard termed them, the Senate refused to give in. The Senate rejection gave Howard a possible trigger for a double dissolution election and opened the possibility of an election based on race.

It was in this atmosphere of heated debate and negotiations over the amendments to the Native Title Act that the High Court was given the opportunity to intervene and shape the nature of the settlement, in effect determining, albeit indirectly, the outcome of the Wik Bill. The Court had to decide the *Hindmarsh Island* case, a claim by Doreen Kartinyeri, Neville Gollan and members of the Ngarridjeri people, that a proposed bridge to Hindmarsh Island, near Adelaide, would desecrate 'secret women's business'. The claim had been discredited by a 1995 royal commission and the federal government had enacted enabling legislation, the *Hindmarsh Island Bridge Act 1997* (Cth), to remove Aboriginal heritage laws and allow the building of the bridge. Kartinyeri and Gollan challenged the constitutional validity of the Act, arguing that the 'race power' in the Constitution, which gives Parliament the power to make laws with respect to 'the people of any race, for whom it is deemed necessary to make special laws' (section 51xxvi) can now be relied on only to enact laws beneficial to Aborigines. They pointed to the very popular 1967 referendum that amended section 51(xxxvi) to allow the federal government to legislate for Aborigines, as well as repealing section 127 of the Constitution and thereby including Aborigines in the census, as evidence of the new way the race power should be employed.

Though the case concerned the specific provisions of the Hindmarsh Island Act, it had more profound implications for the *Wik* debate. A decision that Parliament could only pass laws that favoured Aborigines would raise grave doubts concerning the validity of the government's 10-Point Plan. It would also raise concerns about judicial activism, as the question of whether a law favoured Aborigines would now be determined by the Court, effectively placing it in a supervisory role over Commonwealth Aboriginal policy. The Court, finding itself in a difficult position, declined to decide the issue of whether section 51(xxxvi) now permitted only beneficial legislation. Aware of the delicate nature of the political issues, it decided not to intervene in the political negotiations. The majority resolved the case on the basis that if Parliament had the power to enact the Heritage Protection Act then it also had the power to amend it.

The Court's decision, returning the problem to the political arena and thereby requiring a political solution, appeared to make a double dissolution election based on race a reality. Concerned over the possibility, Senator Harradine 'blinked'; holding the balance of power in the Senate, he resolved the impasse by agreeing to negotiate on the four sticking-points considered unacceptable to the government. For the requirement that the Native Title Act should be subject to the Racial Discrimination Act, some aspects of the Bill were made subject to the Act. Regarding the registration test, where Howard had insisted on the need to prove physical connection with the land, Senator Harradine convinced him to allow members of the 'stolen generation' and others whose parents had connection to the land (the 'locked gates' exception) to appeal to a court and lodge a claim. The contentious sunset clause that would have made the Native Title Act provisions cease after six years was scrapped by Howard. Finally, with respect to the Aboriginal right to negotiate about mining leases on pastoral land, an alternative and lesser form of right to negotiate was adopted.

After a historic debate of 109 hours over a twelve-month period, and two rejections in the Senate, the Bill finally passed the Senate on Wednesday 8 July 1998. Howard welcomed the passage as 'a wonderful outcome for all Australians'.[92] Kim Beazley, Leader of the Opposition, declared that Labor would not campaign the next election on the basis that it would amend the *Wik* amendments to the Native Title Act; any changes would be made after legal challenges to the Act. Senator Harradine justified his decision to compromise with the government as necessary to avoid a race-based election that he believed would have 'torn the fabric of our society and set race relations back forty or fifty years'. According to him, a double dissolution election with the possible election of One Nation senators would have made the Senate anti-indigenous for at least six years.[93] Wik elder Gladys Tybingoompa, who had danced with Harradine on the lawns of Parliament and lobbied him in the final minutes before the vote was taken, felt betrayed by him. She and the Wik people who had travelled to Canberra to sit through the Senate debate walked away from Parliament House and declared that they would turn to the courts for protection. Judicial politics had become an essential aspect of the wider political struggles of indigenous Australians.

Yet as the Court's subsequent decisions would show, judicial politics offered no greater certainty. In *Kruger*, a case dealing with the stolen generation of Aborigines, the plaintiffs who had been taken from their families when they were young pursuant to the Northern Territory

Aboriginal Ordinance and related Acts claimed that those provisions were contrary to the implied constitutional rights and guarantees of legal process, legal equality, freedom of movement and association and freedom of religion. They also argued that the relevant legislation and the actions of the Territory's Chief Protector were unconstitutional because they amounted to genocide. The majority of the Court held that the relevant provisions were not invalid by reason of any rights, guarantees, immunities or freedoms contained in the Constitution.[94] Finally, the High Court in *Fejo* was asked to decide that freehold grants did not necessarily extinguish native title.[95] The case presented the Court with the opportunity of extending the *Mabo* principle beyond *Wik* and leasehold interests to all land in Australia. In holding that native title did not survive freehold grants, the Court signalled the limits of its native title jurisprudence.

New Politics of Native Title

The High Court's native title decisions reveal a profound engagement with the major themes of civilisation and culture, race and identity, justice and history. In the Court's provisional responses and resolutions of these issues it is possible to see the foundations of a regime based on Lockean conceptions of property – a progressive, innovative and technocratic polity that is open to international changes and influence. At the same time, the decisions disclose a deeply spiritual and moral regime, a democracy capable of wrongdoing, that has erred and needs to reconcile itself to past injustices. In this regime the Court becomes the locus for public ethical deliberation and assumes the heavy burden of moral guardian and wise counsellor to guide the nation.

In confronting and articulating these subtle aspects of Australian democracy, the Court reveals the many dimensions to the new politics of the High Court. It also confirms its role as a political institution. We have seen the powerful influence of the Court in setting and demarcating the political agenda in its *Mabo* decision, resulting in the Native Title Act. Yet its *Wik* judgment and the political response in the form of the *Wik* amendments to the Native Title Act show the very real limits to the Court's influence. The judiciary and Parliament working in tandem can be formidable, perhaps unstoppable; opposed by a determined Parliament the Court will always be vulnerable. The dynamic nature of judicial politics is also evident in the increasingly prominent part the Court plays in mediating international changes, accommodating supranational developments within domestic concerns and demands. Its definition of native title, rejection of Aboriginal sovereignty and autochthonous redefinition of statutory leasehold interests are the practical consequences of reconciling practical and immediate political concerns with powerful international legal and jurisprudential developments. Perhaps the Court was not aware of the costs of inaugurating and committing itself to this new native title jurisprudence. It may not have anticipated the larger consequences of its decision, the way the decision would influence its entire jurisprudence. It certainly did not seem prepared for the vehemence and stridency of the new politics that did not hold back from criticising individual judges, questioning the place of judicial independence and separation of powers.

If indeed the Court's native title jurisprudence epitomised the new politics of the High Court, especially its concern with the role of the judiciary within the regime and its delineation of important aspects of Australian democracy, it also underlined the unavoidable and ever-present tension and compromise between justice and politics of the Court.

Notes

1 *Mabo v Queensland (No 2)* (1992) 175 CLR 1; *Wik Peoples v Queensland* (1996) 141 ALR 129.
2 *Attorney-General (NSW) v Brown* (1847) 1 Legge 312; *Cooper v Stuart* (1889) 14 App Cas 286.
3 *Milirrpum v Nabalco* (1971) 17 FLR 141; per Blackburn J at 244–5.
4 *Calder v Attorney-General of British Columbia* (1971) 13 DLR (3d) 64. See generally Brennan, F. 1995, *One Land, One Nation*, Brisbane, University of Queensland Press, 4–7; McRae, H., Nettheim, G. & Beacroft, L. 1997, *Indigenous Legal Issues: Commentary and Materials*, Sydney, Law Book Co., 205–7.
5 See McRae, Nettheim & Beacroft, *Indigenous Legal Issues*, 207, *Administration of Papua v Daera Guba* (1973) 130 CLR 353 per Barwick CJ at 397; *Coe v Commonwealth* (1979) 53 ALJR 403; *Gerhardy v Brown* (1985) 57 ALR 472 per Deane J at 532 regarding the need for 'retreat from injustice'; Whitlam, E.G. 1985, *The Whitlam Government 1972–1975*, Melbourne, Penguin Books, 457–84.
6 The Aboriginal Councils and Associations Bill and the Aboriginal Land Rights (Northern Territory) Bill were enacted by the Fraser government in December 1976: See Whitlam, *The Whitlam Government*, 476–7.
7 See generally Dorsett, S. & Godden, L. 1998, *A Guide to Overseas Precedents of Relevance to Native Title*, Canberra, AIATSIS; Brennan, *One Land, One Nation*, 161–83; Wells, B. & Doyle, J. 1997, 'Reconciliation and the Constitution' in E. Johnston, M. Hinton & D. Rigney (eds), *Indigenous Australians and the Law*, Sydney, Cavendish Publishing.
8 *Calder v Attorney-General of British Columbia* (1973) 34 DLR (3d) 145.
9 *Guerin v R* (1985) 13 DLR (4th) 321; *R v Sparrow* [1990] 1 SCR 1075; *Delgamuukw v ABC* (1991) 79 DLR (4th) 185; *R v Van der Peet* (1996) 137 DLR (4th) 289.

10 *New Zealand Maori Council v Attorney-General* [1987] 1 NZLR 641.
11 The Court divided on the question of whether the Act was inconsistent with s. 10 of the *Racial Discrimination Act 1975* (Cth). Where rights enjoyed by the Meriam people are unique their extinguishment did not leave the same rights in force for other people.
12 Four judgments are given in *Mabo*: Brennan J (with whom Mason CJ and McHugh J agree), Deane and Gaudron JJ, Toohey J, and the dissent by Dawson J.
13 *Mabo v Queensland (No 2)* (1992) 175 CLR 1 at 18.
14 ibid. at 22.
15 See *Attorney-General (NSW) v Brown* (1847) 1 Legge 312; *Randwick Corporation v Rutledge* (1959) 102 CLR 54; *NSW v Commonwealth* (1975) 135 CLR 337.
16 *Mabo v Queensland (No 2)* (1992) 175 CLR 1 at 29.
17 ibid. at 39.
18 ibid. at 40, emphasis added.
19 Velkley, R. 1997, 'The Tension in the Beautiful: On Culture and Civilisation in Rousseau and German Philosophy' in C. Orwin & N. Tarcov (eds), *The Legacy of Rousseau*, Chicago, University of Chicago Press, 67, notes that the use of the term can be traced to Mirabeau. Napoleon uses it in his revolutionary manifestos to describe France's mission as the propagation of the universal rights of man.
20 The 'Great Chain of Being' was a pervasive concept that influenced philosophy, theology and natural science at the time. It attempted to arrange all living matter in a hierarchical pattern. From the late seventeenth century there was a growing tendency to distinguish between different types of human beings and arrange them in hierarchy: see Young, R. 1995, *Colonial Desire*, London, Routledge, 7; Reynolds, H. 1974, 'Racial Thought in Early Colonial Australia', *Australian Journal of Politics and History*, 20: 45–53 at 47. See also Huttenback, R. 1976, *Racism and Empire*, Ithaca, Cornell University Press, regarding the link between race and empire; Kane, J. 1997, 'Racialism and Democracy: The Legacy of White Australia' in G. Stokes (ed.), *The Politics of Identity in Australia*, Cambridge, Cambridge University Press.
21 According to Young, *Colonial Desire*, 11–13, Darwin shifted the dispute between 'monogenists' and 'polygenists' towards the concept of 'type'.
22 For the influence of these views in the Australian colonies see generally Reynolds, 'Racial Thought in Early Colonial Australia'.
23 According to Cole, D. 1971, ' "The Crimson Thread of Kinship": Ethnic Ideas in Australia, 1870–1914', *Historical Studies*, 14, 56: 511–25, ideas of race and blood in Australia were expressed on three levels: on the grounds of colour, excluding all other races; as Anglo-Saxonism; and as the basis for the 'Coming Australian Man'.
24 See Huttenback, *Racism and Empire*, regarding the link between race and empire.
25 *Mabo v Queensland (No 2)* (1992) 175 CLR 1 at 42.
26 For Rousseau's attack on the Enlightenment see the *First* and *Second Discourses*. See also Velkley, 'The Tension in the Beautiful'; Young, *Colonial Desire*.
27 Cicero uses culture to mean cultivation of the soul in philosophy. Pufendorf is the first to use it in the modern non-teleological sense of overcoming the inconveniences of nature: Velkley, 'The Tension in the Beautiful', 69.

28 There are modern notions of culture that preserve a universalist character, such as those of Kant and Wilhelm von Humbolt. See Young, *Colonial Desire*, 36–43; Velkley, 'The Tension in the Beautiful'.

29 To Herder, plurality of cultures contributes to the progressive unfolding of a common humanity. Compare this with Kant's notion in *Universal History* that the moral perfection of the species can be reconciled with progress and enlightenment.

30 *Mabo v Queensland (No 2)* (1992) 175 CLR 1 at 42.

31 ibid. at 29.

32 ibid. at 58.

33 *Case of Tanistry* (1608) 80 ER 516.

34 *Mabo v Queensland (No 2)* (1992) 175 CLR 1 at 61, emphasis added, reference omitted.

35 ibid. at 59–60.

36 ibid. at 64, references omitted.

37 To the extent that property gains value from human labour and endeavour, ie it is 'real estate', a resource that can be exchanged and used, it is consistent with a scientific and commercial notion of land: see Locke, J. 1992, *Two Treatises on Government*, 2nd edn (ed. with intro. and notes by P. Laslett), Cambridge, Cambridge University Press, Second Treatise, ch. v.

38 *Mabo v Queensland (No 2)* (1992) 175 CLR 1 at 29, emphasis added.

39 ibid. at 69, emphasis added.

40 ibid. at 68–9.

41 ibid. at 29, references omitted.

42 ibid. at 42, references omitted.

43 The 1991 Royal Commission into Aboriginal Deaths in Custody recommended that Australia accede to the Optional Protocol of the International Covenant on Civil and Political Rights: Australian Government 1991, *National Report: Royal Commission into Aboriginal Deaths in Custody*, Canberra, Australian Government Publishing Service, 5: 26, Recommendation 333. The federal government accepted the recommendation and acceded to the first Optional Protocol on 25 September 1991. To date, the communication procedures have not been used by indigenous Australians. Cf in this regard the recent concerns of the UN Committee on the Elimination of Racial Discrimination regarding the *Wik* amendments to the Native Title Act (see generally CERD/C/SR.1353).

44 *Mabo v Queensland (No 2)* (1992) 175 CLR 1 at 30.

45 ibid. at 29, 30, 42.

46 ibid. at 29, 30.

47 ibid. at 104.

48 ibid. at 96–7, 105, 108.

49 ibid. at 106, notes omitted.

50 ibid. at 108.

51 ibid. at 109.

52 ibid. at 205.

53 ibid. at 187.

54 ibid. at 188.

55 ibid. at 188–91; 194. See also his extensive discussion of common law Aboriginal title, where he concludes that 'the Meriam people may have acquired a possessory title on annexation. However, as I have said, the

consequences here are no more beneficial for the plaintiffs and, the argument having been put as an alternative, it is unnecessary to reach a firm conclusion' (at 206–14).

56 For an analysis of the case law on fiduciary relationship in America and Canada see Dawson J at 164–70.

57 Dawson J derives these principles from Privy Council decisions. He states that the Canadian cases are relevant due to the common authority of the Privy Council. However, the American cases and those of New Zealand are based on treaties and therefore are less helpful (at 131–7).

58 ibid. at 138.

59 ibid. at 139.

60 ibid. at 149, reference omitted.

61 ibid. at 155.

62 ibid. at 159.

63 ibid. at 145, reference omitted.

64 ibid. at 175.

65 As Mason CJ notes, although the Commonwealth was originally a defendant in the proceedings, it subsequently ceased to be a defendant and became an intervener and ultimately did not participate in the hearing at all: see Virtue, B. 1993, 'Putting Mabo in Perspective', *Australian Lawyer*, July 1993, 23.

66 For criticisms of the High Court's decision see generally McRae, Nettheim & Beacroft, *Indigenous Legal Issues*, 210–18; Goot, M. & Rowse, T. (eds) 1994, *Make a Better Offer: The Politics of Mabo*, Sydney, Pluto Press.

67 See in particular Brennan, *One Land, One Nation*, chs 2, 3; Goot & Rowse, *Make a Better Offer*; Attwood, B. (ed.) 1996, *In the Age of Mabo*, Sydney, Allen & Unwin; Stephenson, M.A. & Ratnapala, S. (eds) 1993, *Mabo: A Judicial Revolution*, Brisbane, University of Queensland Press; Law Book Co. (ed.) 1993, *Essays on the Mabo Decision*, Sydney, Law Book Co.; Bartlett, R. 1993, *The Mabo Decision*, Sydney, Butterworths; Stephenson, M.A. (ed.) 1995, *Mabo: The Native Title Legislation*, Brisbane, University of Queensland Press.

68 Brennan, *One Land, One Nation*, 67–71, outlines the concessions made by both sides.

69 *Coe v Commonwealth (Wiradjuri Claim)* (1993) 68 ALJR 110.

70 *Coe v Commonwealth* (1979) 53 ALJR 403.

71 *Mabo v Queensland (No 2)* (1992) 175 CLR 1 per Brennan J at 31–2, 69, per Deane and Gaudron JJ at 78–9, per Dawson J at 121.

72 *Coe v Commonwealth (Wiradjuri Claim)* (1993) 68 ALJR 110 at 114.

73 *Walker v New South Wales* (1994) 182 CLR 45.

74 ibid. at 50. For an example of other decisions that have an important though indirect bearing on the Native Title Act see *Brandy v Human Rights and Equal Opportunity Commission* (1995) 183 CLR 245.

75 *Western Australia v Commonwealth* (1995) 183 CLR 373.

76 *Wik Peoples v Queensland* (1996) ALR 129.

77 *Mabo v Queensland (No 2)* (1992) 175 CLR 1 per Brennan J at 68. Recall that Mason CJ and McHugh J concurred with Brennan J's judgment.

78 ibid. at 110.

79 Hansard, House of Representatives, No 11 (16 November 1993), 2877–83.

80 A second issue in the case concerned the Wik challenge to the validity of special bauxite mining leases granted by Queensland to certain mining companies. The Court rejected that appeal, upholding the validity of the leases.

81 *Wik Peoples v Queensland* (1996) ALR 129 per Toohey, Gaudron, Gummow and Kirby JJ.
82 Per Brennan CJ; McHugh and Dawson JJ.
83 See his discussion at 140–51.
84 ibid. at 269, 271.
85 Cf Brennan CJ where the majority overrules the law rather than changes its conception.
86 ibid. at 232.
87 For an earlier examination of these issues see Patapan, H. 1999, 'The Howard Government and the High Court' in G. Singleton (ed.), *The Howard Government*, Sydney, University of New South Wales Press.
88 See generally Hiley, G. (ed.) 1997, *The Wik Case: Issues and Implications*, Sydney, Butterworths; Rowse, T. 1994, 'How we got a Native Title Act' in Goot & Rowse, *Make a Better Offer*, 111–32; Hunter, P. 1997, 'The Wik Decision: Unnecessary Extinguishment' in Hiley, *The Wik Case*, 6–18; Horrigan, B. & Young, S. (eds) 1997, *Commercial Implications of Native Title*, Sydney, Federation Press.
89 *Australian*, 19 February 1997, 1.
90 *Courier Mail*, 5 March 1997, 1.
91 See http://www.edime.com.au/nativetitle.
92 *Australian*, 9 July 1998, 6.
93 Bachelard, M., 'Deal "unsticks" Troubled Act', *Australian*, 9 July 1998, 6.
94 *Kruger v Commonwealth* (1997) 190 CLR 1.
95 *Fejo v Northern Territory of Australia* (1998) 195 CLR 96.

CHAPTER 6

Separation of Powers

In this chapter we explore the new politics of the High Court by investigating the way it has shaped the character of separation of powers in Australian constitutionalism. Though the existence of the doctrine of separation of powers in the Constitution is generally acknowledged, insufficient attention has been paid to the Court's pre-eminent role in interpreting the terms of the Constitution and thereby delineating the character of separation of powers and democracy in Australia.[1] By evaluating the extent to which the High Court has directed and influenced the development of the concept of separation of powers in Australia, we can discern the way the Court has defined its place within the Australian regime and its view of the regime as a whole.

The Court's recent statements that it makes the law, combined with its defence of separation of powers as essential for liberty, have posed profound questions concerning separation of powers in Australia. For the courts, the most pressing have been questions of judicial legitimacy and independence. If the judiciary is no different from other law-making institutions, to what extent is it entitled to the independence it has been accorded in the Australian political system? The recent political attacks on the judiciary, the declaration by the Commonwealth Attorney-General that he would no longer speak for the courts and the creation of institutions such as the Judicial Conference of Australia to represent the judiciary in public debate are the most obvious indications of the major changes in the concept of separation of powers in Australia.

These changes can be traced to larger theoretical concerns with the way the Court is formulating the concept of separation of powers. Foremost is the Court's inability to provide a theoretical basis for reconciling the concept of separation of powers with a law-making judiciary. There is also the question of whether the Court is redefining separation of powers away from its traditional English foundations towards an American model of institutional checks and balances. Finally, there is the profound matter of the underlying conceptions of human nature and thereby the competing visions of liberalism and democracy that are being implemented by the Court during its adjudication of the differing notions of separation of powers. Before exploring these questions, however, it is necessary to examine the formulation of separation of powers at Australia's founding.

Separation of Powers and the Founding

Classical political thought recognised different functions of government. For example, Aristotle distinguished between the deliberative, magisterial and judicial aspects of ruling. However, the classic authors did not propose a strict separation of governmental functions, nor did they envisage a balance of these functions as a solution to the political problem of faction. The answer to the formation of factions, especially the competing claims of rich and poor, was the mixed regime or polity, allowing each a share in rule. Thus the Aristotelian or classical regime relied not on institutions but on its citizens; it attempted to cultivate certain human virtues and excellence as a means of moderating the instability caused by the differing demands to rule.[2] Modern political thought emphasised institutional solutions to the problem of rule and therefore separation of powers.[3] At the time of the Australian founding the framers of the Constitution faced competing modern conceptions of separation of powers, the two dominant versions being the doctrine as elaborated in the *Federalist* and given form in the American Constitution, and the common law view articulated in the writings of Blackstone.

The Federalist

The *Federalist* notion of separation of powers was influenced by the most famous modern theorists of the separation of powers, Locke and Montesquieu. Locke, the theoretical defender of liberal constitutionalism, distinguished between three powers – the legislative, the executive and the federative. The legislative power is the supreme power though it is not arbitrary, dispensing justice by promulgated standing laws and known and authorised judges. The executive is ministerial and subordinate to the legislative, having the duty of executing the laws, especially the prerogative. By the federative power Locke means the power of war and peace and all matters concerning international relations. According to Locke, the executive and federative powers are almost always united.

Consequently, in Locke's formulation of separation of powers there is a separation between the legislative and the executive.[4]

The separation of judicial powers becomes prominent in Montesquieu's account of separation of powers. In *Spirit of the Laws* Montesquieu distinguishes between the legislative power, the executive power and what he calls 'the power of judging'. Separation of powers is necessary, according to Montesquieu, to ensure a balance of powers and therefore the liberty of the Constitution. However, a more fundamental reason for the separation of the power of judging is the liberty of the citizen:

> Nor is there liberty if the power of judging is not separate from legislative power and from executive power. If it were joined to legislative power, the power over the life and liberty of the citizens would be arbitrary, for the judge would be the legislator. If it were joined to executive power, the judge could have the force of an oppressor.[5]

The judicial power is separated to keep it independent; it is given only enough power to defend itself from the other two powers. The separation of the judicial is the most important part of the separation of powers because it guards the government against its own lawlessness, preventing any deviation from the rule of law by allowing the legislative and executive powers to be checked by a judicial arm that will interpret the laws and apply them equally to everyone. Therefore, to Montesquieu separation of powers is an institutional arrangement that ensures the rule of law and thereby the liberty and security of the individual.[6]

Though the framers of the American Constitution were influenced by the writings of Locke and Montesquieu, the new Constitution was an innovation, based on principles derived from modern political science. As Alexander Hamilton notes in the *Federalist*:

> The regular distribution of power into distinct departments – the introduction of legislative balances and checks – the institution of courts composed of judges, holding their offices during good behaviour – the representation of the people in the legislature by deputies of their own election – these are either wholly new discoveries or have made their principal progress towards perfection in modern times. They are means, powerful means, by which the excellencies of republican government may be retained and its imperfections lessened or avoided.[7]

The Constitution was devised to address the two-fold political problem outlined in Madison's famous observation in the *Federalist*:

> If angels were to govern men, neither external nor internal controuls [sic] on government would be necessary. In framing a government which is to

be administered by men over men, the great difficulty lies in this: You must first enable the government to controul the governed; and in the next place, oblige it to controul itself. A dependence on the people is no doubt the primary controul on the government; but experience has taught mankind the necessity of auxiliary precautions.[8]

The primary precaution is dependence on the people, or representation. Separation of powers is the main 'auxiliary' precaution which, combined with the 'double security' that arises due to the federal division of powers and the multiplicity of interests, guards against majority oppression.[9]

Two arguments for separation of powers are advanced in the *Federalist*. Separation of powers is needed as a precaution against the encroaching nature of power. As Madison puts it:

> The accumulation of all powers legislative, executive, and judiciary in the same hands, whether of one, a few, or many, and whether hereditary, self-appointed, or elective, may justly be pronounced the very definition of tyranny.[10]

It is based on the 'policy of supplying by opposite and rival interests, the defect of better motives'.[11] But the separation of powers does not mean that power should be kept in isolation from other powers in their branches. The encroaching nature of power demands that each branch have the means to ward off such attempts; independence is secured only by means of mutual checks: 'Ambition must be made to counteract ambition'. In this way, separation of powers provides a precaution against oppression by rulers.[12]

That ambition is to counter ambition reveals the second justification for separation of powers. In describing the three branches of government and the different qualities required for success in each, the *Federalist* speaks to the ambitious as well as to the common people, evoking better motives than mere ambition. Separation makes the powers work better because in vying with each other the ambitious are drawn to better motives, connecting private interest to virtue in carrying out their constitutional duty. But in directing and encouraging the virtue of politicians the *Federalist* subordinates it to liberty; the distribution of power in the Constitution is aimed at liberty, giving all citizens security from fear as well as a share in rule through elections – and for some an opportunity to exercise their ambition.[13]

The final part of the *Federalist* is devoted to the examination of the judiciary.[14] According to Hamilton, 'the judiciary, from the nature of its functions, will always be the least dangerous to the political rights of the Constitution; because it will be least in a capacity to annoy or injure them'. It has 'neither Force nor Will, but merely judgment; and must ultimately depend upon the aid of the executive arm even for the efficacy of its judgments'. Being the weakest of the three departments of power, it is important that it be able to defend itself. Therefore, permanency in office is essential to counter the 'natural feebleness of the judiciary'.[15]

Hamilton defends the need for an independent judiciary on a number of grounds. Independence is essential in a limited Constitution, where specific exceptions to legislative authority are spelled out. Thus the courts are the 'bulwarks of a limited Constitution against legislative encroachment'.[16] As well, the judiciary as the 'faithful guardians of the Constitution' guard it against the 'arts of designing men' and the momentary inclination of the majority. The courts will counter the 'occasional ill humours in the society' in the case of laws generally by 'mitigating the severity, and confining the operation of such laws'. By providing permanent and secure tenure, the judiciary is able to protect the rights of the Constitution and the individual while acquiring skills in the law.[17]

According to Hamilton, 'the courts must declare the sense of the law'; judges should not be disposed 'to exercise Will instead of Judgment', to substitute 'their pleasure to that of the legislative body'. Though he seems to dismiss such a possibility, the subsequent discussion reveals his more considered views on the subject. Strict rules and precedents will avoid an arbitrary discretion in the courts[18] and, even if the will of the legislature is contravened, the nature of judicial power is such that judicial encroachment on the legislative authority is really a 'phantom':

> Particular misconstructions and contraventions of the will of the legislature may now and then happen; but they can never be so extensive as to amount to an inconvenience, or in any sensible degree to affect the order of the political system. This may be inferred with certainty from the general nature of the judicial power; from the objects to which it relates; from the manner in which it is exercised; from its comparative weakness, and from its total incapacity to support usurpations by force.[19]

The constitutional check of impeachment is in itself a 'complete security', according to Hamilton.[20]

Blackstone and the Common Law

It is necessary to contrast the *Federalist* notion of separation of powers with that of Blackstone, who was greatly influential in the development of English common law. His discussion of separation of powers in *Commentaries on the Laws of England* takes place in the context of the king's prerogative, in particular the king as the fountain of justice and conservator of the peace of the kingdom. By this Blackstone understands the king to be not the source of justice, but its reservoir and distributor. Though having the power of judicature the king commits this power to select magistrates. Therefore the entire jurisdiction of the courts derives from the Crown. The delegation of the power of judicature to judges of several courts is described by Blackstone as the outcome of 'long and uniform usage of many ages' which the Crown cannot now alter without an Act of Parliament. Judges' security of tenure – fixed salaries, continuation of office during good behaviour – is designed to maintain their dignity and independence. As Blackstone notes:

> In this distinct and separate existence of the judicial power in a peculiar body of men, nominated indeed, but not removable at pleasure, by the Crown, consists one main preservative of the public liberty which cannot subsist long in any state unless the administration of common justice be in some degree separated both from the legislative and also from the executive power. Were it joined with the legislative, the life, liberty, and property of the subject would be in the hands of arbitrary judges, whose decisions would be then regulated only by their own opinions, and not by any fundamental principles of law, which, though legislators may depart from, yet judges are bound to observe. Were it joined with the executive, this union might soon be an overbalance for the legislative.[21]

Blackstone summarises his position in these terms: 'Nothing, therefore, is more to be avoided, in a free Constitution, than uniting the provinces of a judge and a minister of state'.[22]

To Blackstone, separation of powers means primarily the separation of judicial powers, a principle developed over a long time. There is the suggestion that the judicial separation of powers ensures that the executive power does not 'overbalance' the legislative, that it provides an institutional check on the powers of the executive and the legislature. Yet the core of the argument seems to be that the separation of judicial power preserves the life, liberty and property of subjects by providing for the independence and dignity of judges, allowing them to determine the 'fundamental principles of law'. Judicial separation of powers makes possible what Blackstone had previously described as the 'artificial reason' of the common law, where law is the 'perfection of reason'. In short, separation of powers protects the common law, which is the ultimate security of life, liberty and property.[23]

Australian Founding

To the extent that both the *Federalist* and Blackstone supported the notion of judicial separation of powers and regarded separation of powers as a means of safeguarding liberty, the framers of the Australian Constitution would have found it difficult to distinguish between them. However, as we have seen, there were fundamental differences between them, particularly in the theoretical assumptions underlying each view. To the *Federalist*, separation of powers was designed to address the limitations in human nature. Human beings are not angels, as Madison observes in the *Federalist* 51. On the contrary, humans are ambitious, desiring power. The political problem is that of countering the encroaching nature of power and ambition. This theoretical starting-point determines the character of the political solution: the Constitution is an innovation that would, through institutions that check and balance each other, counter ambition with ambition. In contrast, Blackstone did not start with the conception of human nature that largely informed the political architecture outlined in the *Federalist*. He relied on tradition and the common law to protect liberty: judicial separation of powers was sufficient to secure the artificial reason of the common law and thereby the protection of ancient liberties.

What form of separation of powers did Australia's founders agree upon? It is difficult to discern from the formal records of the Constitutional Convention Debates the theoretical understanding of separation of powers entertained by the delegates, especially those such as Inglis Clark, Barton, Isaacs and Higgins who were familiar with American constitutionalism.[24] Clearly, most founders intended or assumed that courts would have and exercise the power to decide whether Commonwealth and State legislation were unconstitutional.[25] Judicial review and therefore the separation of judicial power were seen as the necessary consequence of a written federal Constitution that would require a disinterested institution to undertake the legal task of interpreting the Constitution and adjudicating disputes between the States and the Commonwealth. Thus the High Court was described as a 'safety valve', the 'guardian' and 'bulwark' of the Constitution. This seems to suggest that the founders accepted, or at least were familiar with, one aspect of the *Federalist* notion of separation of power, but Bryce's *American Commonwealth*, which was the founders' major authority on the American Constitution, is silent regarding the *Federalist* understanding of separation of powers. Moreover, contemporary commentators such as Inglis Clark, Harrison Moore, Quick and Garran also seemed to emphasise the judicial separation of powers.[26] Perhaps the most that can be said, then, given the limited evidence, is that to the framers of the Constitution the common law judicial separation of powers was a familiar concept that could be appropriated and applied to the American innovation of federalism.

The Constitution that was finally enacted did not resolve this ambiguity. Its terms and overall structure appeared to adopt and secure the doctrine of separation of powers as developed in the American Constitution,[27] but the Constitution also required that any minister who was to administer Commonwealth departments be a member of the House of Representatives or the Senate.[28] If these provisions effectively entrenched responsible government in the Constitution, it was clearly at odds with the *Federalist* notion of separation of powers.[29] It seems, then, that the Constitution accommodated an amalgam of political traditions and differing conceptions of separation of powers. Whether and how these different traditions would be reconciled or woven together in practice was a matter that would be influenced significantly by the High Court.

Separation of Powers and the High Court

From the beginning, the High Court interpreted the Constitution as providing separation of judicial powers. Only those courts properly constituted under Chapter III of the Constitution could exercise any part of the judicial power of the Commonwealth.[30] But it was not until *Dignan's* case that the Court considered and ruled on the nature of separation of powers between the legislature and the executive, that is, whether an American conception of separation of powers would be implemented in Australia.[31] In a series of cases prior to *Dignan* the Court had held that Parliament could delegate law-making powers to the executive.[32] The latest of these decisions, *Roche v Kronheimer*, a unanimous decision handed down a year before *Dignan*, decided that Parliament could delegate to the executive power to regulate an aspect of interstate commerce without indicating the standards or principles to be applied.[33] But the question of separation of powers had not been raised in those cases. In *Dignan* the Court had to consider whether it would apply the comprehensive doctrine of separation of powers and thus overrule its recent jurisprudence, or somehow fashion the doctrine to accommodate its previous decisions. It chose to uphold its previous jurisprudence. Chief Justice Gavan Duffy and Justice Starke, in a brief joint judgment, clearly state their preference for upholding the Court's recent decisions on the basis that the existence of separation of judicial power does not mean that the principle also applies to the legislative: 'Legislative power is very different in character from judicial power: the general authority of the Parliament of the Commonwealth to make laws upon specific subjects at discretion bears no resemblance to judicial power'.[34] In a separate judgment, Justice Rich accepts the authority of the previous decisions and agrees with the decision of Justice Dixon. In fact, only Justices Evatt and Dixon consider the substantive argument regarding separation of powers.

Justice Evatt commences his judgment by emphasising the authority of the Court's previous decisions on the issue. He then undertakes a general analysis of separation of powers, suggesting that perhaps not even the notion of judicial separation of powers is conclusive if the Constitution is to be construed by the courts as advancing representative government.[35] Nevertheless, he accepts that there is a separation of judicial powers, based on the High Court's decisions, the 'British Trad- ition' that judicial functionaries should be free from any interference from the legislative or the executive, the 'special nature' of judicial power and the 'elaborate provisions of Chapter III'.[36] But there is a 'great cleavage' between judicial power and legislative and executive power: 'In truth the full theory of "Separation of Powers" cannot apply under our Constitution'.[37] The notion of responsible government and the suprem- acy of Parliament within British parliamentary history means that Parlia- ment has full power to confer the ability to make laws upon authorities other than Parliament. If legislative power were not construed in this way, 'effective government would be impossible'; 'absurd results' would eventuate.[38]

According to Justice Dixon, the founders intended to embody the theory of separation of powers in the Constitution. He refers to Montesquieu, the *Federalist* and US Supreme Court decisions to outline the nature of separation of powers. He then refers to High Court decisions that support the separation of judicial powers, and asks whether the principle can be applied to the separation of legislative power. His conclusion is that *Roche v Kronheimer* determined conclusively that legislative power would not be confined to Parliament. Justice Dixon notes that there appears to be an asymmetry in the Court's interpretation of Chapter III and of Chapters I and II which cannot be justified by referring to judicial precedents. However, 'The existence in Parliament of power to authorise subordinate legislation may be ascribed to a con- ception of that legislative power which depends less upon juristic analysis and perhaps more upon history and usages of British legislation and theories of English law'. He concludes that 'whatever may be its rationale, we should now adhere to the interpretation which results from the decision of *Roche v Kronheimer*'.[39]

The Court's decision in *Dignan* suggests that the American doctrine of separation of powers was not introduced into Australian constitutional- ism by the High Court because of the limitations of the adversarial method of adjudication. The question of separation of judicial powers was determined early and in isolation from the general question of the separation of powers. The decision regarding the separation of legislative and executive powers was also reached without considering the theoret- ical question of separation of powers. When the overarching concept of separation of powers was put to the Court in *Dignan,* the explanations and justifications made it clear that the Court was reluctant to overrule its previous decisions, reconciling 'juristic analysis' with precedent or *stare decisis.* Therefore, separation of powers in Australia was substantially influenced by the way these questions reached the Court and the context in which they were litigated; the institutional limitations of the Court significantly shaped separation of powers in Australia.

It may well be, of course, that the Court would have come to this decision in any case. As the judgments of Justices Evatt and Dixon show, British tradition, responsible government and the reality of legislation by regulation would have overcome what was considered to be no more than a matter of formal 'symmetry' rather than fundamental constitutional design. English constitutionalism and Blackstone's notion of separation of powers would prevail over the innovation of the *Federalist* because, as Sir Owen Dixon put it, 'Legal symmetry gave way to common sense'.[40]

Separation of Judicial Powers

What did the separation of judicial power entail? The Court gave its definitive answer in the *Boilermakers* case, where it held that the Commonwealth Court of Conciliation and Arbitration could not validly exercise the judicial power of the Commonwealth on the grounds that Parliament could not confer upon one body both arbitral and judicial functions. As the Arbitration Court's main functions were non-judicial, Parliament could not validly confer judicial powers on the Court.[41] Though *Boilermakers* has been affirmed by the Court, there has been extensive criticism of the efficacy of the decision.[42] For our purposes the importance of the *Boilermakers* case lies in the valuable insights it provides into the Court's formulation and theoretical justification of separation of powers.

The majority in the *Boilermakers* case reject a strict separation of powers doctrine: 'The fact that responsible government is the central feature of the Australian constitutional system makes it correct enough to say that we have not adopted the American theory of separation of powers'. The character of the division of power is 'determined according to traditional British conceptions'.[43] This conception does not require a strict separation of legislative and executive powers. The majority approves the decision in *Dignan* that history and usages of British legislation may allow the legislature to 'empower the executive Government to make statutory rules and orders possessing the binding force of law',[44] but it does require a strict separation of judicial powers. The reasons for this can be found in the federal character of the Constitution:

In a federal form of government a part is necessarily assigned to the judicature which places it in a position unknown in a unitary system or under a flexible Constitution where Parliament is supreme. A federal Constitution must be rigid. The government it establishes must be one of defined powers; within those powers it must be paramount, but it must be incompetent to go beyond them. The conception of independent governments existing in the one area by law could not be carried into practical effect unless the ultimate responsibility of deciding upon the limits of the respective powers of the governments were placed in the federal judicature. The demarcation of the powers of the judicature, the constitution of the courts of which it consists and the maintenance of its distinct functions become therefore a consideration of equal importance to the States and the Commonwealth.[45]

The Court understands the Constitution in Brycean terms: it is rigid not flexible, federal not unitary. In this light the Court's crucial role is that of an adjudicator of federalism, a 'boundary keeper':

The position and constitution of the judicature could not be considered accidental to the institution of federalism: for upon the judicature rested the ultimate responsibility for the maintenance and enforcement of the boundaries within which governmental power might be exercised and upon that the whole system constructed.[46]

The whole system relies on understanding the Court as the guardian of the federal Constitution. Thus the aim of separation of powers is to preserve the 'essential feature' of the Court as an 'impartial tribunal'.[47]

Reflecting on *Dignan* and *Boilermakers* and their implications for separation of powers in Australia, we begin to discern a preference for British practice and theory over the *Federalist* understanding of separation of powers. This is evident in the Court's rejection of a strict separation of powers and its adoption of a more limited notion of separation of judicial powers.[48] But the Court's adoption of a more limited separation of judicial powers is not, in fact, grounded upon a Blackstonian conception. On the contrary, the Court in *Boilermakers* returns to one strand of the *Federalist* justification to support separation of judicial powers – the view of the judiciary as an essential adjudicator of the boundaries of federalism. Therefore, at the core of the Court's understanding of separation of powers in *Boilermakers* is a federal rather than a liberal-democratic conception of the separation of powers. *Dignan* and *Boilermakers* effectively repudiate the underlying theory of separation of powers as developed in the American founding, producing an Australian conception that sees it as essentially a protection of the judiciary within a federal state.

Shifting Ground?

The Court's recent admission that it 'makes' law has posed profound difficulties for the theory of separation of powers in Australia. A law-making Court is not consistent with the *Federalist* notion of a judiciary that is to exercise judgment rather than 'Will'. It also sits uncomfortably with the Blackstonian understanding of separation of judicial powers since judges, according to Blackstone, declare the law, not make it. As a result, the theoretical uncertainty regarding the Court's place within Australian constitutionalism has raised unprecedented questions concerning the legitimacy of the Court and the nature of separation of powers in Australia.

An important aspect of the High Court's response to these concerns has been the attempt to justify separation of powers by emphasising its importance for the protection of liberty.[49] Accordingly, in the nature of judicial power and the judicial process generally it has discerned a constitutional guarantee of a range of individual rights that are not subject to parliamentary discretion.[50] For example, the Court has held that the legislature may not interfere with the judicial process, particularly with the requirements of natural justice.[51] Similarly, in *Dietrich* the Court has formulated a limited notion of right to counsel from the right to fair trial.[52] The issue in *Dietrich* was whether an accused person charged with a serious crime punishable by imprisonment, who cannot afford counsel, has a right to be provided counsel at public expense. The majority, relying on the common law right of fair trial, held that in such cases a judge should adjourn or stay the trial until legal representation is available. Justices Deane and Gaudron went further by claiming that fair trial was entrenched in the Constitution's requirement of the observance of judicial process and fairness, implicit in the separation of judicial power.[53]

In the *War Crimes* case the High Court decided that the separation of judicial power recognised in the Australian Constitution prevented the Commonwealth Parliament from enacting a Bill of Attainder, an enactment that imposes punishment on a specified person or members of a specified class.[54] Such a declaration of guilt and award of punishment by the legislature was an invalid usurpation by Parliament of judicial power.[55] Although the majority accepted that Parliament may make retrospective legislation, Justices Deane and Gaudron, relying on the separation of judicial powers, went further, stating that Parliament could not enact retroactive criminal laws as they would usurp judicial power.[56]

The wider reach of the implications derived from the separation of powers could be seen in *Leeth*.[57] In that case a narrow majority upheld

Commonwealth legislation which provided that the setting of minimum sentences for Commonwealth offenders was to be done according to the law of the State where the trial took place. Justice Gaudron held the provision invalid because it required the exercise of a power that was inconsistent with the judicial process:

> All are equal before the law and the concept of equal justice – a concept which requires the like treatment of like persons in like circumstances, but also requires that genuine differences be treated as such – is fundamental to the judicial process.[58]

Because the provision required the exercise of a power that necessarily involved impermissible discrimination, it was not part of the judicial power of the Commonwealth.[59] Justice Gaudron's judgment in *Leeth* reveals the extent to which drawing upon constitutional implications – in this case separation of powers – has the potential to introduce substantive judicial review into Australian constitutionalism.

In addition to emphasising the importance of separation of powers for liberty, the Court has addressed the problem of judicial independence and legitimacy by interpreting the notion of separation of judicial powers strictly.[60] In *Wilson* the Court stated that the importance of public confidence in the judicial process justified taking a strict view of the types of non-judicial functions that may be conferred on persons who are federal judges.[61] The Minister for Aboriginal and Islander Affairs appointed a Federal Court judge to prepare a report under the *Aboriginal and Torres Strait Islander Heritage Protection Act 1984* (Cth) concerning the existence of significant Aboriginal areas on and around Hindmarsh Island. At issue was the question of whether the Heritage Act contemplated the nomination of a judge as a reporter, and whether such appointment was contrary to the judicial separation of powers provided by the Constitution. The majority of the Court held that the relevant section in the Act did not authorise the nomination of judges because the function of reporting to the minister was not constitutionally compatible with the office of a judge under Chapter III of the Constitution.[62]

In *Kable* the Court was prepared to extend the principle of incompatibility to State courts.[63] The *Community Protection Act 1994* (NSW) gave the Supreme Court of New South Wales the power to order the detention of a named person, if it was satisfied on reasonable grounds that on balance of probabilities that person was likely to commit a serious act of violence. Though the New South Wales *Constitution Act 1902* did not provide for a separation of judicial power, the High Court held that the separation of judicial power under the Commonwealth Constitution invalidated the Act. This was because the Supreme Court's involvement in the continued imprisonment of the named person would diminish public confidence in State courts that also exercised the judicial power of the Commonwealth.

However, the strict interpretation of the separation of judicial powers has sometimes been at the expense of individual rights. For example, in *Brandy* the High Court struck down provisions of the *Racial Discrimination Act 1974* (Cth) that allowed a determination by the Human Rights and Equal Opportunity Commission to be registered with the Federal Court of Australia and, upon registration, take effect as if it were an order of the Federal Court.[64] The Court held that such provisions were unconstitutional because they purported to invest the Human Rights and Equal Opportunity Commission, a body not properly constituted under sections 71 and 72 of the Constitution, with the judicial power of the Commonwealth.

The Court's decisions on the right to natural justice, fair trial, right to counsel in serious cases, Bills of Attainder and substantive due process suggest that it was shifting its jurisprudence towards an American conception of separation of powers. Its concern with public confidence and the need to protect the independence of the judiciary also appeared to support this view, though in some cases it was at odds with its rights jurisprudence. Having abandoned the declaratory theory of classic common law, was the Court now implementing the *Federalist* concept of power checking power, of the need to have constitutional checks and balances?

A closer look at the Court's decision in *Wilson*, which imposed strict limits on the non-judicial tasks that could be performed by the judiciary, shows the Court's present understanding of the doctrine of separation of powers in Australia.[65] According to the majority, the separation of powers is designed to provide checks and balances, to disperse power and thereby protect the liberty of the individual. Therefore the majority appears to favour a view of separation of powers consistent with the *Federalist*. However, the majority quotes Harrison Moore to the effect that there is a 'great cleavage' between the legislative and executive power on the one hand, and the judicial power on the other – it is the constitutional objective of separation of judicial power that is said to guarantee liberty. Moreover, the majority cites *Boilermakers* to support the view that the Constitution 'reflects the broad principle that, subject to the Westminster system of responsible government, the powers in each category – whose character is determined according to traditional British conceptions – are vested in and are to be exercised by separate organs of government'.[66]

In fact, in tracing the origin of the doctrine of separation of powers it becomes clear that the Court has a different understanding of the principle. According to the majority, the doctrine can be traced back to Montesquieu, as adapted to the 'realities of the British Constitution' by Blackstone.[67] The separation of judicial powers requires not only separate institutions but also the exercise of powers by different people. It is an inheritance of the British tradition and manifested by the *Act of Settlement 1700*.[68] Therefore, to the majority the doctrine of separation of powers is understood essentially as the separation of judicial powers (hence the 'great cleavage' claim). Separation of powers is designed to preserve judicial independence and public confidence in the judiciary, because the legitimacy of the judiciary depends on its reputation for impartiality and non-partisanship. A related argument is that in a federal system the independence of the judiciary is a vital constitutional safeguard: separation of powers is essential for the federal settlement.[69]

Justice Gaudron explores this argument at some length in a separate judgment agreeing with the majority. To Justice Gaudron, 'impartiality and the appearance of impartiality are defining features of judicial power'. The important issue in *Wilson* concerns the special position of the judicature in a federal system, as noted in the *Boilermakers* case. The judicature is required to maintain and enforce the boundaries of federalism and therefore it is essential that judges not perform functions that place them, or appear to place them, 'in a position of subservience to either of the other branches of government'.[70] The function of reporting under the Act would diminish public confidence in the judges concerned and in the judiciary generally, and therefore it should be construed to exclude judges as reporters.

Justice Kirby is the sole dissentient in *Wilson*. His argument is that there is a long-standing practice in Australia of using judges in royal commissions and judicial inquiries, which supports the view that the reference to 'person' in the Act, reading it in its natural sense, includes judges. A limited reading imposes undue restrictions on Parliament and the executive. But his discussion of the doctrine of separation of powers shows that he is largely in agreement with the majority view.[71] Justice Kirby refers to Justice Evatt's judgment in *Dignan* as well as the unique role of the Court in a federal Constitution as noted in *Boilermakers*. The great issue for the courts, according to Justice Kirby, is that of discerning the 'constitutional wall' that separates judicial power from the exercise of other powers. The difference is that the wall is more permeable; there is no express prohibition in the Constitution that forbids a federal judge performing extra-judicial duties.[72]

Wilson provides a number of important insights into the Court's understanding of separation of powers. The *Boilermakers* principle – defending the separation of powers on the grounds of federalism – is retained by the majority and forms the substance of Justice Gaudron's judgment. Judicial separation of powers is a vital constitutional safeguard, essential for the preservation of a federal Constitution. Therefore the federal aspect of separation of powers outlined in the *Federalist* is retained by the High Court.

To the majority, however, the separation of powers is justified primarily on the basis that it protects individual liberty. Though the theoretical source of the doctrine is Montesquieu, it is developed via Blackstone, the Act of Settlement and the British constitutional inheritance, not the *Federalist*. Separation of powers as understood by the framers of the American Constitution is not seen as relevant for Australian constitutionalism – the theoretical justifications for the *Federalist* conception of separation of powers never seriously engage the Court. The animating principles of such constitutionalism would always be fundamentally at odds with the Court's jurisprudence, given the necessity of a pragmatic engagement with the reality of responsible government in Australia. In this light the Court's understanding of separation of powers appears to be a continuation of its previous jurisprudence, where the federal aspect of separation of powers is retained and combined with a Blackstonian notion of separation of judicial powers, except that it now places greater emphasis on the liberal dimension. However, there is no attempt to explain how the Court's adoption of Blackstone's notion of separation of powers is consistent with its rejection of Blackstone's declaratory theory of the common law. Though aware that its new method of interpretation and its law-making role have posed problems for judicial legitimacy and independence, the High Court has not provided a comprehensive theoretical explanation that reconciles a law-making judiciary with the doctrine of separation of powers.[73]

A New Separation of Powers

The High Court's silence on this theoretical question has had major political consequences. It has made the Court vulnerable to political attacks on its legitimacy and independence. It has transformed the role of the Attorney-General and brought into being institutions that will speak for the Court and defend its interests. It has, in short, introduced into the practice of politics the concept of institutional checks and balances. In doing so, it has raised the question of whether the High Court has inadvertently supported or introduced an American conception of separation of powers into Australia.

New Politics of the High Court

The traditional deference to the Court and the judiciary, the tendency to restrain or moderate public criticism of the Court's decisions, seems to have been left behind by the new politics of the High Court. Though aspects of the Court's jurisprudence had been subjected to scholarly and political criticism, the greatest attacks on the Court were occasioned by its decisions on native title – *Mabo* produced unprecedented criticism of the Court. It was *Wik*, however, that exposed the judiciary to the harsh new world of untrammelled, no-holds-barred political attack.[74]

Soon after the Court handed down its decision in *Wik*, holding that the granting of a pastoral lease did not necessarily extinguish all native title rights and interests that might otherwise exist, Queensland Premier Rob Borbidge branded the High Court 'an embarrassment'. He claimed that there were 'virtually no checks and balances' on Australia's supreme legal body, proposing 'constitutional surgery' to allow voters to select and sack judges in a referendum. Other proposals included a Federal Constitutional Court, limiting terms to ten years, and an increased role for the States in selecting judges.[75] According to Borbidge: 'The fact is legislators make the law and the courts – including the High Court – interpret and apply it. Judges are there to apply the law to the community, not to lead it by the nose in directions that community has had no say in choosing'.[76]

Almost a week after the comments by Premier Borbidge, Prime Minister John Howard entered the debate, emphatically rejecting a law-making role for the High Court, declaring 'the laws governing Australians ought to be determined by the Australian Parliament and by nobody else'.[77] Though Howard ruled out any changes to the system of appointing High Court judges, he told federal Parliament that he held the 'strongest possible view' that the only way in which a law could be or should be changed was through Parliament passing a law.[78] Deputy Prime Minister Tim Fischer had also criticised the Court's *Wik* judgment as highlighting a trend toward 'judicial activism'. He stated that if a position on the Bench became available, the Howard government would appoint a new High Court judge who was 'conservative with a capital C', a person who rejected 'the doctrine of judicial activism' and the notion that judges should make the laws.[79]

These extraordinary attacks indicated that the executive and Parliament saw the judiciary in a new light. The Court was now seen as a powerful, financially and administratively independent body no different from other institutions that were ostensibly accountable to the public. The Court's decisions were not interpreted as measures to protect individual liberty, but as a form of institutional muscle-flexing. From this perspective, the Court was clearly exercising its authority in order to extend it, by shaping the political outcomes in each case and gaining greater public respect. Here was an apparently independent, impartial and neutral body that was supposed to interpret and apply the law actually claiming to *make* it. It had discerned constitutional limitations on

Commonwealth and State governments that no one had, until then, seen or anticipated. It had overruled legislation on political advertising, over-turned legislation that had attempted to limit the vast sums expended on election campaigns, and purported to alter State defamation laws. It had compelled the Commonwealth to provide greater funding in serious criminal trials and curtailed the executive's ability to enter into non-binding international Conventions. Finally, it had overturned the common law by recognising native title in Australia, forcing the issue of indigenous rights onto the political agenda. There was no longer any reason to treat the institution differently from other policy-making bodies.[80]

The judiciary was surprised and concerned by the extent and vehemence of the attacks. Though it accepted that the judiciary had a duty to be accountable, to explain publicly the nature of issues judges faced and what judicial work entailed, the courts were unprepared for the new politics.[81] The judicial attempts to respond to the criticisms highlighted the limited avenues open to the Court in such a political struggle of institutions. Responses included a 'letter to the editor' from Professor Stephen Parker, Secretary of the Judicial Conference of Australia, expressing the Conference's concern about the debate and its implications for judicial independence.[82] Chief Justice Brennan wrote a letter to Fischer stating that his recent criticisms of the Court would erode public confidence in the Court. Statements by Chief Justice Brennan and Justice McHugh regarding the law-making role of judges, made during a hearing of submissions on defamation law, were construed by the media as responses to the comments made by Borbidge.[83]

Perhaps the most remarkable judicial response was a 'statement of independence' issued to the media on 10 April 1997 by the Chief Justices of the States and Territories. The statement appeared to be a cross between a legal document and a political declaration. Its intention, as noted in the preamble, was 'to state in more detail in terms applicable to the circumstances of the States and Territories of Australia certain principles relating to judicial appointments and to the exercise of judicial office'. The substance was a series of six principles relating to the appointment of judges to the courts of the States and Territories. The status of the statement, and its intended recipient, was not evident, though given its timing and its content it clearly had the executive in mind.

These attempts to engage the public attested to the judiciary's concern over the potential threat to its independence. The concern was well put by former Chief Justice Sir Anthony Mason in a speech at a New South Wales Law Society dinner, where he stated that the 'violent and abusive' criticism may have left 'a legacy of antagonism to the Court'.[84] The judicial responses also highlighted the problems the courts faced in making public their concerns or responding to political criticism. The difficulty of protecting judicial independence and integrity by entering the political fray without thereby undermining public confidence was exacerbated by the Commonwealth Attorney-General's decision not to defend the courts.

Speaking for the Courts

Traditionally, British judges refrained from commenting on cases before the courts and were especially careful to abstain from comments on government policy; judgments served as a court's most authoritative announcement on matters before it.[85] Where its reputation or independence was in issue the judiciary turned to the Attorney-General to protect its interests.[86] This was because it was not clear who could speak for the judiciary as a whole, and there was a danger that in speaking for itself on political matters the judiciary might appear to jeopardise its impartiality and independence. Thus the need for someone to speak for the courts was justified by the relatively few avenues open to the judiciary in responding to political comments. In this context, the decision of the Commonwealth Attorney-General, Daryl Williams, not to speak for the courts represented a major break from tradition and appeared to leave the High Court without a public defender.

According to Williams, it is time to abandon the notion that the Attorney-General should speak for the courts because such a view, based on a British model, is not appropriate for Australia. In Australia the Attorney-General does not necessarily have legal qualifications and is never excluded from political debate in Cabinet. Nor does the Attorney-General exercise any independent discretion in supervising criminal or contempt of court proceedings. Therefore 'the perception that the Attorney-General exercises important functions independently of politics and in the public interest is either erroneous or at least eroded'.[87] Consequently, Williams argues that there are good practical reasons why neither judges nor the public should look to the Attorney-General 'to take up cudgels for judges in media debate'.[88] There is a risk that in making a substantive reply on an issue the interest of the judiciary may conflict with the interest of the Attorney-General, the government or the party in government. In representing the judiciary the Attorney-General may involve the judiciary in political controversy. Moreover, the demands on a modern Attorney-General are so extensive that a response on behalf of the judiciary may not be adequate or timely; such a response may 'lack impact'.[89]

The Attorney-General's decision not to speak for the courts was criticised by the judiciary. Speaking at the 30th Australian Legal Convention,
Chief Justice Brennan stated that the function of the Attorney-General
was not to justify the High Court's reasons for decision but to defend the
reputation of the judiciary, explain the nature of the judicial process and
repel attacks based on grounds irrelevant to the application of the rule of
law.[90] A speech by Justice Kirby to the American Bar Association meeting
in Hawaii, implicitly criticising the Attorney-General for not protecting
the judiciary from political attacks, received extensive media coverage.[91]
The Attorney-General expressed disappointment with the comments
made by Justice Kirby, reiterating his view that 'Judges are in a very good
position to inform members of the public about what they do and the
constraints there are upon what they can do'.[92]

If the Attorney-General will not 'take up the cudgels' for the judiciary,
who is to speak for the courts? According to Williams, judges should seek
other ways of responding to media criticism and communicating with the
public. In particular he refers to three judicial institutions – the Australian Institute of Judicial Administration (AIJA), the Chief Justices
Council (CJC) and the Judicial Conference of Australia (JCA) – that
might take up the role. The AIJA, which is based in Melbourne, has a vol-
untary membership of judges, magistrates, court administrators, government and practising and academic lawyers. Its main task is to conduct
research in judicial administration; it also provides courses in judicial
administration, seminars and annual conferences. Given the well-defined
nature of its activities and the breadth of its membership, Williams thinks
that the AIJA would not be an appropriate body to speak for the
judiciary.[93]

The creation of bodies similar to the CJC and JCA was first suggested
by Justice McGarvie at the annual Supreme Court and Federal Court
Judges Conference.[94] The CJC is made up of the Chief Justices of the
superior courts of Australia, namely the Chief Justice of the High Court,
Chief Justices of the Federal Court, Family Court and the State and
Territory Supreme Courts, and the Chief Justice of New Zealand. Williams sees two major limitations to the CJC, although it is an important
body. It is not more than generally familiar with the issues affecting
intermediate and magistrates courts in each State and, significantly, a
greater role for the CJC would impose substantial new administrative and
representational burdens on Chief Justices. Thus Williams nominates the
JCA as the appropriate body to speak for the courts, with the potential to
be a potent political force for the judiciary.

The JCA was incorporated in 1993 as an association open to judges and
magistrates in Australia, other judicial officers exercising judicial power

and former members of superior and intermediate courts. A Secretariat with research functions was established with the assistance of the Attorney-General.[95] The JCA's mission statement and strategic plan outline its mission of community education about the proper role of the judiciary, communication with the other arms of government, improvement in the judicial system and research to further these aims. Its goal is to represent the judiciary and promote 'harmonious and constructive relationships with the other arms of government'.[96] Importantly, according to JCA guidelines, it may speak on general matters concerning the judiciary, the administration of justice and upon request of the Chief Justice or the judge or judges of a court, though it will not speak on specific matters without consulting the relevant Chief Justice or judge.

The establishment of the JCA and the Secretariat marks an important development in the separation of powers in Australia. Clearly, the JCA is a representative body that is intended to replace the Attorney-General as the political guardian of the High Court, to speak for and on behalf of the judiciary, especially in the political forum. The establishment of the JCA and its promotion by the Attorney-General are an acknowledgment of the political nature of the judiciary and its potential threat to the government's policy-making ability; it is a concession to the increasing possibility of tension between a law-making judiciary and the executive and Parliament.

The new role of the JCA in Australian politics also indicates a shift away from the British model, where the Attorney-General protected the judiciary, to an American conception of separation of powers as an institutional solution to the problem of ambition, a checking and balancing of equally ambitious and potentially dangerous sources of institutional power. Such a conception will inevitably justify and encourage greater political and partisan attack on the judiciary, on the grounds that it is no different from any other publicly accountable institution and it has the political means to protect itself.

In saying that the separation of powers in Australia is shifting towards the American model, we do not suggest that the American model has been largely adopted. We should not forget that to the *Federalist* the judicial arm was not simply another public institution – it was to be the bulwark of the Constitution, exercising 'judgment'. It would seem that Australian constitutionalism has once more appropriated only some aspects of American constitutionalism, in this case the concept of institutional checks and balances, without acknowledging the importance of the rule of law. This is probably due to the pragmatic and evolutionary changes in the development of Australian constitutionalism. It is also a consequence of the fundamental problem unresolved by the High Court, the theoretical reconciliation of the rule of law and separation of powers.

Democracy and Separation of Powers

By reflecting upon the character of separation of powers in Australia we have come to see the High Court's important role in shaping democracy in Australia. The High Court has consistently understood separation of powers in Blackstone's terms, as a separation of judicial powers, though it has also justified an aspect of separation of judicial powers as a necessary concomitant of federalism. Underlying the Court's view of separation of powers has been the notion of responsible government, representative democracy and a judiciary that, protected from the heat and passion of politics, will declare the law.

The High Court's recent statements that it makes the law have presented it with formidable theoretical and practical problems. Practically, it has exposed the Court to unexpected, sustained and vehement political criticism. This has made the Court fear for its independence and reputation. Theoretically, the Court's abandonment of the declaratory theory has yielded the unresolved problem of reconciling the doctrine of separation of powers with the functions of a law-making judiciary: on what grounds can the separation of powers be justified?

In adopting a new method of interpretation, the High Court has compelled a reconsideration of separation of powers in Australia. In emphasising the importance of separation of powers for individual liberty, the Court has returned to the rhetoric of liberty to justify its independence. This argument has been insufficient, however, to justify the actions of a law-making judiciary, so the Court has also started to speak in terms of checks and balances. In doing so it has contributed to a shift in the conception of separation of powers in Australia, unintentionally encouraging the executive and Parliament to regard the judiciary as no more than any other political institution. Consequently, for the first time political institutions have been created to defend the courts. Importantly, these changes have favoured the introduction of the *Federalist*'s conception of liberal democracy, of limited government made possible by institutional checks and balances rather than responsible government. In these ways the Court has once again significantly shaped and influenced the nature of liberal democracy and the course and direction of constitutionalism in Australia.

Notes

1 See generally Patapan, H. 1999, 'Separation of Powers in Australia', *Australian Journal of Political Science*, 34, 3: 391–407; Thompson, E. 1980, 'The "Washminster" Mutation' in P. Weller & D. Jaensch (eds), *Responsible*

Government in Australia, Melbourne, Drummond; Emy, H. & Hughes, O. 1991, *Australian Politics: Realities in Conflict*, Melbourne, Macmillan, ch. 9; Lucy, R. 1993, *The Australian Form of Government: Models in Dispute*, Melbourne, Macmillan, 321–4; Maddox, G. 1991, *Australian Democracy in Theory and Practice*, Melbourne, Longman Cheshire, 176; Singleton, G., Aitkin, D., Jinks, B. & Warhurst, J. 1996, *Australian Political Institutions*, Melbourne, Addison Wesley Longman Australia, 16; Vile, M.J.C. 1967, *Constitutionalism and the Separation of Powers*, Oxford, Clarendon Press.

2 Aristotle 1984, *Politics* (trans. Carnes Lord), Chicago, University of Chicago Press, 1297b 35; 1295a 25ff. See also Polybius 1979, *Histories* (trans. W.R. Paton), Cambridge, Mass., Harvard University Press, Fragments of Book VI, 3–18, 271–311; Pangle, T.L. 1973, *Montesquieu's Philosophy of Liberalism: A Commentary on The Spirit of the Laws*, Chicago, University of Chicago Press, 107–60.

3 For the earliest formulation of this change in direction see Machiavelli, Niccolo 1996, *Discourses on Livy* (trans. H.C. Mansfield & N. Tarcov), Chicago, University of Chicago Press; Hobbes, Thomas 1981, *Leviathan* (ed with intro. by C.B. Macpherson), Harmondsworth, Middlesex, Penguin.

4 Locke, John 1992, *Two Treatises on Government*, 2nd edn (ed. with intro and notes by P. Laslett), Cambridge, Cambridge University Press, chs xi, xii, xiv.

5 Montesquieu, C. 1989, *The Spirit of the Laws* (trans. and ed. A.M. Cohler, B.C. Miller & H.S. Stone), Cambridge, Cambridge University Press, Bk 11, ch. 6, 18; 157.

6 ibid., Bk 11, chs 1–4.

7 *Federalist*, 9: 38, in Hamilton, A., Madison, J. & Jay, J. 1982 [1787–88], *The Federalist Papers* (ed. G. Wills), New York, Bantam.

8 *Federalist*, 51: 262.

9 Madison, *Federalist*, 10, 51: 264–5.

10 *Federalist*, 47: 244.

11 Madison, *Federalist*, 51: 263.

12 Madison, *Federalist*, 47, 48, 51: 262.

13 Epstein, D. 1984, *The Political Theory of 'The Federalist'*, Chicago, University of Chicago Press; Mansfield, H.M. 1994, 'Separation of Powers in the American Constitution' in B. Wilson & P. Schramm (eds), *Separation of Powers and Good Government*, Lanham, Rowman & Littlefield, 10, 12.

14 Hamilton, *Federalist*, 78–84.

15 *Federalist*, 78: 393–4.

16 ibid., 397.

17 ibid., 398, 399.

18 ibid., 396, 399.

19 *Federalist*, 81: 411.

20 ibid.

21 Blackstone, W. 1884 [1765–69], *Commentaries on the Laws of England* (ed. Thomas Cooley), Chicago, Callaghan & Co., Bk I, 268.

22 ibid., 269.

23 ibid., Introduction, 69.

24 Wheeler, F. 1996, 'Original Intent and the Doctrine of the Separation of Powers in Australia', *Public Law Review*, 7: 96; Sawer, G. 1961, 'The Separation of Powers in Australian Federalism', *Australian Law Journal*, 35: 177; Finnis, J.M. 1967, 'Separation of Powers in the Australian Constitution', *Adelaide Law Review*, 3: 159.

25 The notable exceptions being Holder and Gordon: see Thomson, J. 1988, *Judicial Review in Australia: The Courts and the Constitution*, Sydney, Thesis Publications; Thomson, J. 1986, 'Constitutional Authority for Judicial Review: A Contribution from the Framers of the Australian Constitution' in G. Craven (ed.), *Official Records of the Debates of the Australasian Federal Conventions*, Sydney, Legal Books, Vol. 6, 173.

26 See the discussion in Wheeler, 'Original Intent', 98–99.

27 Chapter I is headed 'The Parliament' and vests legislative power of the Commonwealth in a 'Federal Parliament' (s. 1). Chapter II is headed 'The Executive Government' where the 'executive power of the Commonwealth is vested in the Queen and is exercisable by the Governor-General as the Queen's representative' (s. 61). Chapter III is titled 'The Judicature' and vests the judicial power of the Commonwealth in a 'Federal Supreme Court to be called the High Court of Australia, and in such other federal courts as the Parliament creates, and in such other courts as it invests with federal jurisdiction'. Cf Art. I, s. 1; Art. II, ss 1, 3; Art. III, s. 1 of the American Constitution. See also *Springer v Government of the Philippine Island* (1928) 277 US 189; Zines, L. 1997, *The High Court and the Constitution*, Sydney, Butterworths, ch. 9.

28 Section 44(iv); ss 62, 64; Thomson, J. 1997, 'American and Australian Constitutions: Continuing Adventures in Comparative Constitutional Law', *John Marshall Law Review*, 30: 627, 657.

29 At the founding it was not clear whether responsible government could coexist with federalism. In the words of Hackett, there were two alternatives – 'either responsible government will kill federation or federation in the form in which we shall, I hope, be prepared to accept it, will kill responsible government': Craven, *Official Records* (Sydney Convention Debates, 1891), 280. Griffith wanted to leave the question for the future, providing in the Constitution that the executive *may* sit in Parliament (Inglis Clark agreed: Craven, *Official Records* (Sydney Convention Debates, 1891), 35, 244, 466). However, by the time of the 1897–98 Convention there was strong support for retaining responsible government, Isaacs calling it the 'keystone of this federal arch': Craven, *Official Records*, Adelaide Convention Debates, 1897, 169.

30 See *Huddart, Parker & Co Pty Ltd v Moorehead* (1909) 8 CLR 330; *New South Wales v Commonwealth* (1915) 20 CLR 54; *Waterside Workers Federation of Australia v JW Alexander Ltd* (1918) 25 CLR 434; *In re Judiciary and Navigation Acts* (1921) 29 CLR 257.

31 *Victoria Stevedoring & General Contracting Co Pty Ltd v Dignan* (1931) 46 CLR 73.

32 *Huddart Parker Ltd v Commonwealth* (1931) 44 CLR 492; *Dignan v Australian Steamships Pty Ltd* (1931) 45 CLR 188; *Roche v Kronheimer* (1921) 29 CLR 329.

33 *Roche v Kronheimer* (1921) 29 CLR 329.

34 *Victoria Stevedoring & General Contracting Co Pty Ltd v Dignan* (1931) 46 CLR 73 at 84.

35 ibid. at 116, quoting Isaacs J in *Federal Commissioner of Taxation v Munro* (1926) 38 CLR 153 at 178. It is useful to recall that the separation of powers was not provided for in the Constitutions of the colonies.

36 ibid. at 115, 116.

37 ibid. at 117, 118.

38 ibid.

39 ibid. at 101–2.
40 Dixon, Sir Owen 1935, 'The Law and the Constitution', *Law Quarterly Review*, 51: 590 at 606; Zines, *The High Court and the Constitution*, 155–7.
41 *Attorney-General (Cth) v R; Ex parte Boilermakers Society of Australia* (1956) 94 CLR 254 (the majority consisted of Dixon CJ, McTiernan, Fullagar and Kitto JJ; minority judgments were delivered by Williams J, Webb J and Taylor J); the decision was upheld on appeal to the Privy Council: *Attorney-General (Cth) v R; Ex parte Boilermakers Society of Australia* (1957) 95 CLR 529.
42 For criticisms see Barwick CJ in *R v Joske; Ex parte Australian Building Construction Employees and Builders Labourers Federation* (1974) 130 CLR 87 at 90; Zines, *The High Court and the Constitution*, 212–18; Sawer, 'The Separation of Powers in Australian Federalism'; Lane, P.H. 1981, 'The Decline of the *Boilermakers* Separation of Powers Doctrine', *Australian Law Journal*, 55: 6; Gibbs, H. 1987, 'Separation of Powers: A Comparison', *Federal Law Review*, 17: 151; Gaudron, M. 1995, 'Some Reflections on the *Boilermakers* Case', *Journal of Industrial Relations*, 37: 306. The decision has been affirmed in *Western Australia v Commonwealth* (1995) 183 CLR 373; *Kable v Director of Public Prosecutions for the State of New South Wales* (1996) 189 CLR 51; *Wilson v Minister for Aboriginal and Torres Strait Islander Affairs* (1996) 189 CLR 1.
43 *Attorney-General (Cth) v R; Ex parte Boilermakers Society of Australia* (1956) 94 CLR 254 at 275–6.
44 ibid. at 279.
45 ibid. at 267–9.
46 ibid. at 276.
47 ibid. at 271, quoting Isaacs J in the *Wheat* case, *New South Wales v Commonwealth* (1915) 20 CLR 54.
48 The minority judgments, to the extent that they reject a strict separation of the arbitral and judicial functions of the Court, show even greater reluctance to adopt an American conception of separation of powers. Williams J rejects such a 'rigid demarcation'(at 301); Webb J states that the doctrine of separation of powers 'has never been accepted as applying to the Australian Constitution either by the Privy Council or by this Court' (at 328); Taylor J sees the doctrine of separation of powers as influential but argues that there are 'powers and functions the inherent features of which are not such as to enable them to be assigned, *a priori*, to one organ rather than another' (at 333, 336–7).
49 See generally Williams, G. 1999, *Human Rights under the Australian Constitution*, Melbourne, Oxford University Press; Winterton, G. 1994, 'The Separation of Judicial Power as an Implied Bill of Rights' in G. Lindell (ed.), *Future Directions in Australian Constitutional Law*, Sydney, Federation Press; Zines, *The High Court and the Constitution*, ch. 10; Zines, L. 1994, 'A Judicially Created Bill of Rights?', *Sydney Law Review*, 16: 166; Parker, C. 1994, 'Protection of Judicial Process as an Implied Constitutional Principle', *Adelaide Law Review*, 16: 341; Hope, J. 1996, 'A Constitutional Right to a Fair Trial? Implications for the Reform of the Australian Criminal Justice System', *Federal Law Review*, 24: 173; Brown, J. 1992, 'The Wig or the Sword? Separation of Powers and the Plight of the Australian Judge', *Federal Law Review*, 21: 48.
50 *Chu Kheng Lim v Minister for Immigration* (1992) 176 CLR 1.
51 *Leeth v Commonwealth* (1992) 174 CLR 455 at 470 per Mason CJ, Dawson and McHugh JJ.

52 *Dietrich v The Queen* (1992) 177 CLR 293 per Mason CJ, Deane, Toohey, Gaudron and McHugh JJ; Brennan and Dawson JJ dissenting.

53 ibid. per Deane J at 326, per Gaudron J at 362. See generally Hope, 'A Constitutional Right to a Fair Trial?'

54 *Polyukhovich v Commonwealth* (1991) 172 CLR 501. Historically, a Bill of Attainder referred to an Act that inflicted capital punishment; an Act imposing other forms of punishment was called a Bill of Pains and Penalties. The American Constitution specifically prohibits Congress or the States from enacting a Bill of Attainder: Art. I, ss 9, 10.

55 See also *Chu Kheng Lim v Minister for Immigration* (1992) 176 CLR 1, where Brennan, Deane and Dawson JJ suggest that, subject to certain exceptions, a federal Act which provided for the detention of persons would be in breach of the separation of powers.

56 ibid. per Deane J at 606–29, per Gaudron J at 703–8.

57 *Leeth v Commonwealth* (1992) 174 CLR 455.

58 ibid. at 502.

59 ibid. at 502–3. In their minority judgment Deane and Toohey JJ held that the provision was inconsistent with the doctrine of the underlying equality of the people of the Commonwealth under the law and before the courts (at 486–7).

60 *Brandy v Human Rights and Equal Opportunity Commission* (1995) 183 CLR 245; *Grollo v Palmer* (1995) 184 CLR 348; *Wilson v Minister for Aboriginal and Torres Strait Islander Affairs* (1996) 189 CLR 1; *Kable v Director of Public Prosecutions (NSW)* (1996) 189 CLR 51.

61 *Wilson v Minister for Aboriginal and Torres Strait Islander Affairs* (1996) 189 CLR 1. See *Hilton v Wells* (1985) 157 CLR 57; *Grollo v Palmer* (1995) 184 CLR 348.

62 Brennan CJ, Dawson, Toohey, McHugh and Gummow JJ gave a joint judgment, Gaudron J gave a separate judgment, Kirby J dissented.

63 *Kable v Director of Public Prosecutions (NSW)* (1996) 189 CLR 51.

64 *Brandy v Human Rights and Equal Opportunity Commission* (1995) 183 CLR 245.

65 *Wilson v Minister for Aboriginal and Torres Strait Islander Affairs* (1996) 189 CLR 1, a joint judgment of Brennan CJ, Dawson, Toohey, McHugh and Gummow JJ. In support of this view the majority cite the *War Crimes* case (at 684–5), Kitto J in *R v Davison* (1954) 90 CLR 353 at 368.

66 ibid. at 10, references omitted.

67 The authority for this is said to be the judgments of Windeyer J in *R v Trade Practices Tribunal; Ex parte Tasmanian Breweries Pty Ltd* (1970) 123 CLR 361 at 390–3; Brennan J in *Victoria v Australian Building Construction Employees and Builders Labourers Federation* (1982) 152 CLR 25 at 151; and Vile's *Constitutionalism and the Separation of Powers*, 104–5.

68 *Wilson v Minister for Aboriginal and Torres Strait Islander Affairs* (1996) 189 CLR 1 at 12.

69 ibid. at 9, 12–13.

70 ibid. at 25.

71 ibid. at 39–40.

72 ibid. at 41.

73 See generally Mason, Sir Anthony 1990, 'Judicial Independence and the Separation of Powers: Some Problems Old and New', *University of New South Wales Law Journal*, 13: 173; Kirby, M. 1990, 'Judicial Independence in Australia Reaches a Moment of Truth', *University of New South Wales Law Journal*, 13: 187; Brennan, Sir Gerard 1998, 'The Parliament, the Executive

and the Courts: Roles and Immunities', School of Law, Bond University, 21
February; Marks, K. 1994, 'Judicial Independence', *Australian Law Journal*,
68: 173; Brown, 'The Wig or the Sword?'; Handsley, E. 1998, 'Public
Confidence in the Judiciary: A Red Herring for the Separation of Judicial
Power', *Sydney Law Review*, 20: 5.

74 See Patapan, H. 1999, 'The Howard Government and the High Court' in
G. Singleton (ed.), *The Institutions of Government*, Sydney, University of New
South Wales Press, 44–6.

75 *Australian*, 19 February 1997, 1.

76 *Australian*, 19 February 1997, 2. The statements by Premier Borbidge for the
reform of the High Court were supported by five States and the Northern
Territory, and the issue was set down for discussion at the next Council of
Australian Governments meeting, on 8 March 1997. At that meeting, all
Premiers and Territory chief ministers agreed that the procedure for
appointments to the High Court needed to be overhauled. They were
unanimous in asking the federal government to change legislation so that a
standing committee of Attorneys-General would make the final recommendation of a preferred candidate.

77 *Australian*, 19 February 1997, 2.

78 The next day the Attorney-General, Daryl Williams, and the Minister for
Foreign Affairs, Alexander Downer, jointly issued an executive statement to
counter the High Court 1995 *Teoh* decision that held that ratification of an
international treaty gave rise to a legitimate expectation in administrative law
that a government would act in accordance with the treaty terms even if it
had not been enacted into domestic law.

79 *Courier Mail*, 5 March 1997, 1.

80 See Williams, D. 1995, 'Who Speaks for the Courts?' in Australian Institute of
Judicial Administration, *Courts in a Representative Democracy*, Melbourne, AIJA;
Craven, G. 1999, 'The High Court of Australia: A Study in the Abuse of
Power', *University of New South Wales Law Journal*, 22: 1.

81 Mason, Sir Anthony 1994, 'The State of the Judicature', *Monash University
Law Review*, 20: 1; Mason, Sir Anthony 1994, 'The Australian Judiciary in the
1990s', Address to the Sydney Institute, 15 March; Kirby, M. 1997, 'Judicial
Activism', Lecture to the Bar Association of India, New Delhi, 5 January.

82 *Weekend Australian*, 1–2 March 1997, 20.

83 *Courier Mail*, 5 March 1997, 1.

84 *Australian*, 24 October 1997.

85 Thomas, J.B. 1997, *Judicial Ethics in Australia*, Sydney, LBC Information
Services; Mason, 'Judicial Independence and the Separation of Powers'.

86 There is some ambiguity concerning the status of the Attorney-General. For
a discussion of the view that the Attorney-General should be independent of
and aloof from politics, and the philosophical differences in approach to the
office of Attorney-General, see Edwards, J. 1984, *The Attorney General, Politics
and the Public Interest*, London, Sweet & Maxwell, ch. 3.

87 Williams, 'Who Speaks for the Courts?', 183.

88 ibid., 190–2.

89 ibid.

90 Brennan, Sir Gerard 1997, 'The State of the Judicature', 30th Australian
Legal Convention, Melbourne, 19 September.

91 *Age*, 6 January 1998, A3; Kirby, M. 1998, 'Attacks on Judges: A Universal
Phenomenon', American Bar Association, Winter Leadership Meeting, Maui,

Hawaii, 5 January. It is interesting to note that in its recent decision on standing, *Bateman's Bay Local Aboriginal Land Council v Aboriginal Community Benefit Fund Pty Ltd* (1998) 155 ALR 684, the High Court accepts the quasi-political role of the Australian Attorney-General.

92 *Age*, 7 January 1998, A4.
93 Williams, 'Who Speaks for the Courts?'; Williams, D. 1997, 'Judicial Independence and the High Court', Monash University Law School Foundation lecture, 1 May, paras 37–46.
94 McGarvie, R. 1992, 'The Ways Available to the Judicial Arm of Government to Preserve Judicial Independence', *Journal of Judicial Administration*, 1: 236; Marks, 'Judicial Independence'.
95 See generally *Judicial Conference News*, May 1997, Vol. 1.1.
96 *Judicial Conference News*, November 1997, Vols 1.2, 3.

CHAPTER 7

Judging Democracy

This book has sought to examine and evaluate the way the Australian High Court is judging democracy. Each chapter has considered a different strand of the Court's jurisprudence to discern the nature and character of the new politics of the High Court. What has emerged from this investigation is a Court that has openly and self-consciously redefined itself as more than an arbitrator of the boundaries of federalism, as a Court that is prepared to adjudicate constitutive questions – matters that go to the very make-up of the regime. Many factors have contributed to, and made possible, the new politics of the High Court. The increasing importance of the judiciary in Australia can be traced to the steady and gradual evolution of Australia into an independent and sovereign state. Facilitated by the Court's decisions on federalism and external affairs, Australia's evolving international standing had, in turn, far-reaching consequences for the place of the High Court in Australian constitutionalism. The incremental restrictions on the jurisdiction of the Judicial Committee of the Privy Council paralleled the ascendancy of the High Court as the court of final appeal in Australia. Combined with the creation of a federal court structure to bear the substance of ordinary litigation and the requirement of leave to appeal, which allowed the High Court to control its docket, the Court secured its place at the apex of the Australian legal system and thereby its authority within the regime.

These changes took place during major developments in international politics and law. Increasingly, human rights became the moral *lingua franca* of international law: political, social and cultural rights and freedoms became matters of international concern. Though these changes contributed to the increasing authority of the judiciary in a number of countries, the situation in Australia was more complicated. Australia had an enviable international reputation in promoting and supporting international human rights instruments, treaties and Conventions, but showed a continuing reluctance to enact those provisions into Australian law. Coupled with the fact that Australia did not have an entrenched Bill of Rights, the High Court, now the most powerful legal authority in Australia, had difficulty negotiating international changes – and increasing international scrutiny – without the constitutional or legislative authority to do so. Thus the new politics of the High Court can be understood partly as a judicial response to the impasse created by Australia's reluctance to implement a rights regime; it is a defence of the Court's institutional position as well as an attempt to step into the breach left by political inaction.

On a more theoretical level, the Court assumed the task of mediating international and domestic changes in constitutionalism – the uncharted waters of judging democracy – because of its perception that parliamentary government was no longer capable of checking executive power. Facilitated by a new hermeneutical principle of sociological jurisprudence, the new politics of the High Court was justified on the grounds that the previous settlement, the old politics (assuming it existed), was no longer sufficient to protect liberty. The question was what would take its place. If the *Australia Acts 1986* marked the start of a new independent Australia, was it appropriate to have the judiciary trace and inscribe its new features, anticipating the coming republic? Or should we see the apparent judicial advances not so much as leadership by the Court but as the relative diffidence, intractability, even conservatism of Australian politics?

Having examined the many facets and different dimensions to the new politics of the High Court, we are better placed to reflect on these questions, especially regarding the extent to which the High Court can be said to be judging democracy or, through its decisions, putting into place a comprehensive vision of Australian democracy. Our task is to look at the arguments discerned in the various jurisprudential formulations of the new politics of the High Court, to bring together the themes that have threaded their way through the Court's judgments, to discern in the warp and weft of its legal adjudication an emerging notion of an Australian democracy.

We do so with Tocqueville's observation in mind, that the courts that exercise judicial review – hold laws to be unconstitutional – wield immense political power. As we have seen, developments in Australian constitutionalism have augmented the High Court's political power. The Court has become the final court of appeal in Australia and may select the cases it will hear on appeal. It has announced that it is more than an 'arbitrator', it makes the law by formulating general principles. Significantly, because it is difficult to amend the Australian Constitution the

Court's constitutional decisions are (for all practical purposes) final. But Tocqueville went further, discerning in the judiciary and lawyers generally an aristocracy that would temper and moderate democracy, a power that 'enwraps the whole of society, penetrating each component class and constantly working in secret upon its unconscious patient, till in the end it has molded it to its desire'.[1] Is the new Australian High Court such an aristocracy? The major claim of the new High Court is that its workings are no longer 'secret'. It now prides itself on its openness to public scrutiny, discussion and critique – its democratic credentials. But this claim to openness implicitly affirms the Court's ability to mould society, restating an even more compelling case for attempting to delineate the boundaries and character of its 'desire' to shape society.

Indeed, is it not possible to make an even stronger Platonic case for a judiciary that is the Guardian of the Law, that is protected from the few and the many and therefore moderates the partial justice of both democrat and oligarch, that deliberates and decides after argument, handing down a reasoned defence of its decisions, that interprets the Constitution and in doing so renews and refounds the regime – in short, to borrow J.S. Mill's formulation, a commission that embodies intelligence where Parliament represents will?[2] How else are we to account for, and justify, the forms and practices of the Court, its emphasis on argument and precedent, its independence and security of tenure, its power and authority? It is with these highest expectations and standards in mind, encouraged by the High Court's own claims, that we return to the new politics of the Court to discern its vision of the Australian regime, expressed in its decisions. When we do so, however, we are confronted not with a comprehensive, consistent delineation and presentation of a regime, but with a mosaic of differing and often competing and contradictory formulations.

Competing Views of Australian Democracy

Our discussion and analysis of the principles of interpretation relied upon by the Court showed that it had abandoned the declaratory theory of the common law – the view that judges merely declare not make the law – and therefore the strict demarcation and distinction between the legal and the political. Because this conflicted with the fundamental and underlying concept of the rule of law, the Court turned to 'community values' and the sociological jurisprudence of Pound and Stone. But the reference to, and reliance on, community values seemed to lead to conflicting notions of the regime. On the one hand, community values introduced into Australian constitutionalism the idea of sovereignty of the people and thereby the idea of the polity as a rational entity, founded upon contract and consent, seeking to protect and perpetuate core human rights and freedoms – a liberal-democratic constitutionalism founded upon human rights. More ambitiously and ambiguously, this view supported a larger but undefined republican constitutionalism. But the notion of a judiciary that openly determined policy, contributing to deliberative democratic politics, also reinforced the long-established view of the Australian regime as a progressive democracy, where a representative and responsible Parliament considered and determined all political questions, leaving the specialised legal role of 'boundary keeper' and umpire to the courts.

A similar tension could be discerned in the Court's jurisprudence of rights and freedoms. As we noted, the Court's implied rights decisions did not represent an innovation in Australian constitutionalism. The rights that were discerned were not natural or human rights, derived from the individual. They were rights implied from the institutions secured in the Constitution, negative or residual rights derived from the representative and responsible government. The limited range and scope of the rights indicated the nature of the political settlement that guided and was reinforced by the judiciary – a Millian parliamentary sovereignty. At the same time, however, the Court's adoption of the Bangalore Principles, allowing it access to international legal principles in its determination of the common law and constitutional ambiguities, anticipated a judiciary open to a range of democratic and republican regimes founded upon individual rights and popular sovereignty.

But the Court's understanding of the regime, as seen in its judicial reflections and observations on the nature of citizenship, the franchise and one-vote–one-value in Australia reasserted the primacy of parliamentary sovereignty and a Millian progressive regime. It returned to the 'political' and 'legal' dichotomy, with the political to be resolved and settled by Parliament. A major consequence of the Court declining to define citizenship is that the concept of representative democracy remains contested and contestable, subject to the determination of Parliament. Therefore citizenship is potentially indeterminate, assuming different dimensions and multiple layers: the extensive power and freedom of States and the Commonwealth to construe and define citizenship is unaffected. The judiciary plays a minimal role, ensuring that the channels of representation and institutions of governance function efficiently.

It is true that the Court's new native title jurisprudence clearly rejected a racially discriminatory Australia. In doing so, however, it retained a notion of civilisation based not on culture but on scientific and technological advances; in agreement with Locke, labour gave right to property, relegating the spiritual and religious to the precincts of the private. However, the refounding of regime on this apparently secular and progressive foundation is made possible by the reintroduction of a version of the declaratory theory of common law. The common law as the conscience of the regime, or as an aider or abettor in its misdeeds, introduces a moral and ethical regime that needs to be made whole again. This view elevates the ambitions of the regime beyond comfortable self-preservation, acknowledging the possibility of virtuous citizenship in the recognition of a just regime. The cleansing of the regime that is attempted in *Mabo* and *Wik* seeks to identify the judiciary as the heart and conscience of the polity, and appears to relegate the problem of the definition of property to the demands of justice.

Finally, our examination of the Court's formulation of separation of powers revealed a judiciary that has consistently understood separation of powers as separation of judicial power in the Blackstonian sense, presupposing a powerful plenary Parliament guided by the artificial reason of the common law. Yet its rejection of the declaratory theory has presented the Court with the difficulty of reconciling a law-making judiciary with separation of powers. In seeking to resolve this tension and defend and justify judicial independence, the Court has been prepared to accept a regime that limits government by institutions that check and balance each other. In addition, as a protector of individual rights it has defined a liberal-democratic or republican regime that approximates American constitutionalism, subject to the necessary autochthonous accommodation of responsible government.

Competing Roles of the High Court in Australian Democracy

These tensions and differences in the Court's democratic vision can be seen most clearly in the Court's understanding and definition of the common law and its own role within the regime. The new politics of the High Court gives a strong impression that it has abandoned the 'fairy-tale' of the declaratory theory of the common law. But when we examine the different aspects of the Court's jurisprudence this view of the common law proves to be inaccurate, or at least partial. It is hard to reconcile the apparent rejection of the declaratory theory with the Court's reference to a 'moral' common law in its native title and rights jurisprudence. That the moral and ethical aspect of the older view of the common law, the 'enduring values' of the common law, is retained by the Court challenges the assertion that the declaratory theory was no more than a noble lie to mask the Court's opinions and make its decisions palatable, to sweeten the bitter herb of its judgments. Moreover, abandoning the declaratory theory presents major obstacles for the Court's claims of judicial independence, founded on a Blackstonian notion of separation of powers. Therefore, in seeking to reconcile separation of powers and a law-making judiciary the Court continues to entertain elements of the artificial reason of the common law. Indeed, in the idea of *void ab initio* the Court retains in its jurisprudence as a whole an important aspect of the declaratory theory. There is no reason why judge-made law should necessarily be retrospective, but the High Court has rejected the possibility of progressive overruling. The Court's decisions claim to reach into the past and reorder history to accord with the correct interpretation of the law. As noted in our discussion of *McGinty*, *Mabo* and *Wik*, this principle imposes significant burdens on the judiciary. It assumes that there is a transcendent notion of what is just and correct. It also assumes that it is always possible and appropriate to reorder and arrange the past into its correct pattern. The more immediate practical problem with such an approach includes the awkward and unpersuasive anachronism of interpreting provisions as if they assumed and anticipated future developments.

These varying notions of the common law allow different room and scope for judicial intervention. Indeed, a general overview of the new politics of the High Court shows that fundamentally different notions of its proper place in the regime have been put forward by the Court. There is the Court as 'umpire' or keeper of rules, taking no active part in politics (understood as making policy and defining core concepts such as the nature of representative democracy and citizenship). The Court as umpire that polices the rules, ensuring the health of democratic processes, exercises a form of representation-reinforcing judicial review that seems to locate the judiciary 'above' politics. Similar to this role is that of the Court as 'renovator', bringing laws up to date with community values and expectations, an essential counterpart to the democratic and deliberative politics of the legislature. The Court is a facilitator and support for a Parliament which necessarily relegates specialist legal questions to the judiciary. Although the Court takes part in politics it is as legal factotum rather than rival. In contrast to both those roles is the Court as 'adversary', perhaps the least dangerous branch but still a powerful political institution that challenges and checks the other arms of government. It is an active political contender, vying for political power and authority. But this self-interest and ambition, manifesting in an institutional struggle for power, indirectly protects liberty by limiting the encroachment of the other institutions. In stark contrast to all these roles is that of the Court as 'guardian' or 'protector'. The guardian intervenes in politics not only to uphold the Constitution and fundamental rights and freedoms, but also to protect the weak and vulnerable. The Court as moral guardian employs natural rights, human rights, popular sovereignty or even the common law as its Archimedean point to lever and shift the political landscape. The Court intervenes in politics, but only to do justice. We have encountered each of these views of the common law and these justifications of the judicial politics in the Court's decisions, sometimes in the competing views of majority and minority decisions, at other times in different strands of the Court's jurisprudence. In each instance they have suggested, or combined with, a notion of a regime which the Court has implicitly delineated in its judgment.

Limits to Judging

This conclusion suggests that the Court does not hold a comprehensive view or understanding of Australian democracy. Its decisions are a palimpsest of different constitutive ambitions or, to adopt a Blackstonian metaphor, an ancient rambling castle with new, foreign additions to old, weak foundations, a mass of renovations and abutting rooms, awkwardly mixing the dark and spacious, the disused and modern. But perhaps we were too ambitious in looking for a comprehensive and consistent depiction of Australian democracy in the Court's judgments. True, of all institutions the Court seems the most sheltered from the arbitrary and powerful, the fleeting and passionate. In the manner of its workings, its consistency, we discern an order most conducive to persuasive speech, debate, reasoning, considered will and deliberate judgment. Yet perhaps the very requirements of an institutional form limit these aspirations, undermining in important respects these goals and ideals. Can any institution, especially a major institution of governance, hope to achieve such ambitions?[3]

The nature of this difficulty becomes evident when we step back and ask what we mean by the High Court. There are many different dimensions and aspects to the Court. There is the institution of governance established and secured in Chapter III, sections 71–79 of the Constitution. There are the justices who have held office since the *Judiciary Act 1903* (Cth) established the Court. There is even the very substantial edifice that was officially opened near Parliament House in Canberra in 1975 and is now a popular tourist destination. But, encouraged by the way the Court views itself, we have concentrated upon the High Court that decrees and declares, that decides, that *judges*; we have concentrated upon its mind, reasoning and opinion as shown in law reports spanning a century of decisions. This perspective favours the notion of a single unified Court, issuing decrees and judgments. It is true that the Court sometimes speaks in one voice, in the form of a unanimous judgment. But more often its decisions are handed down in the form of separate judgments with many and varied reasons, differing or disagreeing in shade or emphasis if not in substance. The difficulty of reconciling these opinions points to the general problem of establishing the 'Court's' reasoning and justifications, its opinion or judgment. This problem is formidable when there are dissenting opinions. To some extent these dissenting arguments articulate powerful alternative positions; they facilitate the Court's role as a deliberative institution where ideas and concepts are contested and challenged. The possibility of dissent marks the Court as a forum that anticipates, confronts and reconciles profound arguments – a court of reason. We have seen something of this in our analysis of the Court's judgment in *Mabo*. But on another level the existence of these alternative positions points to the potentially irreconcilable character of arguments. This aspect of adjudication is confirmed by the way conflicting judgments are determined into conclusive reasons and decisions – the democratic principle of counting, majority in numbers, decides the outcome of a close case.

To the extent that mere counting appears to endorse will over reasoning and persuasion it seems to suggest that ultimately the Court and its judgments are determined by the individual wills and desires of the justices and the coalitions they can muster to secure a particular outcome. It is this view that has inspired extensive analysis of the backgrounds and upbringing of judges – jurimetrics – and raised to greater prominence the process of judicial appointments. This opinion has also encouraged some to regard the Court as no different from other democratic institutions and therefore as subject to the claims and demands of representation noted in our discussion of citizenship, for example representation of territory (justices should be appointed from all States, not just New South Wales and Victoria) and representation of interest (justices should be women or minorities).

Though the strength of this claim should not be underrated, it is important to note that in some instances the minority opinion has appeared, over time, to be more persuasive, compelling the Court to distinguish or even overrule its previous judgment. This indicates that in some instances even the democratic element of majority judgments can give way to the force of argument or persuasion. Nevertheless, though we speak of a Court, it is also true that we refer to the 'Dixon Court' or the 'Mason Court'. Although precedent may overcome the contingencies of time and place to allow the Court to be identified as an entity (decisions will form a precedent that will, more or less, bind and limit the discretion of future judges), the very possibility of many judgments, of minority and majority views, entertains the promise of dissent and thereby legitimates the possibility of overruling. That the Court may reject its previous decision, albeit rarely and reluctantly, presents the awkward possibility of many Courts, even a right and a wrong Court, a better or worse Court, a Court that is more or less legitimate.

These considerations are an important reminder of the significant limitations on the Court's ability to articulate its democratic vision.[4] The Court cannot simply declare its opinion: there must be a dispute before it can hear a matter and determine the question at issue. Consequently the Court is largely at the mercy of the litigation offered it. Yet through hints, suggestions and appropriate silences in judgments the Court is able to communicate indirectly with prospective litigants regarding cases that may profitably be brought before it. For example, the Court's initial decisions on freedom of political speech encouraged a number of litigants to use that defence in a wide range of cases that allowed the Court to broaden the principle. Similarly, the Court's formulation of native title and rejection of Aboriginal sovereignty gave clear guidelines for the success of future cases. Therefore the Court has a measure of success, although awkward and slow, in influencing the nature of dispute before it.

But the existence of a dispute does not allow the Court unbridled freedom to develop and formulate its understanding of the nature of the regime. Each case involves unique facts and circumstances, special features that may aid, but more likely limit, the Court's ability to articulate general principles. Thus the specificity and therefore partiality of judgments reduce the horizon of problems and issues that may be examined. In short, because the Court does not simply declare principles, some cases will be better than others as a vehicle for the Court's political endeavours.

In fact, a review of the Court's jurisprudence suggests that it relied on the incremental, piecemeal nature of litigation to develop its jurisprudence: concepts are developed step by step, taken up, tried, evaluated and either rejected or refined. There are significant decisions that appear to be major innovations or apparent breaks from the past, such as the *Political Advertising* case. There are decisions such as *Theophanous* that seem to stretch the jurisprudential fabric, relying on an inappropriate theoretical premise or advancing too far, too quickly. Then there are decisions such as *McGinty* that reconsider and reassess the previous decisions, imposing limits on the development of the principle or establishing it on new foundations. Finally there are decisions that consolidate, clarifying the lines of the arguments, unequivocally defining the new position and establishing the foundation for future developments. The Court's *Lange* decision appears to be one of these decisions. Such decisions are followed by cases that will define the extent to which the Court will favour innovation, rejecting some developments as in *Kruger*, and leaving open others, as in *Levy*. Throughout these changes and developments there is the subtle but crucial interplay of majority and minority opinions. Minority judgments often act as scouts of a possible future path, advancing the jurisprudence; at other times they are the corrective, rejecting such advances. There is no assurance that they will be successful and form a part of the majority in subsequent judgments.[5]

These developments are influenced by the comparable development of legal principles in different cases. Sometimes there is merely the connection of temporal proximity, in other cases there may be a cross-over. For example, the Court developed its implied rights jurisprudence at the same time it was determining its contentious native title decisions. In *Kruger* there was a cross-over – the plaintiffs sought to rely on implied rights to gain monetary compensation for harm they claimed they suffered as part of the 'stolen generation' of Aboriginal children that had forcibly been removed from their parents. Inevitably, the Court's previous formulation of native title as the proper means for compensating indigenous Australians affected the implied rights that would be recognised in *Kruger*.

These observations on the evolving nature of legal doctrine hint that the Court may not be aware of the full scope and reach of its decisions. As we saw in the early cases on separation of powers, the Court had already decided the question of the separation of legislative and executive powers before the proposition was formally put in *Dignan*. In other cases, for example *Theophanous*, the Court will advance too far, necessitating a return not only in terms of specific outcome but also in theoretical formulation. Accordingly, in *McGinty* and later *Levy*, the Court rejects the notion of representative democracy as an independent principle for constitutional interpretation. In certain fundamental cases the Court will propose a major innovation and, depending upon its reception and success, will advance further. The *Political Advertising* case and *Mabo* are obvious examples. Importantly, in formulating each step the Court is concerned with the reception of its decision, acutely aware of the comments, criticisms and remarks by lawyers and academics who closely attend to (and in some instances lead) the Court's jurisprudence, and by the politicians and larger policy community whose intervention will be more specific and selective. In this light the Court is no longer the simply powerful entity that is shaping Australian constitutionalism; it forms part of a larger body of legal practitioners, academics and policy-makers who frame and mould opinion, indirectly influencing and guiding the Court's jurisprudence.

Even if the Court could break from this body of advisers, as it arguably did in inaugurating its new politics, there are strong invisible boundaries to the Court's discretion and independence. One of the most powerful is that of *stare decisis*, or precedent. A Court that decided each question afresh, that took little or no account of its previous decisions, that immersed itself in the particular without the guidance of a general principle would be respected solely because it had the power to decide. Hence the importance of precedent as a foundation of judicial authority and equality before the law. But precedent is not an inviolable principle: the High Court has held that it will, in appropriate circumstances, over-rule its decision. Leaving aside the little-examined theoretical implic-ations of such self-overruling or correcting, it is clear that in most cases the Court can avoid precedent by more subtle means, such as distinguish-ing a precedent on the grounds that it did not decide the question, limiting the precedent to its own particular circumstances, or simply not recognising it. These possibilities were demonstrated in the majority judgments in *Wik*, which sought to limit the opinions expressed in *Mabo* regarding leasehold interests and native title. But to the extent that the Court's decisions are cumulative, precedent forms a powerful and binding force on future discretion.

Yet it is not precedent as much as the powerful ideas that underlie decisions that raise barriers against judicial discretion. Attempted changes in the Court's jurisprudence will inevitably meet well-established and firmly entrenched ideas and concepts such as the rule of law, equality before the law, separation of powers, parliamentary sovereignty, federalism, individual rights and freedoms. Though expressed in general and perhaps vague terms, these concepts manifest in specific and precise ways and are interlocked and sustained in a complex theoretical archi-tecture. For example, in raising questions regarding the law-making responsibilities of the judiciary, we meet not only the concept of the rule of law but also the related notion of separation of power. If the judicial task is not distinctly different from the legislative, is a separation of powers justified? If judicial authority is to be justified by a republican notion of sovereignty of the people, how should this be reconciled with representative democracy and parliamentary sovereignty secured in the Constitution? How are fundamental rights reconcilable with a progres-sive constitutionalism? Is the notion of individual human rights consis-tent with a representative system that relies on the representation of territory and interests?

In so far as the Court can decide individual cases without recourse to these complex and profound questions, they may not present such an obstacle to its jurisprudence. But because the High Court has under-taken to articulate and justify its decisions by relying on such concepts in developing its new jurisprudence, it will have to rework, renegotiate and reconcile its innovations with the complex theoretical structures that support such concepts. In doing so, it will have to concern itself with principles and ideas that are increasingly removed from the conventional understanding of the law: having entered the province of politics, political theory, philosophy, sociology and economics, to name a few, the Court's judgments now have to meet the higher requirement of theoretical exegesis as well as legal argument to dispose of a dispute. Each judgment is now examined as a political and theoretical tract, its intention and purpose examined for consistency and subtle nuances and shifts in thought. But are the Court's judgments suitable vehicles for such cogitations and demonstrations? Importantly, should the judiciary be expected to combine such rare and remarkable skills? Consider the difficulties the judges in *Wik* had in outlining their understanding of the relationship between truth and history. Was such an undertaking necessary for the judgment? Was it persuasive?

Models of Democracy

There is a danger that the limitations outlined above – that the Court is made up of seven justices who may have diametrically opposed views on a subject, the incremental nature of judicial law-making, and the limits imposed by theoretical principles such as the rule of law – may have persuaded us that the Court has little or no discretion, that its decisions are simply *ad hoc* or dictated by the practical exigencies of each case, that what looks like judging democracy is in fact an accidental collage of thoughts and observations rather than a complete picture of the regime. The new politics of the High Court refutes this proposition: the disjunction and in some cases break from the Court's previous decisions, and the extra-curial claims of the justices themselves, indicated and promised a more ambitious plan. At least the judiciary itself believed it had greater freedom than we have presented in the limits to judging. So perhaps what is needed is a more subtle evaluation of the Court's intentions, an examination that will pay due regard to the limits elucidated while discerning in the Court's jurisprudence an overarching view of Australian democracy. Let us return, then, to the Court's decisions, not to paint a sharp picture but to trace trends and tendencies, to look at transformations, evolutions and transitions in the Court's jurisprudence.

This starting-point yields a different answer to the question of the Court's democratic vision. The view of the regime that has exercised the most powerful and persistent hold on the Court is the one that it developed from the beginning. We are familiar with the main features of this picture. The most important aspect is the centrality of parliamentary government. Parliamentary and therefore representative and responsible government is the institution that represents and mediates interests, deliberates on the common good, corrects grievances and formulates policy. It is the political centre, checking executive excess while integrating subjects and citizens into the political process. As the voice of the people, Parliament must have practically unlimited powers and discretion – it would appear undemocratic and theoretically inconsistent to limit Parliament. The extensive powers of Parliament are also essential for the crucial feature of parliamentary democracy – its inherently progressive nature, made possible by the free and open debate at the heart of the parliamentary process. The judicial task in such a regime is to adjudicate disputes and maintain the democratic processes mandated by Parliament. The courts also declare the common law, but such elaboration is subject to parliamentary discretion. In such a regime the judiciary implements the rule of law as it is determined by Parliament: the judiciary is in a very real sense ministerial.

This picture was complicated in Australia by the establishment of a federal commonwealth. The innovation of federalism sat uneasily with the essential theoretical principles of parliamentary responsible government. This could be seen clearly in the new Constitution that established the Senate and the House of Representatives, limited State and federal Parliaments, and divided sovereignty and responsible government. The judiciary sought to accommodate these innovations within the previous political settlement. Within each sphere – State or federal – Parliaments retained full sovereignty. Provisions limiting the powers of States or the federal government were to be interpreted strictly. In adjudicating the boundaries of federalism the Court did not overrule legislatures but interpreted the enacted will of Imperial Parliament. Federal judicial review was no more than an exercise in the interpretation of a legal provision – ordinary rules of statutory interpretation were a sufficient guide in constitutional contests. Finally, progress and innovation were the province of State and federal Parliaments and ultimately the people through referendum.

Compare this ideal with the model towards which, we can say, the Court has directed Australian constitutionalism. The regime is founded upon republican ideals, though popular sovereignty expresses its will through representative institutions such as Parliament that are subject to liberal-democratic ideals. Therefore certain core or fundamental principles are entrenched expressly or implicitly in the Constitution. These fundamental rights, which include freedom of speech and movement, of equality and non-discrimination, are jealously guarded by the judiciary which will supervise with suspicion – check and balance – other institutions such as Parliament and the executive who continually seek to augment their power and authority. The regime provides the greatest room for the play of human innovation and endeavour, assuring progress and prosperity. On the whole the polity is outward-looking, taking its cues and direction from international developments.

These roughly sketched alternatives seem to depict a Court that is moving from a regime founded upon English parliamentarianism towards a modern American republicanism based on human rights. It is obvious that the Court will not, indeed cannot, implement all aspects of the American model. In fact, what we have defined as American constitutionalism is actually a more subtle, dynamic and sophisticated evolution in constitutionalism that is occurring worldwide, facilitated by courts of final jurisdiction, with countries like Canada and Australia at the forefront of innovation. Though difficult to predict the long-term implications of these innovations, they support the international trend towards a more powerful judiciary.[6] The Canadian experience indicates that the developments in Australia will be unique; innovations in constitutionalism will be adjudicated and adjusted to accord with special aspects and requirements of the Australian practice. Nevertheless, there is a clear picture of the overall direction: the Court is in a sense completing Australia's break from the UK, the war of independence that Australia never had, readying the country for the challenges of the new millennium.

Great Expectations

The picture of the High Court is that of a composite entity, an aristocracy that is limited by procedural, institutional and theoretical elements, a powerful body that appears remarkably limited in crucial respects. The Court that relies on reasoning, argument and deliberation, that is protected from undue influence and bias, is also slow, incremental in its formulation of policy, retrospective in its judgments, limited by the facts before it, bound in general by its previous decisions, often divided in its own views and influenced by the opinions of others.

This reassessment of the Court provides an important corrective to the ambitious and potentially misleading claims regarding the Court's new jurisprudence. For example, the claim that the Court now makes the law is potentially misleading when we take into account the complexities of the declaratory model of common law adjudication, the requirement of the rule of law, and the fundamental differences between common law and constitutional adjudication and between judicial and parliamentary law-making. Similar ambiguities exist in the idea that the Court protects rights and freedoms by relying on sovereignty of the people, or that the Court is somehow a more representative institution. It is not that these claims are incorrect; rather, it is the complexity and subtlety of such propositions that make them of limited practical import in wider political debate. Although the Court's attempt to open its processes and deliberations to the public, to make itself more accountable and claim that it is undeniably a political body, is necessary and commendable, the reality is that the substance of the Court's undertakings – the specialised knowledge and complexity of ideas – cannot be popularised without some distortion and therefore misrepresentation. The *Mabo* and *Wik* debates show the potentially serious implications of deliberately exploiting this limitation.[7]

We are tempted to conjecture that the Court is aware of this, and the real audience of such announcements is the 'shadow court' – legal practitioners, academics, commentators and students. Arguably, that is the audience the Court needs to persuade because it is the most concerned with the Court's judgments, and because it translates and therefore represents the Court's decisions to the larger community. But it is precisely in this context that the more ambitious view of the Court's capabilities presents a serious danger for the Court. The available information suggests that an unprecedented number of young Australians are forsaking a generalist education in the arts and sciences to pursue law degrees: legal education is supplanting liberal education in Australia. Whether it is an adequate replacement need not be taken up here. What is evident is that the best and keenest students, encouraged by the achievements of their colleagues in Canada and America, will seek to fulfil their great ambitions and noble aspirations through the law. Thus as Tocqueville observed in America, the power and influence of lawyers is increasing in Australia. But 'an elite body can never satisfy all the ambitions of its members; if talents and ambitions are always more numerous than places, there are bound to be many who cannot rise quickly enough by making use of the body's privileges and who seek fast promotion by attacking them'.[8] It is not injustice but the powerful desire that regards law as a hindrance to achieving complete justice that presents the greatest threat to the judiciary; it is the example and ambitions of the 'Great Dissenter' on the Bench that will be emulated by the young. A clear-sighted restatement of the limits to judicial politics is crucial for the well being of the Court and the health of the regime.

Finally, this increasing judicialisation of politics in Australia prompts us to consider the various attempts that have been made to limit it, particularly the proposals for altering the appointment or tenure of justices to the High Court.[9] But attempts to make the Court and thereby its judgments more political by making judges more representative, however defined, reveal the limitations of that proposal – the judicialisation of politics will not be fundamentally altered by changing the make-up or the means of selecting the judiciary. If such attempts are more than a corrective to judicial politics and are seen as influencing the outcome of the Court's judgments, then they reveal a misunderstanding of the different functions of the judiciary, which include the tendency to review, check and limit the untrammelled ambitions of popular politics.

Nevertheless, our overview of the increasingly complex and profound duties and obligations of High Court judges in judging democracy does present a strong case for appointing individuals who are more than excellent legal advocates, individuals who have the stature and experience, the breadth of vision, to assume the considerable burdens of office.

Few would deny that the new politics of the High Court demands much more from the judiciary: statesmanship is essential for a Court that seeks to determine the character of constitutionalism and influence the nature of democracy in Australia. But the burdens of office weigh not only on the shoulders of the judges. Democratic and republican government requires – indeed demands – a sharing of this burden, if not directly then through our own exercise of judgment and debate, deliberation and prudent choice. This book has sought to contribute to this form of active healthy citizenship by examining the new politics of the High Court and its democratic vision for Australia.

Notes

1 Tocqueville, Alexis de 1969, *Democracy in America* (ed. J.P. Mayer), New York, Doubleday, Part II, 270.
2 Plato 1980, *The Laws of Plato* (trans. with commentary by T.L. Pangle), Chicago, University of Chicago Press (references to Guardian of the Laws, 551); Mill, J.S. 1972 [1861], *Considerations on Representative Government* in H.B. Acton (ed.), *Utilitarianism, On Liberty, Representative Government*, London, Dent & Sons, 256. In making this observation we are aware of the modern political and philosophical predisposition to understand 'reason' as an aspect of 'will': see Strauss, L. 1989, 'On Classic Political Philosophy' in L. Strauss (ed.), *The Rebirth of Classical Political Rationalism*, Chicago, University of Chicago Press, ch. 4.
3 For an overview of American writings see Tucker, D.F.B. 1995, *The Rehnquist Court and Civil Rights*, Aldershot, Dartmouth; Rosenberg, G.N. 1991, *The Hollow Hope: Can Court Bring about Social Change?*, Chicago, University of Chicago Press; Horowitz, D. 1977, *The Courts and Social Policy*, Washington DC, Brookings Institution.
4 ibid. See also Mason, Sir Anthony 1996, 'The Judge as Law-maker', *James Cook University Law Review*, 3: 1 at 7.
5 For a discussion of theories of decision-making in the context of the judiciary see Snortland, N.E. & Stanga, J.E. 1973, 'Neutral Principles and Decision-making Theory: An Alternative to Incrementalism', *George Washington Law Review*, 41: 1006, referred to in Etzioni, A. 1998, 'Mixed Scanning Revisited' in A. Etzioni (ed.), *Essays in Socio-economics*, Berlin: Springer-Verlag, 121.
6 See generally Holland, K.M. (ed.) 1991, *Judicial Activism in Comparative Perspective*, London, Macmillan; Jacob, H.E.B., Krittzer, H.M., Provene, D.M. & Sanders, J. 1996, *Courts, Law, and Politics in Comparative Perspective*, New Haven, Yale University Press; Waltman, J.L. & Holland, K.M. (eds) 1988, *The Political Role of Law Courts in Modern Democracies*, London, Macmillan;

Tate, N. C. & Vallinder, T. (eds) 1995, *The Global Expansion of Judicial Power*, New York, New York University Press.

7 Williams, G. 1999, 'The High Court and the Media', *University of Technology Sydney Law Review*, 1: 136, examines in detail the relationship between the High Court and the media, recommending the appointment of a public information officer, changing the way the Court writes its judgments and providing summaries of its judgments. See also Lane, B. 1999, 'Silence at the Court', *Australian*, Media 7, 13–19 May.

8 Tocqueville, *Democracy in America*, Bk II, 265; see also Lincoln, A. 1943 [1838], 'Address before the Young Men's Lyceum of Springfield, Illinois' in T.H. Williams (ed.), *Selected Writings and Speeches of Abraham Lincoln*, New York, Hendricks House, 4–10.

9 See in general the papers presented at the *Third Annual Colloquium of the Judicial Conference of Australia*, Surfers Paradise, 6–8 November 1998, at http://www.law.monash.edu.au/JCA.

Bibliography

Ackerman, B. 1985, 'Beyond Carolene Products', *Harvard Law Review* 98, 713.

Aristotle 1984, *Politics* (trans. Carnes Lord, Chicago, University of Chicago Press).

Attwood, B. (ed.) 1996, *In the Age of Mabo* (Sydney, Allen & Unwin).

Bagger, R. 1985, 'The Supreme Court and Congressional Apportionment: Slippery Slope to Equal Representation Gerrymandering', *Rutgers Law Review*, 38: 109.

Bailey, P. 1990, *Human Rights: Australia in an International Context* (Sydney, Butterworths).

Bartlett, R. 1993, *The Mabo Decision* (Sydney, Butterworths).

Barwick, Sir Garfield 1964, 'The Australian Judicial System: The Proposed New Federal Court', *Federal Law Review*, 1: 1.

Barwick, Sir Garfield 1979, 'The State of the Australian Judicature', *Australian Law Journal*, 53: 487.

Barwick, Sir Garfield 1983, *Sir John did his Duty* (Sydney, Serendip Publications).

Barwick, Sir Garfield 1995, *A Radical Tory: Garfield Barwick's Reflections and Recollections* (Sydney, Federation Press).

Beiner, R. 1992, *What's the Matter with Liberalism?* (Berkeley, University of California Press).

Bennett, J.M. 1980, *Keystone of the Federal Arch: A Historical Memoir of the High Court of Australia to 1980* (Canberra, AGPS).

Bennett, S. 1971, *The Making of the Commonwealth* (Melbourne, Cassell).

Berger, R. 1979, 'Government by Judiciary: John Hart Ely's "Invitation"', *Indiana Law Journal*, 54: 277.

Birch, A.H. 1964, *Representative and Responsible Government: An Essay on the British Constitution* (London, Unwin University Books).

Blackshield, A.R. (ed.) 1983, *Legal Change: Essays in Honour of Julius Stone* (Sydney, Butterworths).

Blackshield, A.R. 1994, 'The Implied Freedom of Communication' in G. Lindell (ed.), *Future Directions in Australian Constitutional Law* (Sydney, Federation Press).

Blackshield, G.S. & Chubb, P. 1988, *Judging the World* (Sydney, Butterworths).

Blackstone, W. 1765, *Commentaries on the Laws of England* (Oxford, Clarendon Press).

Booker, K. & Glass, A. 1997, 'What Makes the *Engineers* Case a Classic' in M. Coper & G. Williams (eds), *How Many Cheers for Engineers?* (Sydney, Federation Press).

Brennan, F. 1995, *One Land, One Nation* (Brisbane, University of Queensland Press).

Brennan, Sir Gerard 1991, 'Courts, Democracy and the Law', *Australian Law Journal*, 65: 32.

Brennan, Sir Gerard 1992, 'The Impact of a Bill of Rights on the Role of the Judiciary: An Australian Response', Paper delivered at a Conference on Human Rights, University House, Canberra, 16 July.

Brennan, Sir Gerard 1993, 'A Critique of Criticism', *Monash University Law Review*, 19: 1.

Brennan, Sir Gerard 1997, 'The State of the Judicature', Paper delivered at the 30th Australian Legal Convention, Melbourne, 19 September.

Brennan, Sir Gerard 1998, 'The Parliament, The Executive and the Courts: Roles and Immunities', Lecture at School of Law, Bond University, 21 February.

Brown, J. 1992, 'The Wig or the Sword? Separation of Powers and the Plight of the Australian Judge', *Federal Law Review*, 21: 48.

Bryce, J. 1901, *Studies of History and Jurisprudence* (Oxford, Clarendon Press).

Bryce, J. 1919, *The American Commonwealth*, 2nd edn (New York, Macmillan).

Campbell, E. 1994, 'Unconstitutionality and its Consequences' in G. Lindell (ed.), *Future Directions in Australian Constitutional Law* (Sydney, Federation Press).

Castles, A. 1982, *An Australian Legal History* (Sydney, Law Book Co.).

Charlesworth, H. 1991, 'Australia's Accession to the First Optional Protocol to the International Covenant on Civil and Political Rights', *Melbourne University Law Review*, 18: 428.

Charlesworth, H. 1993, 'The Australian Reluctance about Rights', *Osgoode Hall Law Journal*, 31: 195.

Charlesworth, H. 1995, 'Australia's Split Personality: Implementation of Human Rights Treaty Obligations in Australia' in P. Alston & M. Chiam (eds), *Treaty-Making and Australia: Globalisation versus Sovereignty* (Sydney, Federation Press).

Chesterman, J. & Galligan, B. 1997, *Citizens without Rights* (Melbourne, Cambridge University Press).

Cole, D. 1971, '"The Crimson Thread of Kinship": Ethnic Ideas in Australia 1870–1914', *Historical Studies*, 14, 56: 511.

Coper, M. & Williams, G. 1997, *How Many Cheers for Engineers?* (Sydney, Federation Press).

Coper, M. & Williams, G. (eds) 1997, *Justice Lionel Murphy: Influential or Merely Prescient?* (Sydney, Federation Press).

Craven, G. 1986, *Official Records of the Debates of the Australasian Federal Conventions* (Sydney, Legal Books).

Craven, G. 1990, 'Original Intent and the Australian Constitution: Coming to a Court Near You', *Public Law Review*, 1: 166.

Craven, G. 1992, 'After Literalism, What?', *Melbourne University Law Review*, 18: 874.

Craven, G. 1992, 'The Crisis of Constitutional Literalism in Australia' in H.P. Lee & G. Winterton (eds), *Australian Constitutional Perspectives* (Sydney, Law Book Co.).

Craven, G. 1993, 'Cracks in the Facade of Literalism: Is there an Engineer in the House?', *Melbourne University Law Review*, 19: 540.

Craven, G. 1999, 'The High Court of Australia: A Study in the Abuse of Power', *University of New South Wales Law Journal*, 22, 1: 216.

Creighton, P. 1994, 'Apportioning Electoral Districts in a Representative Democracy', *Western Australia Law Review*, 24: 78.

Crisp, L.F. 1983, *Australian National Government* (Melbourne, Longman Cheshire).

Cristaudo, W. 1993, 'Republic of Australia? The Political Philosophy of Republicanism', *Current Affairs Bulletin*, 69: 4.

Davidson, A. 1991, *The Invisible State: The Formation of the Australian State 1788–1901* (Cambridge, Cambridge University Press).

Davies, M. 1994, *Asking the Law Question* (Sydney, Law Book Co.).

Dawson, Sir Daryl 1990, 'Intention and the Constitution: Whose Intent?', *Australian Bar Review*, 6: 93.

Detmold, M.J. 1985, *The Australian Commonwealth: A Fundamental Analysis of its Constitution* (Sydney, Law Book Co.).

Dicey, A.V. 1915, *Introduction to the Law of the Constitution*, 8th edn (London, Macmillan).

Dicey, A.V. 1926, *Lectures on the Relation between Law and Public Opinion in England*, 2nd edn (London, Macmillan).

Dixon, Sir Owen 1935, 'The Law and the Constitution', *Law Quarterly Review*, 51: 590.

Dixon, Sir Owen 1942, 'Address at the Annual Dinner of the American Bar Association', *Australian Law Journal*, 16: 192.

Dixon, Sir Owen 1965, 'The Common Law as the Ultimate Constitutional Foundation' in Sir Owen Dixon, *Jesting Pilate: And Other Papers and Addresses by Sir Owen Dixon* (Melbourne, Law Book Co.).

Dixon, Sir Owen 1965, *Jesting Pilate: And Other Papers and Addresses by Sir Owen Dixon* (Melbourne, Law Book Co.).

Dorsett, S. & Godden, L. 1998, *A Guide to Overseas Precedents of Relevance to Native Title* (Canberra, AIATSIS).

Doyle, J. 1993, 'Constitutional Law: "At the Eye of the Storm"', *University of Western Australia Law Review*, 23: 15.

Edwards, J. 1984, *The Attorney-General: Politics and the Public Interest* (London, Sweet & Maxwell).

Else-Mitchell, R. (ed.) 1961, *Essays on the Australian Constitution* (Sydney, Law Book Co.).

Ely, J. & Ely, R. 1986, *Lionel Murphy: The Rule of Law* (Sydney, Akron Press).

Ely, J.H. 1980, *Democracy and Distrust: A Theory of Judicial Review* (Harvard, Harvard University Press).

Emy, H. & Hughes, O. 1991, *Australian Politics: Realities in Conflict* (Melbourne, Macmillan).

Epstein, D. 1984, *The Political Theory of 'The Federalist'* (Chicago, University of Chicago Press).

Etzioni, A. 1998, 'Mixed Scanning Revisited' in A. Etzioni, *Essays in Socio-Economics* (Berlin, Springer-Verlag).

Evans, G. 1996, 'The Impact of Internationalisation on Australian Law: A Commentary' in C. Saunders (ed.), *Courts of Final Jurisdiction: The Mason Court in Australia* (Sydney, Federation Press).

Finnis, J.M. 1967, 'Separation of Powers in the Australian Constitution', *Adelaide Law Review*, 3: 159.

Fraser, A. 1990, *The Spirit of the Laws: Republicanism and the Unfinished Project of Modernity* (Toronto: University of Toronto Press).

Fraser, A. 1995, 'In Defence of Republicanism: A Reply to George Williams', *Federal Law Review*, 23: 362.

Fullagar, I. 1993, 'The Role of the High Court: Law or Politics?', *Law Institute Journal*, 67: 72.

Gageler, S. 1987, 'Foundations of Australian Federalism and the Role of Judicial Review', *Federal Law Review*, 17: 162.

Galligan, B. 1987, *The Politics of the High Court* (Brisbane, University of Queensland Press).

Galligan, B. 1989, 'Realistic Realism of the High Court's Political Role', *Federal Law Review*, 18: 40.

Galligan, B. 1990, 'Australia's Rejection of a Bill of Rights', *Journal of Commonwealth and Comparative Politics*, 28: 344.

Galligan, B. & Nethercote, J. (eds) 1989, *The Constitutional Commission and the 1988 Referendums* (Canberra, Centre for Research on Federal Financial Relations and Royal Australian Institute of Public Administration).

Galligan, D. 1983, 'Judicial Review and Democratic Principles: Two Theories', *Australian Law Review*, 57: 69.

Gaudron, M. 1995, 'Some Reflections on the Boilermakers Case', *Journal of Industrial Relations*, 37: 306.

Gibbs, H. 1987, 'Separation of Powers: A Comparison', *Federal Law Review*, 17: 151.

Gleeson, A.M. 1999, 'Legal Oil and Political Vinegar', Address to the Sydney Institute, Sydney, 16 March.

Gleeson, M. 1997, 'The Role of the Judiciary in a Modern Democracy', Judicial Conference of Australia Annual Symposium, Sydney, 8 November.

Glendon, M. 1991, *Rights Talk: The Impoverishment of Political Discourse* (New York, Free Press).

Goldsworthy, J. 1989, 'Realism about the High Court', *Federal Law Review*, 18: 27.

Goldsworthy, J. 1995, 'The High Court: Implied Rights and Constitutional Change', *Quadrant*, March: 46.

Goldsworthy, J. 1997, 'The Path to Engineers' in M. Coper & G. Williams (eds), *How Many Cheers for Engineers?* (Sydney, Federation Press).

Goldsworthy, J. 1997, 'Commentary' in M. Coper & G. Williams (eds), *Justice Lionel Murphy: Influential or Merely Prescient?* (Sydney, Federation Press).

Goldsworthy, J. 1997, 'Originalism in Constitutional Interpretation', *Federal Law Review*, 25: 1.

Goot, M. & Rowse, T. (eds) 1994, *Make a Better Offer: The Politics of Mabo* (Sydney, Pluto Press).

Gregor, M. 1988, 'Kant's Approach to Constitutionalism' in A. Rosenbaum (ed.), *Constitutionalism: The Philosophical Dimension* (New York, Greenwood Press).

Gruen, F. & Grattan, M. 1993, *Managing Government* (Melbourne, Longman Cheshire).

Hamilton, A., Madison, J. & Jay, J. 1982 [1788–88], *The Federalist Papers* (ed. G. Wills, New York, Bantam).

Handsley, E. 1998, 'Public Confidence in the Judiciary: A Red Herring for the Separation of Judicial Power', *Sydney Law Review*, 20: 5.

Hanks, P. 1992, 'Constitutional Guarantees' in H.P. Lee & G. Winterton (eds), *Australian Constitutional Perspectives* (Sydney, Law Book Co.).

Hiley, G. (ed.) 1997, *The Wik Case: Issues and Implications* (Sydney, Butterworths).

Hobbes, T. 1981, *Leviathan* (ed. with intro. by C.B. Macpherson, Harmondsworth, Penguin).

Hocking, J. 1997, *Lionel Murphy: A Political Biography* (Cambridge, Cambridge University Press).

Hogg, P. 1992, *Constitutional Law of Canada* (Scarborough, Ont., Carswell).

Holland, K.M. (ed.) 1991, *Judicial Activism in Comparative Perspective* (London, Macmillan).

Hope, J. 1996, 'A Constitutional Right to a Fair Trial? Implications for the Reform of the Australian Criminal Justice System', *Federal Law Review*, 24: 173.

Horowitz, D. 1977, *The Courts and Social Policy* (Washington DC, Brookings Institution).

Horrigan, B. 1995, 'Is the High Court Crossing the Rubicon? A Framework for Balanced Debate', *Public Law Review*, 6: 284.

Horrigan, B. & Young, S. (eds) 1997, *Commercial Implications of Native Title* (Sydney, Federation Press).

HREOC 1997, *Bringing Them Home: Report of the National Inquiry into Separation of Aboriginal and Torres Strait Islander Children from their Families* (Sydney, Human Rights and Equal Opportunity Commission).

Hudson, W. & Carter, D. 1993, *The Republicanism Debate* (Sydney, New South Wales University Press).

Hunt, A. 1978, *The Sociological Movement in Law* (London, Macmillan).

Hunter, P. 1997, 'The Wik Decision: Unnecessary Extinguishment' in G. Hiley (ed.), *The Wik Case* (Sydney, Butterworths).

Huttenback, R. 1976, *Racism and Empire* (Ithaca, Cornell University Press).

Irving, H. 1997, *To Constitute a Nation: A Cultural History of Australia's Constitution* (Cambridge, Cambridge University Press).

Jacob, H., Blankenburg, E., Krittzer, H.M., Provene, D.M. and Sanders, J. 1996, *Courts, Law, and Politics in Comparative Perspective* (New Haven, Yale University Press).

Kane, J. 1997, 'Racialism and Democracy: The Legacy of White Australia' in G. Stokes (ed.), *The Politics of Identity in Australia* (Cambridge, Cambridge University Press).

Kant, I. 1991, *Metaphysics of Morals* (Cambridge, Cambridge University Press).

Kercher, B. 1995, *An Unruly Child: A History of Law in Australia* (Sydney, Allen & Unwin).

Kerr, Sir John 1978, *Matters for Judgment* (Melbourne, Macmillan).

Kirby, M. 1983, 'Law Reform as "Ministering to Justice"' in A.R. Blackshield (ed.), *Legal Change: Essays in Honour of Julius Stone* (Sydney, Butterworths).

Kirby, M. 1990, 'Judicial Independence in Australia Reaches a Moment of Truth', *University of New South Wales Law Journal*, 13: 187.

Kirby, M. 1995, 'The Role of International Standards in Australian Courts' in P. Alston & M. Chiam (eds), *Treaty-Making and Australia: Globalisation versus Sovereignty* (Sydney, Federation Press).

Kirby, M. 1997, 'Judicial Activism', Bar Association of India Lecture, New Delhi, 5 January.

Kirby, M. 1998, 'Attacks on Judges: A Universal Phenomenon', Paper delivered at American Bar Association Winter Leadership Meeting, Maui, Hawaii, 5 January.

Kirk, J. 1995, 'Constitutional Implications from Representative Democracy', *Federal Law Review*, 23: 37.

La Nauze, J.A. 1972, *The Making of the Australian Constitution* (Melbourne, Melbourne University Press).

Lane, P. 1996, 'The Changing Role of the High Court', *Australian Law Journal*, 70: 246.

Lane, P.H. 1981, 'The Decline of the *Boilermakers* Separation of Powers Doctrine', *Australian Law Journal*, 55: 6.

Latham, Sir John 1961, 'Interpretation of the Constitution' in R. Else-Mitchell (ed.), *Essays on the Australian Constitution* (Sydney, Law Book Co.).

Lavarch, M. 1995, 'The Role of International Law-Making in the Globalisation Process' in P. Alston and M. Chiam (eds), *Treaty-Making and Australia: Globalisation versus Sovereignty* (Sydney, Federation Press).

Lee, H.P. 1992, 'The High Court and External Affairs Power' in H.P. Lee & G. Winterton (eds), *Australian Constitutional Perspectives* (Sydney, Law Book Co.).

Lester, A. 1993, 'English Judges as Law Makers', *Public Law.* 269.

Lincoln, A. 1943, 'Address before the Young Men's Lyceum of Springfield, Illinois' in T.H. Williams (ed.), *Selected Writings and Speeches of Abraham Lincoln* (New York, Hendricks House).

Lindell, G. 1994, 'Recent Developments in the Judicial Interpretation of the Australian Constitution' in G. Lindell (ed.), *Future Directions in Australian Constitutional Law* (Sydney, Federation Press).

Lindell, G. (ed.) 1994, *Future Directions in Australian Constitutional Law* (Sydney, Federation Press).

Lobban, M. 1991, *The Common Law and English Jurisprudence, 1760–1850* (Oxford, Oxford University Press).

Locke, J. 1992, *Two Treatises on Government*, 2nd edn (ed. with intro. and notes by P. Laslett, Cambridge, Cambridge University Press).

Loughlin, M. 1992, *Public Law and Political Theory* (Oxford, Clarendon Press).

Lucy, R. 1993, *The Australian Form of Government: Models in Dispute* (Melbourne, Macmillan).

Lumb, R.D. 1991, *The Constitutions of the Australian States* (Brisbane, University of Queensland Press).

Machiavelli, N. 1996, *Discourses on Livy* (trans. H.C. Mansfield & N. Tarcov, Chicago, University of Chicago Press).

Maddox, G. 1991, *Australian Democracy in Theory and Practice* (Melbourne, Longman Cheshire).

Malleson, K. 1999, 'A British Bill of Rights: Incorporating the European Convention on Human Rights', *Choices*, 5: 1, 21.

Mandel, M. 1989, *The Charter of Rights and the Legalization of Politics in Canada* (Toronto, Wall & Thompson).

Mansfield, H.M. 1994, 'Separation of Powers in the American Constitution' in B. Wilson & P. Schramm (eds), *Separation of Powers and Good Government* (Lanham, Rowman & Littlefield).

Marks, K. 1994, 'Judicial Independence', *Australian Law Journal*, 6: 173.

Mason, Sir Anthony 1986, 'The Role of Constitutional Court in a Federation: A Comparison of the Australian and the United States Experience', *Federal Law Review*, 16: 1.

Mason, Sir Anthony 1989, 'A Bill of Rights for Australia?', *Australian Bar Review*, 5: 79.

Mason, Sir Anthony 1990, 'Judicial Independence and the Separation of Powers: Some Problems Old and New', *University of New South Wales Law Journal*, 13: 173.

Mason, Sir Anthony 1993, 'The Role of the Judge at the Turn of the Century', Fifth Annual AIJA Oration in Judicial Administration, Melbourne, 5 November.

Mason, Sir Anthony 1994, 'The Australian Judiciary in the 1990s', Address to the Sydney Institute, Sydney, 15 March.

Mason, Sir Anthony 1994, 'The State of the Judicature', *Monash University Law Review*, 20: 1.

Mason, Sir Anthony 1995, 'Trends in Constitutional Interpretation', *University of New South Wales Law Journal*, 18: 237.

Mason, Sir Anthony 1996, 'An Australian Common Law', *Law in Context*, 14: 81.

Mason, Sir Anthony 1996, 'Courts and Community Values', *Eureka Street*, 6: 32.

Mason, Sir Anthony 1996, 'The Judge as Law-Maker', *James Cook University Law Review*, 3: 1.

Mason, K. 1989, 'Prospective Overruling', *Australian Law Journal*, 63: 526.

Mathew, P. 1995, 'International Law and the Protection of Human Rights in Australia: Recent Trends', *Sydney Law Review*, 17: 177.

Mayer, J.P. (ed.) 1969, *Democracy in America* (New York, Doubleday).

McCamish, C. 1996, 'The Use of Historical Materials in Interpreting the Commonwealth Constitution', *Australian Law Journal*, 70: 648.

McGarvie, R. 1992, 'The Ways Available to the Judicial Arm of Government to Preserve Judicial Independence', *Journal of Judicial Administration*, 1: 236.

McHugh, M. 1988, 'The Law-making Function of the Judicial Process', *Australian Law Journal*, 62: 18.

McRae, H., Nettheim, G. & Beacroft, L. 1997, *Indigenous Legal Issues: Commentary and Materials* (Sydney, Law Book Co.).

Meale, D. 1992, 'The History of the Federal Idea in Australian Constitutional Jurisprudence: A Reappraisal', *Australian Journal of Law and Society*, 8: 25.

Menzies, Sir Douglas 1968, 'Australia and the Judicial Committee of the Privy Council', *Australian Law Journal*, 43: 79.

Menzies, Sir Robert 1967, *Central Power in the Australian Commonwealth* (London, Cassell).

Mill, J.S. 1972 [1861], 'Considerations on Representative Government' in H.B. Acton (ed.), *Utilitarianism, On Liberty, Representative Government* (London, Dent).

Montesquieu, C. 1989, *The Spirit of the Laws* (trans. and ed. A.M. Cohler, B.C. Miller & H.S. Stone, Cambridge, Cambridge University Press).

Mullins, A. 1994, 'Women and the Text of the Australian Constitution', *Constitutional Centenary*, March: 18.

O'Brien, D. 1996, *Special Leave to Appeal: The Law and Practice of Application for Special Leave to Appeal to the High Court of Australia* (Sydney, Law Book Co.).

Opeskin, B. & Rothwell, D.R. (eds), *International Law and Australian Federalism* (Melbourne, Melbourne University Press).

Pangle, T.L. 1973, *Montesquieu's Philosophy of Liberalism: A Commentary on The Spirit of the Laws* (Chicago, University of Chicago Press).

Parker, C. 1994, 'Protection of Judicial Process as an Implied Constitutional Principle', *Adelaide Law Review*, 16: 341.

Patapan, H. 1996, 'Rewriting Australian Liberalism: The High Court's Jurisprudence of Rights', *Australian Journal of Political Science*, 31: 2, 225.

Patapan, H. 1997, 'The Liberal Politics of Rights: Changing Constitutionalism and the Bill of Rights Debate in Canada and Australia', PhD thesis, University of Toronto.

Patapan, H. 1997, 'Competing Visions of Liberalism: Theoretical Underpinnings of the Bill of Rights Debate in Australia', *Melbourne University Law Review*, 21: 497.

Patapan, H. 1997, 'The Dead Hand of the Founders? Original Intent and the Constitutional Protection of Rights and Freedoms in Australia', *Federal Law Review*, 25: 211.

Patapan, H. 1997, 'The Author of Liberty: Dicey, Mill and the Shaping of English Constitutionalism', *Public Law Review*, 25: 211.

Patapan, H. 1999, 'The Howard Government and the High Court' in G. Singleton (ed.), *The Howard Government* (Sydney, University of New South Wales Press).

Patapan, H. 1999, 'Separation of Powers in Australia', *Australian Journal of Political Science*, 34(3): 391.

Pitkin, H.F. 1967, *The Concept of Representation* (Berkeley, University of California Press).

Plato 1980, *The Laws of Plato* (trans. with commentary by T.L. Pangle, Chicago, Basic Books/University of Chicago Press).

Pocock, J.G.A. 1987, *The Ancient Constitution and the Feudal Law* (Cambridge, Cambridge University Press).

Polybius 1979, *Histories* (trans. W.R. Paton, Cambridge, Mass., Harvard University Press).

Postema, G. 1986, *Bentham and the Common Law Tradition* (Oxford, Clarendon Press).

Preston, K. & Sampford, C.J.G. (eds) 1996, *Interpreting Constitutions: Theories, Principles and Institutions* (Sydney, Federation Press).

Pryles, M. 1981, *Australian Citizenship Law* (Sydney, Law Book Co.).

Reid, Lord 1972, 'The Judge as Lawmaker', *Journal of the Society of Public Teachers of Law*, 12: 22.

Reynolds, H. 1974, 'Racial Thought in Early Colonial Australia', *Australian Journal of Politics and History*, 20: 45.

Rosenberg, G.N. 1991, *The Hollow Hope: Can Court Bring about Social Change?* (Chicago, University of Chicago Press).

Rowse, T. 1994, 'How We got a Native Title Act' in M. Goot & T. Rowse (eds), *Make a Better Offer: The Politics of Mabo* (Sydney, Pluto Press).

Rubenstein, K. 1995, 'Citizenship in Australia: Unscrambling its Meaning', *Melbourne University Law Review*, 20: 503.

Sandel, M. 1982, *Liberalism and the Limits of Justice* (Cambridge, Cambridge University Press).

Sandoz, E. (ed.) 1993, *The Roots of Liberty* (Columbia, University of Missouri Press).

Saunders, C. 1994, 'Concepts of Equality in the Australian Constitution' in G. Lindell (ed.), *Future Directions in Australian Constitutional Law* (Sydney, Federation Press).

Saunders, C. (ed.) 1996, *Courts of Final Jurisdiction: The Mason Court in Australia* (Sydney, Federation Press).

Sawer, G. 1956, *Australian Federal Politics and Law 1901–1929* (Melbourne, Melbourne University Press).

Sawer, G. 1961, 'The Separation of Powers in Australian Federalism', *Australian Law Journal*, 35: 177.

Sawer, G. 1963, *Australian Federal Politics and Law 1929–1949* (Melbourne, Melbourne University Press).

Scutt, J. (ed.) 1987, *Lionel Murphy: A Radical Judge* (Melbourne, McCulloch Publishing).

Shearer, I. 1995, 'The Implications of Non-Treaty Law-Making: Customary Law and its Implications' in P. Alston & M. Chiam (eds), *Treaty-Making and Australia: Globalisation versus Sovereignty* (Sydney, Federation Press).

Simpson, A.W. 1973, 'The Common Law and Legal Theory', *Oxford Studies in Jurisprudence* (Oxford, Oxford University Press).

Singleton, G., Aitkin, D., Jinks, B. & Warhurst, J. 1996, *Australian Political Institutions* (Melbourne, Addison Wesley Longman Australia).

Snortland, N.E. & Stanga, J.E. 1973, 'Neutral Principles and Decision-Making Theory: An Alternative to Incrementalism', *George Washington Law Review*, 41: 1006.

Solomon, D. 1992, *The Political Impact of the High Court* (Sydney, Allen & Unwin).

Solomon, D. 1999, *The Political High Court: How the High Court Shapes Politics* (Sydney, Allen & Unwin).

Star, L. 1992, *Julius Stone: An Intellectual Life* (Melbourne, Oxford University Press in association with Sydney University Press).

Stephenson, M.A. (ed.) 1995, *Mabo: The Native Title Legislation* (Brisbane, University of Queensland Press).

Stephenson, M.A. & Ratnapala, S. (eds) 1993, *Essays on the Mabo Decision* (Sydney, Law Book Co.).

Stephenson, M.A. & Ratnapala, S. (eds) 1993, *Mabo: A Judicial Revolution* (Brisbane, University of Queensland Press).

Stokes, M. 1986, 'Federalism, Responsible Government and the Protection of Private Rights: A New Interpretation of the Limits of the Legislative Powers of the Commonwealth', *Federal Law Review*, 16: 135.

Stone, J. 1961, *The Province and Function of Law, Law as Logic, Justice and Social Control* (Sydney, Maitland Publications).

Stone, J. 1965, *Human Law and Human Justice* (Stanford, Stanford University Press).

Stone, J. 1966, *Social Dimensions of Law and Justice* (Sydney, Maitland Publications).

Stoner, J. 1992, *Common Law and Liberal Theory* (Lawrence, Kan., University of Kansas Press).

Strauss, L. 1989, 'On Classic Political Philosophy' in L. Strauss, *The Rebirth of Classical Political Rationalism* (Chicago, University of Chicago Press).

Sturgess, G. & Chubb, P. 1988, *Judging the World* (Sydney, Butterworths).

Sugarman, D. 1983, 'The Legal Boundaries of Liberty: Dicey, Liberalism and Legal Science', *Modern Law Review*. 102.

'Symposium on Constitutional Rights for Australia' 1994, *Sydney Law Review*, 16: 1.

'Symposium on the High Court of Australia 1960–1993' 1993, *Western Australia Law Reports*, 23: 11.

'Symposium on the Internationalisation of Australian Law' 1995, *Sydney Law Review*, 17: 1.

Tate, N. & Vallinder, T. (eds) 1995, *The Global Expansion of Judicial Power* (New York, New York University Press).

Tenbensel, T. 1996, 'International Human Rights Conventions and Australian Political Debates: Issues Raised by the "Toonen Case"', *Australian Journal of Political Science*, 31: 7.

Third Annual Colloquium of the Judicial Conference of Australia 1998, Surfers Paradise, 6–8 November.

Thomas, J.B. 1997, *Judicial Ethics in Australia* (Sydney, Law Book Co.).

Thompson, E. 1980, 'The "Washminster" Mutation' in P. Weller & D. Jaensch (eds), *Responsible Government in Australia* (Melbourne, Drummond).

Thomson, J.A. 1982, 'Principles and Theories of Constitutional Interpretation and Adjudication: Some Preliminary Notes', *Melbourne University Law Review*, 13: 597.

Thomson, J. 1986, 'Constitutional Authority for Judicial Review: A Contribution from the Framers of the Australian Constitution' in G. Craven (ed.), *Official Records of the Debates of the Australasian Federal Conventions* (Sydney, Legal Books).

Thomson, J. 1988, *Judicial Review in Australia: The Courts and the Constitution* (Sydney, Thesis Publications).

Thomson, J. 1997, 'American and Australian Constitutions: Continuing Adventures in Comparative Constitutional Law', *John Marshall Law Review*, 30: 627.

Tocqueville, A. de 1969, *Democracy in America* (ed. J.P. Mayer, New York, Doubleday).

Toohey, J. 1993, 'A Government of Laws, and Not of Men?', *Public Law Review*, 4: 158.

Tribe, L. 1980, 'The Puzzling Persistence of Process-Based Constitutional Theories', *Yale Law Journal*, 89: 1063.

Tucker, D. 1994, 'Representation-Reinforcing Review: Arguments about Political Advertising in Australia and the United States', *Sydney Law Review*, 16: 274.

Tucker, D.F.B. 1995, *The Rehnquist Court and Civil Rights* (Aldershot, Dartmouth).

Twining, W. (ed.) 1986, *Legal Theory and Common Law* (Oxford, Blackwell).

Uhr, J. 1998, *Deliberative Democracy in Australia: The Changing Place of Parliament* (Melbourne, Cambridge University Press).

Velkley, R. 1997, 'The Tension in the Beautiful: On Culture and Civilization in Rousseau and German Philosophy' in C. Orwin & N. Tarcov (eds), *The Legacy of Rousseau* (Chicago, University of Chicago Press).

Vile, M.J.C. 1967, *Constitutionalism and the Separation of Powers* (Oxford, Clarendon Press).

Virtue, B. 1993, 'Putting Mabo in Perspective', *Australian Lawyer*, July: 23.

Walker, G. 1988, *The Rule of Law: Foundation of Constitutional Democracy* (Melbourne, Melbourne University Press).

Walker, K. 1996, 'Treaties and the Internationalization of Australian Law' in C. Saunders (ed.), *Courts of Final Jurisdiction: The Mason Court in Australia* (Sydney, Federation Press).

Waltman, J.L. & Holland, K.M. (eds) 1988, *The Political Role of Law Courts in Modern Democracies* (Basingstoke, Macmillan).

Warden, J. 1993, 'The Fettered Republic: The Anglo–American Commonwealth and the Traditions of Australian Political Thought', *Australian Journal of Political Science*, 28: 83.

Wells, B. & Doyle, J. 1997, 'Reconciliation and the Constitution' in E. Johnston, M. Hinton & D. Rigney (eds), *Indigenous Australians and the Law* (Sydney, Cavendish Publishing).

Wheeler, F. 1996, 'Original Intent and the Doctrine of the Separation of Powers in Australia', *Public Law Review,* 7: 96.

Whitlam, G. 1979, *The Truth of the Matter* (Melbourne, Penguin).

Whitlam, E.G. 1985, *The Whitlam Government 1972–1975* (Melbourne, Penguin).

Williams, D. 1995, 'Who Speaks for the Courts?' in *Courts in a Representative Democracy* (Melbourne, Australian Institute of Judicial Administration).

Williams, D. 1997, 'Judicial Independence and the High Court', Monash University Law School Foundation Lecture, Melbourne, 1 May.

Williams, G. 1995, 'A Republican Tradition for Australia?', *Federal Law Review,* 23: 133.

Williams, G. 1995, 'What Role for Republicanism? A Reply to Andrew Fraser', *Federal Law Review,* 23: 376.

Williams, G. 1999, *Human Rights under the Australian Constitution* (Melbourne, Oxford University Press).

Williams, G. 1999, 'The High Court and the Media', *University of Technology Sydney Law Review,* 1: 136.

Williams, G. 1999, '*Engineers* is Dead, Long Live Engineers!', *Sydney Law Review,* 17: 62.

Williams, J. 1996, 'Race, Citizenship and the Formation of the Australian Constitution: Andrew Inglis Clark and the "14th Amendment"', *Australian Journal of Politics and History,* 42: 1, 11.

Williams, J. 1997, 'Revitalizing the Republic: Lionel Murphy and the Protection of Individual Rights', *Public Law Review,* 8: 27.

Williams, T.H. (ed.) 1943, *Selected Writings and Speeches of Abraham Lincoln* (New York, Hendricks House).

Windeyer, Sir Victor 1962, '"A Birthright and Inheritance": The Establishment of the Rule of Law in Australia', *Tasmanian Law Review,* 1: 635.

Winterton, G. 1986, 'Extra-Constitutional Notions in Australian Constitutional Law', *Federal Law Review,* 16: 223.

Winterton, G. 1994, 'The Separation of Judicial Power as an Implied Bill of Rights' in G. Lindell (ed.), *Future Directions in Australian Constitutional Law* (Sydney, Federation Press).

Winterton, G. 1998, 'Popular Sovereignty and Constitutional Continuity', *Federal Law Review,* 26: 1.

Wright, H.G.A. 1998, 'Sovereignty of the People: The New *Grundnorm?*', *Federal Law Review,* 26: 165.

Young, R. 1995, *Colonial Desire* (London, Routledge).

Young, S. 1998, 'The Long Way Home: Reparation for the Removal of Aboriginal Children', *University of Queensland Law Review,* 20: 1, 70.

Zines, L. 1994, 'A Judicially Created Bill of Rights?', *Sydney Law Review,* 16: 166.

Zines, L. 1997, *The High Court and the Constitution,* 4th edn (Sydney, Butterworths).

Index